The Power of
Religious Publics

The Power of Religious Publics

Staking Claims in American Society

Edited by
William H. Swatos, Jr. and
James K. Wellman, Jr.

Religion in the Age of Transformation
Anson Shupe, Series Adviser

Westport, Connecticut
London

BL
2525
.P68
1999

Library of Congress Cataloging-in-Publication Data

The power of religious publics : staking claims in American society /
   edited by William H. Swatos, Jr. and James K. Wellman, Jr.
      p.   cm.—(Religion in the age of transformation, ISSN
   1087–2388)
   Includes bibliographical references and index.
   ISBN 0–275–96478–7 (alk. paper)
   1. United States—Religion—20th century.   2. Religion and
sociology.   3. Sociology, Christian.   I. Swatos, William H.
II. Wellman, James K.   III. Series.
BL2525.P68   1999
200′.973—dc21   98–53393

British Library Cataloguing in Publication Data is available.

Library of Congress Catalog Card Number: 98–53393
ISBN: 0–275–96478–7
ISSN: 1087–2388

First published in 1999

Praeger Publishers, 88 Post Road West, Westport, CT 06881
An imprint of Greenwood Publishing Group, Inc.
www.praeger.com

Printed in the United States of America

The paper used in this book complies with the
Permanent Paper Standard issued by the National
Information Standards Organization (Z39.48–1984).

10 9 8 7 6 5 4 3 2 1

Contents

Preface

This book has its origins in a consultation sponsored by the Public Religion Project, then barely in its infancy, held in Chicago in the fall of 1996. Martin Marty and his colleagues called together the executive officers of about a dozen academic societies dedicated in one way or another to the study of religion. Bill Swatos attended as executive officer of the Religious Research Association (RRA). While driving to dinner one evening, Marty mentioned that he had a child living in the San Diego area; since the RRA was meeting in conjunction with the Society for the Scientific Study of Religion (SSSR) in San Diego in the fall of 1997, Swatos suggested that this was an excellent venue for a deeper exploration of the "public religion" concept.

Jim Wellman was the RRA program chair for 1997. We worked together from that point on to build a session that yielded eight of the chapters in this volume. One person whom we invited but had to decline our offer, because he had just accepted an offer to speak at the American Academy of Religion (AAR) meeting to be held in San Francisco only two weeks after the RRA/SSSR meeting, was Robert Bellah. Fortuitously, Marty, Wellman, and Swatos were all at the AAR meeting, and upon hearing Bellah's presentation we agreed that if possible it should be included. Close to the same time the AAR's *Religious Studies News* published two companion pieces on teaching religion. One was by Marty; the other was by Jacob Neusner on teaching religion in a public institution. The goodness of fit of Neusner's work to our theme prompted us to invite him to elaborate on it further, and he has done so with William Scott Green. The final two chapters are from each of us.

Our collaboration represents the good fellowship that has characterized the RRA over many decades, and we are grateful to it for providing the context whereby such projects as this may fruitfully develop. We also appreciate the support of our friend and fellow RRA colleague Anson Shupe, the editorial director of this series.

James K. Wellman, Jr.
William H. Swatos, Jr.

Chapter 1

The the *Public and the Public's Publics*

Martin E. Marty

The Power of Religious Publics addresses three main areas of concern:

- How do the concepts of "public" and "religion" interrelate in American society today?
- What kinds of power do "religious publics" assert, and what are the limits to such power?
- Is there or should there be such a thing as the public—as in "the general public"—or is society made up of numberless "subpublics," and how do the answers to this bear on the question of asserting power?

Each contributing author addresses these questions from perspectives shaped by his or her own experiences, curiosities, and areas of expertise. In my case, this calls for reflection on how the historian might deal with the concept of what I call "the *the* public" and "the public's publics." To do so, I conflate the first two questions and then deal with the third.

THE CONCEPTS OF "PUBLIC" AND "RELIGION"

The construct "public religion" itself combines two constructs. The word *public,* a term no longer to be taken for granted, is regularly employed by philosophers, politicians, social scientists, humanists, including theologians, and others. They apply it as an adjective to collectives of people who, from other angles, including their own, merely go about the business of being people, perhaps citizens. These people become a public or become aware of being a public when, for example, debates over "public opinion" reveal them to exist as a public. Similarly, there are "public schools" and debates over "public access."

At times talk of the public tends to overlook the role of what we might call "subpublics" as well as the role of the individuals that make up it and them. Thus to understand citizens and believers in their various roles, including as elements in a public, the observer does and to some degree must categorize or typify them. In such endeavors, the careful social scientist remains aware that when observing or inventing a public, the social scientist is dealing with a *construct*. This also means that each person who participates in what this person chooses to discern and define as a public can be viewed from many angles, again, including his or her own. Thus any use of the term *public* can be costly to the integrity of the individual agent. A thoughtful anthropologist takes pains to note "the agent's description" of reality before applying observers' terms of reference. Thus the philosopher William James recognized that the intellect—with some hazard—inevitably classifies any object with something else. But that object or individual must first be seen as *sui generis* and unique: "Probably a crab would be filled with a sense of personal outrage if it could hear us class it without ado or apology as a crustacean, and thus dispose of it. 'I am no such thing,' it would say; 'I am MYSELF, MYSELF alone.'"[1]

Whoever therefore keeps in mind the interests of extreme individuality, particularity, and subjectivity will remain aware of how relative, how plastic, and how fluid are the applications of the concept of the "public" to various publics. This is the case even before it gets linked as an adjective with nouns, as in the tandem "public religion."

Similarly, *religion* is a term employed and applied by philosophers, politicians, social scientists, humanists, including theologians, and other classifiers and typifiers. They apply this second-order term to individuals—though such persons will also appear in collectives—who go about their own business as believers and behavers, as being just ordinary people when they are not being classified by those who have reason to define and create constructs.

Very little of what most social scientists say about the religious person may match the individual agents' descriptions of what they are about. In the American Academy of Arts and Sciences's Fundamentalism Project, scholars found it valuable to speak of fundamentalists around the world in ways that they intended to be precise but were necessarily not confined to "agents' descriptions." Fundamentalists, in their summary view, were people who had found it necessary to react against modernity's erosive force and who were concerned about threats to personal and social identity. In their reaction they engaged in selective retrieval of presumed religious "fundamentals."[2]

None of those observed or written about in the Fundamentalism Project would think of himself or herself in precisely the terms used by scholars. When the voice of the religiously fundamentalist HIMSELF, HERSELF was heard, it was not in a speech about his or her religion, but in references to "I found God!" or

"I'm born again!" or "Allah has spoken!" or "God said it. I believe it. That settles it." In order to keep such agents' descriptions in mind, the scholars involved in this and similar projects spend much energy on interviewing, listening, tape-recording, and reproducing images of such adherents.

In the essays that follow, we will be arguing about how the constructs "public," "subpublics," and individual "agents" relate to each other, especially in respect to issues of power—well aware that such impositions cannot do full justice to the dynamic and idiosyncratic character of life in a free society made up of 260 million people. To assert that these terms are social scientific constructs compels the authors to provide at least an outline of their own definitions of these.

Aware of the "MYSELFs" and of the metaphorical crabs and crustaceans that make up the necessary human constructs "public" and "religion," I could consume all the allotted space merely in launching definitional tasks. Instead, I am going to hurry past extensive definitions and merely, if precariously, point to commonsense applications of the two key terms.

First, *public:* Most dictionaries simply define this by contrasting it with "private." In the present context, therefore, every word about "public religion" is going to imply its relation to and contrast with something like "private religion." Some scholars today caution lest referring to this polarity suggest that the simple contrast might exhaust the possibilities of definition. Yet a commonsense approach, against the background of American experiences, leads me to say in respect to religion—which is "a private affair" in much of the American heritage and colloquial usage—that "public religion" represents both the otherwise private reality "going public" and religion conceived *ab origine* as public. Along the way, in both cases, religion takes on distinctive forms that would have remained latent, suppressed, or invisible if they were seen as being confined to the private realm. These forms, it is in place to remember, may even be in some ways in tension with, or appear contradictory to, some religion-in-private or private-religion impulses.

Second, *religion:* Scholars can present and have presented hundreds of definitions of religion. A book-length struggle with definition, for example, appears in Wilfred Cantwell Smith's *The Meaning and End of Religion.* Its second chapter is an extensive treatment of the subject of definitions, and its 160 footnotes offer a rich feast of miniature essays on how others have defined or, in Smith's terms, have misdefined, religion.[3] When time is short and I am asked what I mean to include under the category of religion, I simply point to the enormous sixteen-volume *Encyclopedia of Religion* and say, "Religion is a word we use for the kinds of phenomena that you write about and can look up in a work of this sort with that sort of name."[4] Many of those hundreds of religious phenomena can be addressed as private expressions, but most of them also have public dimensions or find public expressions.

A third definition: *Public religion* combines the two other words into one construct. As such it finds its place alongside cognates developed by social scientific and humanistic observers, terms such as *civil religion, invisible religion, political religion,* and *societal religion.*

That most Americans could get along without such a construction as "public religion" is obvious from the fact that for a long time the majority of them did. In most places and among most people, the term would remain unfamiliar. It might be seen as local, confined to its place in certain kinds of society. I do not know whether "public religion" has cognates or would make sense in the worlds formerly called "primitive" and "archaic." Similarly, it is unclear whether non-Western places have, or have the same kind of need and place for, such abstractions and applications. In what we today call the West, however, one can find anticipations of this combination in the ancient Greek and then especially the Roman worlds. Such concepts have appeared wherever and whenever there was devotion to "public" concerns and when these concerns displayed a religious cast or involved religious implications.

THE RISE OF THE CONCEPT IN THE UNITED STATES

In American culture, the first trace of the combination that I have found, and one that remains determinative, occurred in Benjamin Franklin's advocacy in 1749. He spoke of "the Necessity of a *Publick Religion.*"[5] Such religion was to be useful for morals and intellectual development. William Lee Miller has remarked that for the American founders, influenced by the Enlightenment, religion was often seen as a "public utility." Just as there are "water works" there had to be "religion works." Whatever they may have believed in their private worlds—and some of them, such as James Madison, were extremely reticent to testify concerning their own faith—most of them argued the case for something like public religion at considerable length and with significant diversity.[6]

Needless to say, most of those who profess religion would not have been content to have their relation to the divine reduced to anything like what Franklin, Madison, and other founders had in mind when talking about public and republican religion. However, many who today advocate a public place for religion, be they believers and practicers of particular faiths or not, still stand in the tradition of those founders who advertised it as commendable or even necessary for virtue and morals in the republic.

In my understanding as a historian, sensitive to what Franklin had in mind, "publick religion" complements the construct "civil religion."[7] But the latter term, as reintroduced by Robert N. Bellah in a deservedly famous essay in 1967, derives from Jean-Jacques Rousseau and Emile Durkheim and appears to be more of a top-down creation that relates congenially to governmentally based "collective representations."[8] Franklin's "publick religion" was based more on a bottom-up awareness. That is, he looked out the window at the many sects and churches and saw most of them to be contributing to virtue and morals while also clinging to idiosyncratic particular features. He then asked how what they stood for at their best and in common might contribute to the larger public and republic.

"Public religion" did not have the field to itself among the enlightened founders. Nor would it have been immediately comprehensible or fully satisfying as a faith in the minds of the particularist religious leaders of the time. They wanted to preach the truth, save souls, build subcommunities, inspire the fear of hell and the hope of heaven, or minister to hungry souls. All the while most of them evidenced the conviction that an important but still secondary by-product of these endeavors might be a more moral citizenry and a virtuous republic. The separate faiths and their leaders might support the common good as participants in a public, but they would not give up their salvific peculiarities or specialized ways of going about the practice of faith.

RELEGATING MOST RELIGION TO THE PRIVATE SPHERE

It is ironic that much "public philosophy" in America has often relegated religion to the private sphere, even in the case of some of the founders who spoke of "publick religion." Franklin's own more or less Deist faith, which he regularly expressed, dealt only incidentally with civil, political, or public and republican corporate life; his virtues were relevant to private life. Thus in his *Autobiography* he wrote:

I was never without some religious principles. I never doubted, for instance, the existence of the Deity; that he made the world, and govern'd it by his Providence; that the most acceptable service of God was the doing of good to men; that our souls are immortal; and that all crime will be punished, and virtue rewarded, either here or hereafter. These I esteem'd the essentials of every religion; and, being to be found in all the religions we had in our country, I respected them all, tho' with different degrees of respect, as I found them more or less mix'd with other articles, which, without any tendency to inspire, promote, or confirm morality, serv'd principally to divide us, and make us unfriendly to one another.[9]

Similarly, in the years and expressions of the American Enlightenment, Franklin's younger contemporary Thomas Jefferson and the stormier revolutionary Tom Paine both confessed and declaimed "my own mind is my own church" (Paine) and "I am of a sect by myself, as far as I know" (Jefferson), which meant that religion was to be nurtured apart from community and from a public place.[10] When in 1802 Jefferson contended for a "wall of separation between church and state," and when he excluded theology and ministry training from the University of Virginia, confining it to "the Confines," he was seeking to render and keep religion private and was showing disdain for most of its communal expressions.[11]

As in politics, so in philosophy religion was often a private affair. Thus William James defined religion as "the feelings, acts, and experiences of individual men in their solitude, so far as they apprehend themselves to stand in relation to whatever they may consider the divine."[12] There was in James's work little positive appraisal of communal, societal, or public religion. Similarly, the philosopher Alfred North Whitehead saw religion to be what one did with his or her "solitariness."[13]

All the while, however, there were also public philosophers who included the idea of religion, however marginal it might appear to be, in the *the* public. John Dewey treated it thus in *The Public and Its Problems,* and Walter Lippmann did something similar in his *The Public Philosophy.*[14] Dewey repudiated his Protestantism and its God but spoke up for *A Common Faith,* assigning a public role not to religion, as he saw it defined institutionally and creedally, but to religiousness.[15] Lippmann generally ignored and was unmoved by his inherited Judaism or by the surrounding Christian churches. He spoke up instead for a public "religion of the spirit" that had more direct social bearings than did sectarian and creedal faiths.[16]

The Jefferson/Paine and James/Whitehead schools had little difficulty with private religion as they defined it. But they were critical of, or at least wary about, public religion whenever they had the whole *the* public in mind. The Dewey/Lippmann schools, on the other hand, had some difficulty with private or, to them, sectarian religion. But they saw a need for a publicly conceived, confessed, and celebrated religion whenever they had the *the* public in mind.

Some theologians, as interpreters of both faith and the public order, have sought a language to address a variety of publics. Thus David Tracy notes and calls for one kind of language for "The Public of the Academy," another for "The Public of the Church," and a third for "The Public of Society," which we are here calling the *the* public, or the public's public.[17]

THE NOTIONS OF A *THE* PUBLIC AND THE PUBLIC'S PUBLICS

The problem of the *the* public is that, once the construct is proposed, the proposer or observer must fill it with content. Who is this *the* public? Who feeds it intellectually? Who represents it? What discourse does it develop for propagation? Does it leave out anyone?

In the last third of this century, challenges to the very notion of a *the* public, or to the idea that there could be integrity in attaching any kind of religion to such, have been frequent, persistent, and often well aimed. Sometimes they score. During this time the challenges have come from those who spoke up for (and were thus typed or categorized in company with) feminists; voices for and of other gender designations (e.g., gay, lesbian, and bisexual); the "ethnic pentagon" of hyphenated Native-, Euro-, Afro-, Hispanic-, and Asian-American religions; plus the several hundred variations, combinations, and innovations that appear when citizens represent their distinctive MYSELFs, MYSELFs: social and economic classes, those who speak up for victims and the abused, generations, groups formed on aesthetic and taste grounds, professions and vocations, and the like—including, of course, religion.

In terms of the present topic, each of these references represents either subpublics or agencies that present alternative perspectives on the power of what was presumed to be, quite inaccurately, an undifferentiated *the* public. At issue is the hegemony of one set of articulators and embodiments or observers of this *the* public. It seems clear that at midcentury one set of people—men, more often than not of Protestant population cohorts if not confessors or belongers; white, again, more often than not of Angloid background—dominated and had access to the agencies of management and control. Whole shelves full of documentation by historians, humanists, and social scientists published in the most recent four decades reinforce that observation and point.

Time and space here permit but one reference. Catherine Albanese, in the widely used textbook *America: Religions and Religion,* would be the last among religious historians to be accused of slighting religious movements once seen by many as belonging to "outsider," "marginal," "esoteric," or "alternative" subpublics. Yet she is among the first to note how pervasive what she calls "public Protestantism" was at establishing what she calls "the Protestant code," which is "a large part of the body of connecting religious characteristics" in the nation. "Present nearly everywhere in Protestant America [which, for Albanese, means virtually anywhere and everywhere], the code has expressed itself as clear conditions, institutions, and underlying patterns for behavior within the mainstream."

Among the features of this "public Protestantism," in Albanese's eyes, are these as chapter subheads:

The Conditions: Religious Liberty, Democratic Equality, Separation of Church and State
The Institutions: Denominationalism and Voluntaryism
The Patterns: Activism and the Search to Simplify Moralism

Later, under the category of "The Protestant Cultus," she adds "Revivalism," and under "The Protestant Creed," "Individualism . . . Higher Law . . . Millennialism." Then: "To sum up, public Protestantism was and is the dominant religion of the United States," and in a way, as a result of historical processes, the nation saw "the ascendancy of public Protestantism as the 'one religion.'" In our terms: This was the religion of the *the* public.[18]

Of course, one can question the categories Albanese and others like her present in summary. At first glance, for example, many would restrict "revivalism" to Protestantism. Yet there have been studies of Catholic revivalism, and in the competitive American religious market, even Eastern religions have overcome the passivity with which it was believed that they arrived and have made revivalistlike moves. "Millennialism" looks like a motif of certain kinds of Protestantism, but once again, many religious movements and certainly "civil religion" and "public religion" have acquired millennial casts. But let Albanese do her own summarizing:

Not only were there many religious traditions within the geographical boundaries of the United States, but there was manyness *within* traditions. [She illustrates both by reference to American Indians, Catholics, occult, metaphysical, and New Age forms that represent "subpublics."] . . . By the same token, even as we immersed ourselves in the religious pluralism, from time to time we could not fail to notice the ways in which different traditions and movements seemed to take on some of the characteristics of the Protestant mainstream. Reform Jews of the late nineteenth century moved their Sabbath services to Sunday morning and imitated the style of Protestant worship. Catholics after Vatican II adopted a leaner and simpler version of the Mass, closer to the demands of the Protestant Reformation. Mormons and Adventists, who affirmed the good life in this world, resembled liberal Protestants in their optimism, while Japanese Buddhists in America spoke of churches, acknowledged bishops, and initiated Sunday services. Meanwhile, blacks who became middle class often gravitated toward congregations that were integrated or that resembled in their style the churches of white mainline Protestantism. In these and other instances, manyness was still thriving, but there were numerous ways in which the boundaries of the separate traditions overlapped the boundaries of Protestantism.[19]

In my terms, "the *the* public" and the subpublics, the "public's publics," in many ways were in confluence to form a new kind of mainstream. We shall return to this motif shortly, since it comes to the main point of my plot and contradicts what is often offered as a vision of American religion at century's end.

The medieval Muslim thinker Al Ghazali once said, "There is no hope of returning to a traditional faith after it has once been abandoned, since the essential condition in the holder of a traditional faith is that he should not know he is a traditionalist."[20] Among observers of American religion, myself included, there has been a fall into relativity, if not relativism; into a field of perspectives, if not perspectivalism. One can never look at the old *the* public and its power and canons in the same naive, unguarded ways that one could in, say, 1950. I am not saying that the people of 2000 will be wiser or more virtuous than were their grandparents because of the perspectives the people of 2000 have acquired and now will bring. They simply have the advantage of having been born later and can put to work the hindsight and experiences that make new perspectives possible. They have lost at least one set of innocences. Yet they still have to keep their "hermeneutics of suspicion" antennae alert lest they see no remaining traces of the *the* public in American religion and fail to notice how the religion of its sort influences and is influenced by the "subpublics," something leaders of such publics often obscure or against which notion they are sometimes militant.

POWER, THE *THE* PUBLIC, AND THE PUBLIC'S PUBLICS

If my contention that the religion of the *the* public influences the subpublics, and vice versa, and that they are not in simple competition for hegemony when "staking claims" on American power has merit, the critical social scientist or the social-scientifically informed critic does well in his or her probes to be a hermeneut of suspicion about the claims of both the *the* public and the public's publics. Whoever reads the advocacies of the latter with even minimal care will see that the contentions of our decade do not represent simply an issue between those who have and who want to hold power versus those who do not have it and do not want it.

The moment one enters the political realm, as most religious groups do these years, even if one does so as a representative of the victims of abuse or as an heir of slaves or of people confined to reservations, one deals with what politics is about: power. Not that all contenders want to replace one old monopoly or hegemony with another—their own. Many of them are true re-publicans, which means they know that in a republic power is shared, balanced, and kept in tension between the aggregates, the subpublics, each of which brings its own interests and may also seek to promote a common good.

The subpublics do indeed bring different perspectives from those associated with Albanese's pictured "public Protestants" in their midcentury prime. The *the* public in the writings of John Dewey and Walter Lippmann, published just before the challenges posed in the last third of the twentieth century, gave voice to and found expression in premier agencies of publicness as it was then conceived and experienced. These include national newsmagazines and other popular journals, metropolitan newspapers, mainstream church body leadership, network radio and early network television, *Who's Who* connections, corporate and often labor union leadership, and the like.

The presumed coherence of that midcentury world waned along with the demise of *Collier's* and *Look* and the weekly *Life* magazine. In recent decades, magazines specialize through a process called "twigging." Scores of television channels compete in the era of cable; it is harder for the dominant voices to dominate. Radio stations attract highly focused listening subcultures.

What had been "marginal" religions—Mormon, Pentecostal, fundamentalist, Hispanic Catholicism, African American—came to the center and stood a better chance of being represented at public office inaugurations than the clergy of mainstream Catholicism or Protestantism. The celebrities of the "marginal" groups have replaced the leadership of standard-brand Protestantism in the public eye. Who can name more than one—or even one—of the bishops or other leaders of such Protestant churches, though they are heirs of those whose elections and careers would have been followed in *Time* and *Newsweek* only decades ago. Historians pay far more attention to Mormons than to Methodists, to Shakers than to many mainstream bodies. Jews are now presidents and key faculty on prestigious university campuses where still toward midcentury there had been quotas limiting the enrollment of Jewish students. Asians will soon dominate the public universities in the most populated state. In the worlds of entertainment, athletics, and popular culture, what had been the many "public's publics" now dominate.

This is not to argue that the power of the older *the* public has entirely disappeared. The personnel pools of the corporate world leadership, for example, still reflect what appear to be secularized versions—religion is private, not public, in the boardroom—of the old standard-brand male people of power, white "Judeo-Christians."

When individuals or groups, such as the Public Religion Project of the University of Chicago, are given the charge to make "efforts to bring to light and interpret the forces of faith within a pluralistic society" by "finding ways to help assure that religion in its many voices is well represented in North American public life," they inevitably find the concept of "public" to be as problematic as "religion" itself had been.[21] There are hundreds of denominations in the *Yearbook of the American and Canadian Churches,* thousands of religions in the encyclopedias, millions of variations in the population.

How then do we conceive of the "public"? Is there a mandate to reach and represent every manifestation of inquiries represented at a convention of the Society for the Scientific Study of Religion or the Religious Research Association? Must Yoruban and Wiccan, Turkish Judaism and Louisiana Folk Saints congregants be given as much attention as one might give to Theosophy and Pentecostalism, to say nothing of Judaism and Catholicism? Each in the former set represents a subpublic in search of its own kind of power, devoted to its own canons, manifesting worlds and worldviews of its own.

Does postmodern social scientific study of religion commit one to the study of religion reduced to "nothing but" the mathematics of proliferations, prolificity, and market-oriented inventions? If such study has among its purposes the endeavor to help people find their way around in a culture, to make sense of a society, to learn how to prophesy or act in a society, the vision of such "mere multitudinousness" would quite likely render one helpless. Better to have stayed content with studying groups in the Yellow Pages of the telephone book. There at least some kind of coherence prevails, even if it derives from little more than an alphabet of institutions.

Two provocative things should be said if one wants to advance debate on the theme of the *the* public, the public's publics, and the study of religion.

First, to chronicle the loss of power among the dominant midcentury groups that had presumed to speak to and for the only "public" there was or to criticize its representatives for presuming that they exhaust what is involved in "public religion" is not to leave the scene desolate, so that no power is evident. However one defines power, it is clear that *all religious responses involve people in some form of assertion of power.* This is as true of Wiccans and Theosophists as it was of Episcopalians and Southern Baptists. To see an inherited public religion metanarrative questioned or subverted, as it often is today, is not necessarily to concede that no common narratives can appear or have appeared. To demolish the existing canons of public religion, with their orthodoxies established by winners, is not to say there will be no more canons. The proposed countercanons—see Ronald Takaki's *Another Shore* and its counterparts—turn out to be as predictable as were the first editions of Commager on *The American Mind.*[22] In these books that collect the religious expressions of subpublics, one expects to find Sojourner Truth and early Asian immigrants, slave narratives and addresses by Native American chiefs, accounts of pioneer feminists and of Hasidic rabbis. Martin Luther King, Jr., and Frederick Douglass are certainly more acceptable and evident in the broader canons today than are Jonathan Edwards or Horace Bushnell. The abused and the victimized, the heirs of those who overcame slavery and segregation, do not speak only out of and back to their own subpublics. They "belong" to other publics that, taken together, represent durable and emergent elements of a new *the* public.

The second provocation connects with and derives from that theme and is an extension of the previous sentence. That is, with all the attacks on hegemony, exercises of the hermeneutics of suspicion, and deconstructionist reconstructions in play, there is still a measurable *the* public. Refined and pop survey research alike turn up surprising orthodoxies about what it is to be American, religious, and public. As one sample, a special Independence Day report, "The Beliefs We Share," finds Stephen Covey saying, "In the debate over values and culture, it's easy to forget an important fact: On many core issues, Americans agree with each other." To illustrate:

- 95 percent believe freedom must be tempered by personal responsibility
- 89 percent believe it's their responsibility to help those less fortunate
- 86 percent believe that, despite our mobile society, family ties are more important than ever
- 83 percent believe the United States is the greatest nation on Earth

- 81 percent believe a spiritual or religious belief is essential to a fulfilling life
- 80 percent believe personal responsibility has more to do with success in life than do personal circumstances[23]

These points of agreement tend to be "secular" in orientation, though even the only slightly informed and sophisticated historian can trace the old *the* public religion of Protestant provenance in their shaping. And opinion surveys on religious opinions tend to show a great deal of consensus on key issues, surprising those who believe that subpublics alone represent the world to those who make them up. Also, old notions of "overlapping consensus" among groups can be matched by concepts of "overlapping publics" and "overlapping subpublic perceptions and interests." To overlook that fact would be to situate oneself so far removed from the American powers that it would be as hard to report on them as it would be to change any part of them.

What is different near 2000, from the situation around 1950, is neither that there was then only a *the* public of the sort Dewey and Lippmann, Reinhold Niebuhr, John Courtney Murray, or Will Herberg addressed, nor that the "public's publics" or subpublics with their interests, perceptions, and powers did not then exist. It is that we have become aware of some of the ways they interplay in the constantly shifting juxtapositions of powers in American life, including in its public religion, whatever it will be seen to be as those shifts occur.

THE HISTORIAN'S EQUIPMENT FOR DEALING WITH THE INTERACTION

Since the old "consensus" has been called into question, has putatively disappeared, or is fighting a defensive war of survival against the identity and interest groups, today many historians question whether there can ever again be common stories—since the metanarrative that went with the religion of the *the* public is no longer so easily available, if it is available at all.

So the issue is often posed as, must one be a relic, an ancient, who survives with residues of a consensus that never should have existed or a reminiscence of a domain of power that has disappeared? In other words, is one condemned to die with "the mainstream"? Must one be committed to emergent and lately discovered elements of dissensus that are acquiring power in religion today? How do we observe the two in interrelation?

Since I was asked to keynote these essays, I assume that there is some curiosity about my own position, how I have attended to both, and how I picture doing so in the future. I have always worked to relate the one and the many, the "one" representing the *the* public and the many, the public's publics. These might appear religiously in the form of a "communion of communions," as they do in *The*

Public Church: Mainline–Evangelical–Catholic, or republicanly, as a "community of communities" (after Johannes Althusius), or "an association of associations" (after Alexis de Tocqueville), or "an aggregate of aggregates" (after Aristotle), or a republic of "e pluribus unum" (after James Madison), or a "free society" with all "agencies of mind and spirit" interacting.[24]

So much for the past. How do we refine this double interest in programs and prospectuses for future writing on American religious history? The framework that I have found most congenial is posited in Peter Burke's *Varieties of Cultural History,* in the chapter "Unity and Variety in Cultural History." Burke deals in complex ways with "tradition," a concept that can get the student of American culture in trouble if all accent falls on the progenitors and transmitters of traditions, be they of the *the* public or the public's publics. Burke relies instead, as have I, on what has come to be called "reception" theory, which considers the replacement of "the traditional assumption of passive reception by the new assumption of creative adaptation." The accent then falls not just on what Jonathan Edwards or Benjamin Franklin passed down to later generations. Now the interest is in what happens to tradition as it is received by subpublics with great varieties of interests.

As we study the racial, ethnic, cultural, identity, gendered, class, taste, and ideological, among others—each of which is somehow, usually by design, distanced from any religious complex of the *the* public—reception theory teaches us to be alert to the kinds of accommodations that go on and the transformations along the way. Burke, at once ponderously and puckishly, provides a catalog of names for options:

A great variety of terms are used in different places and different disciplines to describe the processes of cultural borrowing, appropriation, exchange, reception, transfer, negotiation, resistance, syncretism, acculturation, enculturation, inculturation, interculturation, transculturation, hybridization (*mestizaje*), creolization, and the interaction and interpenetration of cultures. . . . Some of these terms may sound exotic, and even barbarous. Their variety bears eloquent witness to the fragmentation of today's academic world. They also reveal a new conception of culture as *bricolage,* in which the process of appropriation and assimilation is not marginal but central.[25]

I believe that these processes are at work in most of the essays collected in five typical recent symposia, collections whose existence gives some indication of the vitality and freshness evident in American religious history. All five are conceived to be in many ways "deconstructive" and "decentering" efforts, designed to show how captive of a *the* public paradigm the historians through midcentury and until the recent past have been. Titles such as *Retelling U.S. Religious History, Minority Faiths and the American Protestant Mainstream, Religious Diversity and American Religious History, New Directions in American*

Religious History, and the less revealing title but just as deconstructive plot *Religion and American Culture* prepare one for overdue critiques of the way the American religious story was told back when "public religion" was too often equated with what Albanese called "public Protestantism" and shaped into a synthesis that appeared to be the religion of the *the* public.

A quick scan of the topics shows how the historians reach beyond Puritanism and Catholicism, the Protestant mainstream, and the civil religion as conceived shortly after midcentury. For example, the accent falls on sexuality, ritual sites, women's history, supply-side approaches, Asian-rim Eastern religion, Indians, the Canadian border, "exchange," Mormon "otherness," African American, "minority faiths," the South, "sectarian religious movements," Muslims, Lakota Sioux, "the Easter parade," Victorian fraternal rituals, feminist black Baptists, Pentecostalism, Haitian voodoo, California, and southern civil religion. Few words turn up more consistently in titles and essays than "marginal" to go with "mainstream."[26]

Even when these essays deal with traumas to the old "mainstream" groups or the story of their own accommodations to change, and especially when they deal with "marginal" and "outsider" groups, as these were once conceived, they effectively show how it would be pointless and futile, both substantively and methodologically, to tell the story of the *the* public religion as if there were a consensus, a dominant institutional form and single cultural influence in American religion of the recent past.

Implicit in many of the essays, however, is the assumption that the margins and the outsiders, while being agents of "reception" of cultural influences among each other and from the "public Protestantism" and its kin, really go their own ways, stay intact, and are not transformed. Instead, in my rereading—and I invite others to read or reread the books with Peter Burke's elaborations in view—what is apparent is the social scientific and historical description of processes not of mutually exclusive phenomena but of, once more, "cultural borrowing, appropriation, exchange, reception, transfer, negotiation, resistance, syncretism, acculturation, enculturation, inculturation, interculturation, transculturation, hybridization (*mestizaje*), creolization, and the interaction and interpenetration of cultures."

To have this pointed out often infuriates spokespersons for exclusivist subpublics or those who see themselves not enriched, but tainted, by anything that flows from a changed mainstream *the* public religious complex or who refuse to recognize what each contributes to the former. But can there be such isolation? The Nation of Islam and many Muslim assemblies, the Mormons, the gay and lesbian churches, Hispanic Catholicisms, Buddhisms, and all retain some of their integrity—one hopes!—and their texture, color, particularity, and even exclusive and unsharable features. But they also get pulled to a new congeries of centers, if not a center.

Once one entertains this reception-theory understanding, one finds on all hands evidences of how the process works. The person on the street of Honolulu drops into the Buddhist "church" and sees pews, evidences of stewardship campaigns, "Sunday bulletins," and other receptions of Christian religion. To take a totally random but revelatory example, the columnist Bob Greene recently wrote about Wonder Bread as the symbol of the old *the* culture, as once "epitomizing America the Non-Ethnic," dominant, homogenizing, bland, central, as "the national icon of the white-bread America of nostalgic memory: plain and standard and obedient and home before dark. . . . If Wonder Bread were a person, that person would shine those shoes every morning and go to church every Sunday."

Back then, Greene notes, bagels represented exclusive and distinctive Jewish food from the "margins" and the "outsiders." They belonged to one of the public's publics, but not to the *the* public. "Bagels were Jewish food . . . found at bar mitzvahs, not in public school cafeterias; bagels were served after synagogue services, not after Cub Scout meetings. . . . The U.S. was not as homogenized as it pretended to be," Greene continues, "and bagels represented the great divide."

Now, "bagels have gradually crossed over. Protestants, Catholics, every denomination of every religion eat bagels these days." They are part of African American, Hispanic American, Asian American culture, "the ethnic background no longer matters." And, the shocker: "Wonder Bread now has a new division: Wonder Bagels." A spokesman asked and answered: "Are Wonder Bagels mainstream bagels? I think you could make that conclusion."[27]

Quoting *USA Weekly* and a Bob Greene column may mean reaching so far into the "public" that I might risk scholarly credentials. But to make or try to make points about publics one reaches into the literatures of public spread and intent. Let me illustrate the reception-theory point with three more references, each of which I think is congruent with the point Catherine Albanese makes as she deals with oneness and manyness or with Burke, with adaptation.

The first is by K. Anthony Appiah, a Ghanaian-born intellectual now at Harvard, as he reviews two books on toleration and multiculturalism. "Is it not, indeed," he asks, "one of the most pious of the pieties of our age that the United States is a society of enormous cultural diversity?"

Appiah begins his answer historically by noting how out of the mainstream were shtetl Jews on Ellis Island not too long ago. "They transplanted a religion with specific rituals, beliefs, and traditions" along with other untranslatable cultural elements. Now "the rich immigrant gumbo has become thin gruel." Yiddish is gone, and its phrases survive in everyone's vocabulary. So, too, with the one-time distinctives of Italian Catholics.

There are still seders and nuptial masses, still gefilte fish and spaghetti, but how much does an Italian name tell you, these days, about church attendance, or knowledge of Italian, or tastes in food or spouses? Even Jews, whose status as a small non-Christian group in an overwhelmingly Christian society might have been expected to keep their "differences" in focus, are getting harder to identify as a cultural group. (At the seder I go to every Passover, nearly half of those in attendance are gentiles.)

Appiah, a black, sees Italians and Jews—once perceived as racially different—and almost everyone else becoming "white." Even blacks, forced into subcultures and then retaining some elements and improvising new ones while borrowing others, have very much in common with whites. The English language is pervasive; 97 percent of adult Americans speak it. They share sports, consumer culture, consumer goods, and movie stars.

Even the supposedly persisting differences of religion turn out to be shallower than you might think. American Judaism is, as is often observed, extraordinarily American. Catholics in this country are a nuisance for Rome just because they are . . . well, so Protestant. Unlike Catholics in many other countries, for example, even the most devout tend to celebrate the separation of Church and State. They also claim individual freedom of conscience—so they don't automatically take the Church's line on contraception and divorce.

Albanese's subtitles and theses about the pervasiveness and proteanism of public Protestantism here get corroborated. "American religion, whatever its formal sectarian designation, is decidedly Protestant," and America Islam, "for example, is as happy with the separation of Church and states as most Muslims elsewhere are resistant to change."[28]

A second foray into semipopular journalism finds Richard Brookhiser, who likes to write in the language of the WASP snob, condescending in criticism of a synagogue service in New York, one marred—in his eyes and ears—by the sight and sound of the guitar in the hand of a rabbi and ending in moves "from blasphemy to fatuity. In its past efforts, "Reform Judaism was once a different package," when Jews "were trying to bring their faith in line with modernity, which, in this country, meant the Protestant establishment. One earnest, verbal culture converged with another"—into a mainstream. Catholics have also moved as the Jews did, says guitar-hater Brookhiser.

Meanwhile, "Protestantism was once a force in New York," but "now you could probably fit all the white Protestants in New York into the Felt Forum, but they still set the tone." And what a tone it is. "The guitars, the folk songs, the folksiness—that is all ours. The tone is transtheological, infecting Unitarians and evangelicals alike. The music of megachurches is as bad as any hippie cleric sing-along." So, "look what WASPS have accomplished. We have destroyed ourselves and American Catholicism. I saw the smoking wreck of Judaism. Let the Moslems set up shop here, we'll get them too." The public Protestantism blended into the *the* public religion and ethos now infects the public's publics, almost none of whom seem out of reach in Brookhiser's vision.[29]

The critic Louis Menand in "Being an American," subtitled "How the United States Is Becoming Less, Not More, Diverse," joined Appiah in his conclusions as he reviewed a book about America. He takes on the questions of diversity and multiculturalism in the public's publics. He sampled American multicultural expression as of 1992 and offered a list that would not be hard to match nearly a decade later: Madonna, *Dances with Wolves, Iron John,* Bill Cosby, Eddie Murphy, Anita Hill, Clarence Thomas, *Chutzpah,* Michael Jordan, Magic Johnson, the AIDS crisis, hip-hop, Robert Mapplethorpe, *Sexual Personae,* Tawana Brawley, the Palm Beach case, the Mike Tyson case, Spike Lee, Soon-Yi—"America's popular culture and America's media events over the past few years have been a multiculturalist's dream." However,

when the whole culture is self-consciously "diverse," real diversity has disappeared. Real diversity is what the United States *used* to have—when women and men, black and white Americans, Christians and Jews, gays and straights, and the various ethnic communities of recent immigrant groups led, culturally, largely segregated lives. The notion that this means that the melting-pot was once really melting, and that it no longer does, is perverse. Assimilation does not come from suppressing difference; it comes from mainstreaming it.

To Menand this means that people in the United States still want to become "American": "It is just that being American is now understood to mean wearing your ethnicity, religion, gender and sexual history—your 'difference'—on your sleeve. You would be naked, in fact, without them—which is why one meets, for example, Americans with one non-observant Jewish grandparent who describe themselves as 'Jewish.' If you didn't advertise your differences, then you really would be different." And, notes Menand, "the more the marginal, the exotic and the new become central to the culture, the more everything begins to send the same messages. This is, after all, the way capitalism works." And that is why "the self-consuming, ephemeral, sensationalist, polymorphous, magpie popular culture of the United States is at bottom remarkably conservative." Menand also cites Tocqueville: "The United States is a country in which people, permitted to say whatever they like, all somehow end up saying the same thing," for better or for worse.[30]

One need not agree with all details of the observations made by Bob Greene, K. Anthony Appiah, Richard Brookhiser, and Louis Menand in order to be ready to face the interplay of religion and religious power in the *the* public and the public's publics. What I have described has nothing to do with nostalgia for an old consensus or the suggestion that we might find a new one in the *the* public. It has much to do with rejecting the notion that exclusive subpublics have only been abused and victimized by the *the* public culture and religion or that the "public's publics" are indigenous and can exist as isolated entities.

Instead, the observation centers in the mutual borrowings and constant transformations of each and all, when the accent is less on those who formed and
passed on a set of traditions and more on reception theory in respect to traditions
and the observation of many constant, surprising, and both deadening and
promising exchanges.

Chapter 2

Can Religion Be Religious in Public?

Phillip Hammond

The rhetorical question that is my title must be answered with a qualified "Yes," but that qualification is a crucial one. It depends upon how one answers this question: Is the essence of religion thought to be its public *authority?* Since religion's public authority is precisely what must be relinquished when religion engages in public debate, persons who answer positively to this second question will look upon religion in public as tamed to the point of becoming nonreligion. Others, however, see the matter in a different way. They can imagine religion having authority over individuals if, in a society such as our own, such individuals voluntarily accept it. What is prohibited is the use of *governmental* authority to enforce *religion's* authority. To do that would be to violate the First Amendment's Establishment Clause.

Religion, then, can be religious in public by following the rules implied in the Establishment Clause, which, as we shall see, are by no means obvious. Indeed, they are the subject of much debate and, as Justice Rehnquist's testy dissent in *Wallace v. Jaffee* (1985) demonstrates, even incoherent in operation. That situation need not be, however, and I advance here an argument that would bring clarity in the realm of Establishment Clause jurisprudence and, in so doing, show how religion can be religious in public.

FOUR HISTORIC STEPS

I begin with four historic steps in the history of First Amendment decision making.

The First Step

In 1879, in *Reynolds v. United States,* the United States Supreme Court found that, although the First Amendment prohibited restrictions on government control of religious *belief,* it could restrict *action* based on that belief. Reynolds was Mormon with two wives living in the Utah territory. The United States Congress, which had jurisdiction over Utah, had passed a law making plural marriages in United States territories illegal, and Reynolds challenged that law. He lost, but what makes the case noteworthy is the fact that for the first time the Supreme Court employed the so-called belief–action distinction. The distinction was common enough even in colonial times, but now it became constitutional doctrine. The idea is simple: The Free Exercise Clause gives absolute freedom to *believe* as one chooses, but *actions* reflecting those beliefs are subject to government restraint. "Congress was deprived of all legislative power over mere opinion," wrote Chief Justice Waite, "but was left free to reach actions which were in violation of social duties or subversive of good order."[1] The Court claimed that polygamy was indeed destructive of good order and therefore upheld the law in the face of Reynolds's challenge.

The Second Step

This belief–action distinction operated pretty much unchanged until 1940. In 1940, however, in *Cantwell v. Connecticut,* the Supreme Court reversed the conviction of a Jehovah's Witness who was clearly violating a breach-of-the peace ordinance by playing in public a religious message on a portable phonograph. It was, in fact, a strongly anti–Roman Catholic message in a predominantly Roman Catholic neighborhood. Until 1940, courts would have rendered a guilty verdict—as the lower court did in this case—noting simply that it was a secular regulation being violated, a regulation that did not target Jehovah's Witnesses, or any religious group, but was applicable to all citizens.

In *Cantwell* the Supreme Court reversed the lower court's verdict, acknowledging that *religiously* motivated behavior can be constitutionally protected even though the same behavior, otherwise motivated, is not. It is important to note here that not only was the belief–action distinction being amended, but also—since obviously *some* religiously motivated actions are impermissible (for example, human sacrifice at the sacred altar) even as others are allowable—the Court had now to find some way to balance the interests on both sides of disputed actions.

The Third Step

In *Cantwell,* however, the Court also uncovered another troubling question that it could not dodge: What *is* religious? The evolution of the answer to this second question began in 1944 in *United States v. Ballard*. Guy Ballard and his family led the I AM movement, which, among other things, made claims of being able to cure diseases that doctors called incurable. These claims were made in mailings to people, asking for the payment of money in exchange for the spiritual cure. Because the United States Post Office was involved, the government brought suit against the Ballards, charging fraud. In effect, then, the government was saying that the I AM movement's doctrines were not true and that the Ballards knew they were not true. The trial judge, however, instructed the jury that they were to decide not whether the doctrines were true but only whether the Ballards *believed* them to be true. On that basis the defendants were acquitted, and the government appealed to the Supreme Court.

The *Ballard* case is vitally important for the story here because it argued the point that government must not get involved in determining the truth or falsity of any religion—indeed, must not even define religion. Justice Douglas, for the majority, wrote: "Heresy trials are foreign to our Constitution. Men may believe what they cannot prove. . . . The religious views espoused by respondents might seem incredible, if not preposterous, to most people. But if those doctrines are subject to trial before a jury charged with finding their truth or falsity, then the same can be done with the religious beliefs of any sect."[2]

The Fourth Step

Two decades later, the Court made explicit that intensely held convictions playing the role in people's lives that religion as commonly understood plays in other people's lives are entitled to be treated in the same way that religion is treated. That is to say, conviction equals religion (*United States v. Seeger*, 1965). Conscientious objection has long been recognized in American law. At one point, membership in a so-called peace church (often Mennonite or Quaker) determined one's eligibility for that status, but over the years eligibility rules loosened somewhat in recognition of the great variety of religious beliefs found in the United States. In 1948, Congress amended the Selective Service Act again, declaring that, for the purposes of draft boards, eligibility would be determined by one's "religious training and belief [which] means an individual's belief in a relation to a Supreme Being involving duties superior to those arising from any human relation, but does not include essentially political, sociological, or philosophical views or merely personal moral code."[3]

In the 1965 case, Seeger contended that, though he did not believe in a Supreme Being, he did have a "faith in a purely ethical creed" and thus was entitled to conscientious objector status. The Supreme Court agreed. His creed, the justices said, was the equivalent of a religion, which they characterized in the phrase "a sincere and meaningful belief which occupies in the life of its possessor a place parallel to that filled by the God of those admittedly qualifying for the exemption."[4] Five years later, in *Welsh,* the majority opinion went even further in declaring eligible for exemption from military service "all those whose consciences, spurred by deeply held moral, ethical, or religious beliefs, would give not rest or peace if they allowed themselves to become a part of an instrument of war." The Court, as one legal scholar put it some years later, left "no room for any residual doubt." It "viewed deeply and sincerely held moral or ethical beliefs as the functional, and thus the legal, equivalent of religious beliefs. The Justices had obfuscated any distinction between religion and all other belief systems."[5]

IMPLICATIONS FOR THE ESTABLISHMENT CLAUSE

In the Free Exercise realm, this development is not particularly complicated; it means simply that people with more broadly defined convictions are entitled to First Amendment protection when it comes to actions their conscience tells them they should or should not do despite what the law says.

In the Establishment realm, however, a quite different—and more complex—situation arises. If conviction, irrespective of content, is what the Free Exercise Clause protects, what does the Establishment Clause prohibit? Put differently, if convictions that are not religiously couched are accorded the same protection as religiously couched convictions, what implication does this have for laws that, in the Supreme Court's words, have "no secular purpose" but merely reflect society's past conventions? Some of these laws are simply quaint, such as so-called blue laws, but others are very serious. All of them, however, reflect past convictions that may be held by some, but by no means all, persons today.

I offer three examples—much in the center of contemporary cultural debate—that in my view illustrate the *improper* role of religion in public. The first example is Missouri's legislation outlawing tax-supported abortion, at least that part of the legislation declaring that life begins at the moment of conception. The second is the widespread legislation, recently upheld by the Supreme Court, that prohibits terminally ill patients from seeking medical assistance in ending their lives. The third example involves same-sex marriage, a matter that has been under consideration in several states but is destined to play out in the nation's courts as well as its editorial pages.

It is clear from these three examples that "religion" is involved in the issues in question not because religious doctrine proclaims when life begins or ends or declares what is a real marriage. Rather "religion" is involved as conviction, and the state in these examples has lent its authority to prefer one conviction over another. But in the minds of many, it has done so without a secular purpose. It has said in Missouri that people who are convinced that life does not begin until a fetus can be sustained outside the womb cannot act on that conviction. It has said in New York and Washington State that terminally ill persons must continue to endure their pain or indignity even if they believe that what they regard as "life" is already over for them. And many states, by passing legislation denying recognition to any same-sex marriage solemnized in another state, are using the government's authority to honor one conviction and deny another.

But surely, some will object, government can override at least *some* convictions and pass legislation declaring *some* actions to be legal and others to be illegal. It may indeed, but—and here is a key point—only when it has a *secular* purpose in doing so. Homicide is thus illegal not because one of the Ten Commandments prohibits killing but because society reasons that violence is disruptive, and anarchy would prevail if violence were not curtailed. This "translation step" is the lesson that religion must learn and follow if it wants to be religious in public. It must identify a secular purpose, even if its own reasons are religiously inspired. This is Richard John Neuhaus's meaning when he writes, "Those who want to bring religiously based values to bear in public discourse have an obligation to 'translate' those values into terms that are as accessible as possible to those who do not share the same religious grounding."[6]

It would appear, then, that for religion to be religious in public it must know how to translate its religious values into secular language. What does that mean? I suggest that it means that claims—whether religiously motivated or not—must, if they are to be made in public and carry authority, have an empirical, logical, or rational basis, including those claims that may also have a religious basis. Claims having an empirical, logical, or rational basis are, in principle, claims that can receive unanimous agreement.

Thus, for example, after the *N*th week of a pregnancy, a fetus can be shown to have a probability greater than zero of surviving outside the womb. On an *empirical* basis, therefore, a state may declare that life has begun in the *N*th week and extend legal protection to that life. It may also, on *rational* grounds, decide that even after the *N*th week, a fetus may be aborted if doing so will save the life of the mother. Having thus rationally judged a life-not-yet-born as less valuable than that of an already living mother-to-be, a state may *logically* extend its reasoning and also conclude that a fetus known to be so ill developed as to make life after birth impossible may likewise be aborted after the *N*th week.

TWO EXAMPLES

Perhaps some real-life examples will illustrate the general point. In 1980 the United States Supreme Court struck down Kentucky's law requiring the posting of the Ten Commandments in every public school classroom in that state. Recognizing that such a law could not be justified on the grounds, for example, that the Ten Commandments were handed down by God, the legislature of Kentucky stipulated that the posters include the following sentence: "The secular application of the Ten Commandments is clearly seen in its adoption as the fundamental legal code of Western Civilization and the common Law of the United States" (*Stone v. Graham*). Here, obviously, the Kentucky lawmakers imagined themselves to be "translating" religious claims into claims having an empirical, logical, or rational basis. And, in the case of the last six commandments, regarding honoring parents, murder, adultery, stealing, lying, and coveting, perhaps the legislators had a point. But the first four commandments—to remember the Sabbath, not to honor other gods, not to make graven images, nor to take God's name in vain—because they are incapable of translation into empirical, logical, or rational terms, could be justified only on grounds of conviction.

It is conceivable, in other words, that Kentucky might have prevailed had only the last six commandments been posted. If, in addition, selections from Hammurabi's Code, the Magna Carta, and the like, been included, the display almost certainly would pass constitutional muster. Kentucky, however, was attempting to piggyback four clearly impermissible commandments onto a poster that otherwise might well be said to have a rational purpose: to show the cultural sources of contemporary law.

An Alabama judge recently vowed to keep a display of the Ten Commandments on his courtroom wall despite a circuit court ruling that the display is unconstitutional. The circuit court judge who made the ruling is quoted as saying, "It is obvious that the sole purpose of the plaques hanging in the courtroom in such a fashion is purely religious." The circuit court judge even suggested that his opinion might change if the Ten Commandments were displayed differently, "perhaps with other historic or cultural items."[7] The Alabama judge, however, had forthrightly declared that his motive was religious, and the basis for the display lies in his conviction that the laws he administers are in turn based on a belief in God.

So, it must be said in this case, the judge's beliefs were the *only* basis for bringing religion into the public arena. And that is not enough. As Justice Harry Blackmun wrote in his dissent in a case upholding a Georgia law prohibiting sodomy, "The legitimacy of secular legislation depends . . . on whether the State can advance some justification for its law beyond its conformity to religious doctrine."[8] That is what those who bring religious motives and religious agendas to the public table must recognize. Those motives and agendas are admissible, of course, but there must be "some justification . . . beyond" their "conformity to religious doctrine."

SECULAR VERSUS RELIGIOUS PURPOSES

David A.J. Richards, in his *Toleration and the Constitution,* points to what might be called "public reason" to get at this issue. Public reasons involve rational principles that give "necessary and indispensable protection to the interests of adult persons in life, bodily security and integrity, security in institutional re-lationships and claims arising therefrom, and the like." Public reasons, in other words, identify what Richards calls "neutral goods—things all persons could rea-sonably accept as all-purpose conditions of pursuing their aims, whatever they are."[9] For Richards, therefore, laws that prohibit the sale or use of contraceptives, that outlaw all abortions or homosexual relations, are unconstitutional not be-cause some religions have moral codes declaring these activities to be sins, but because they reflect no "neutral goods" that public reason can identify.

Edward B. Foley also utilizes the concept of public reason, which he claims has two components: "The epistemological component is, essentially, the meth-ods and conclusions of logic and science. The ethical component . . . is the fun-damental idea that the interests of all persons count equally for purposes of determining their rights and duties as citizens."[10] For Foley also, therefore, pub-lic reason involves the employment of concepts, principles, and cause–effect re-lations that all persons can reasonably be expected to accept.

Kyron Huigens advocates another path to much the same end. In a 1989 law review article, "Science, Freedom of Conscience and the Establishment Clause," Huigens borrows the insight of Karl Popper, the philosopher of science who gave us the notion of "falsifiability." "Popper's key insight," Huigens writes, "was to notice that scientific experiments are persuasive, not when they verify hypothe-ses, but when there is a substantial risk that they will have the opposite effect: falsification." Huigens would apply the falsifiability test to governmental actions and declare invalid under the Establishment Clause any actions having the "ef-fect of advancing belief not falsifiable in principle."[11]

Huigens's proposal may seem radical to some, but it conforms nicely to the ar-gument of this chapter. The strong separationist position involved in his proposal views the decisions in *Engel v. Vitale* (outlawing school prayer), *Abington Town-ship v. Schempp* (outlawing school Bible reading), *Epperson v. Arkansas* (per-mitting the teaching of evolution), *Stone v. Graham* (outlawing the posting of the Ten Commandments), and all other cases involving religion in the public schools as fundamentally decisions that involve the *protection of conscience.* All these cases bar government from "advancing dogmatic belief, not because dogma is the product of an established church or because it might lead to persecution but for reasons having to do with dogma itself."[12] In other words, dogma by defini-tion is not falsifiable and therefore, for Establishment reasons, cannot be ad-vanced by the state.

Huigens's proposal goes considerably beyond any accommodationist position. In fact, "accommodation" of religion *as such* would disappear under his scheme, allowing for no governmental benefits to religion except those *required* by the Free Exercise Clause. Thus, under the Huigens doctrine, parochial schools would receive police and fire protection; to deny such protection would burden the Free

Exercise rights of parochial school students and their parents. But tax-supported bus transportation (*Everson v. Board of Education,* 1947) would not be allowed, since the state should not assist in the promulgation of sectarian dogma. Similarly, tax-supported military chaplains are constitutional because many military personnel, away from home, are otherwise unable freely to exercise their religious rights. The legislative chaplain in the Nebraska legislature, on the other hand, would be disallowed, contrary to *Marsh v. Chambers* (1983), because it makes the state the sponsor or promulgator of dogma.

Huigens revisits the creation vs. evolution cases (*Epperson v. Arkansas,* 1968; *Edwards v. Aguillard,* 1987) to illustrate his falsifiability principle. Any proposal to have public schools teach creationism (or "creation science") is unconstitutional not because a possibility exists that such teaching would become an "establishment" but simply because—unlike evolutionary theory, which offers falsifiable propositions—creation theory offers only immutable-truth dogma. For public schools to teach creationism, then, is for the state to use its power to assault the freedom of conscience. For the state to use its "power to inculcate, strengthen or perpetuate belief not falsifiable in principle violates deeply held convictions about the state, belief, and the injunction to use others as ends, not means."[13] Huigens's proposal, read one way, appears hostile to religion, but read another way, it gives priority precisely to religious liberty; it requires the state to give a wide berth to the free exercise of conscience.

SACRED PURPOSE AS A RESIDUAL CATEGORY

It is notable that in the several methods just reviewed for determining what is religious or secular for Establishment Clause purposes—and thus what is and is not constitutional—religion is essentially a residual category. That is, the decisive distinction involves finding what is "secular," with all else being "religious" in the eyes of the law. This makes for some surprising outcomes, of course, because much that is nonsecular is not, in the ordinary sense, religious. We see this vividly in Justice Stevens's dissent in the 1989 Missouri abortion decision. The Preamble portion of the Missouri legislative bill declared that the life of each human being begins at conception. That Preamble, wrote Stevens, happens to coincide with the tenets of one or another religion, but that is not what disqualifies it in his view. Rather, only if the state had a *secular* purpose in adopting the Preamble would that part of the bill be constitutional. Stevens could find no secular purpose and held therefore that the Preamble of the Missouri bill violated the Establishment Clause. (I admit that Justice Stevens's opinion was the minority view.)

It bears repeating, however, that Justice Stevens is not arguing that life does *not* begin at conception, for that statement, like its opposite, also has no secular purpose. And that is exactly the point; since no known reliable and valid way exists to determine just when "life" begins, people are allowed—up until fetal viability *is* determined—to answer the question however they wish.

What is the dividing line between the two beliefs—one dealing with fetal viability, which all persons are expected to accept, and the other, dealing with the origin of life, which persons are free to answer as they choose? The best answer to this question I have encountered is Peter S. Wenz's *Abortion Rights as Religious Freedom.* His book's argument (coincident with the argument of this essay) is that up until the time of fetal viability—which itself is subject to change, of course, by technological advance—a woman must, on the basis of her free exercise of conscience, have a right to terminate her pregnancy. Wenz thus devotes a great amount of attention to this issue of the dividing line between the two kinds of belief—between secular beliefs and religious beliefs. Like the authors already reviewed on this issue, Wenz defines as religious any beliefs that are not secular. Unlike secular beliefs, Wenz says, religious beliefs

cannot be established solely by appeals to generally accepted methods of coming to know what is true and right. This is the epistemological standard for distinguishing religious from secular belief. Additionally, religious beliefs are those on which agreement is unnecessary for the cooperation required to sustain our society. They are matters on which people sharing our current way of life can agree permanently to disagree. They are not among the threads needed to hold our social fabric together.[14]

Wenz's epistemological standard is the standard Huigens called falsifiability. It is scientific in the sense of employing normal canons of reason and evidence. Secular beliefs, in this light, do not in fact have to obtain 100 percent agreement, but at least in principle they could.

Beliefs judged to be religious by the fact that differing positions, even contradictory positions, on those beliefs need not be disruptive of social life represent a quite different category. Included are some obvious instances, such as the capacity of the unitarian, trinitarian, and atheist to live together in harmony if they choose to do so; their dogmatic differences need not interfere in their interactions. The fact that quarrels over religious beliefs *do* occur does nothing to disqualify that statement.

In sharp contrast are those beliefs about matters for which agreement *is* necessary for a smoothly functioning society. They are therefore secular beliefs. These range from seemingly simple beliefs that nobody claims are religious rather than secular (e.g., which side of the road on which to drive), to those beliefs whose origins or legitimation can be found in religion, such as beliefs about the immorality of murder, robbery, battery, and so on. Many, of course, might regard these kinds of beliefs to be religious, and in one sense they are for those persons who conceive of their own beliefs about morality as rooted in their religion. From the legal standpoint, however, whether these beliefs are regarded by persons as rooted in their religion is immaterial; society expects people to behave in accordance with these beliefs anyway, as necessary for a stable society.

A SPECIAL CLASS

There is a class of activities involving the state and religious organizations worthy of special note. These are cases in which a government agency, in pursuit of its religiously neutral goals, utilizes religious organizations as its agents. Unlike government subsidies—for example, in the form of vouchers, salary assistance, or building maintenance—for parochial schools to aid those schools in achieving *their* goals, government in these cases is not assenting to requests from religious communities but asking those communities to help government achieve *its* goals. In most instances, no doubt, those goals overlap those of the religious communities, but that is for them, not the state, to decide.

Take, as a vivid example, the case of refugee relief following the Vietnam War, when thousands upon thousands of Vietnamese, Laotians, and Cambodians sought refuge in the United States and elsewhere. Because some churches already had in place the facilities for "processing" refugees, the United States government found it convenient (and cheaper) to use those facilities to conduct health examinations, fill out migration forms, and so forth—activities those facilities had been doing earlier, but on a smaller scale and without government financial support.

Before this cooperative endeavor began, the religious organizations could decide whom they would accept and what would be done with those accepted. Now the United States government made those decisions, which may have caused some frustration or curtailed some behavior by religiously motivated personnel. Presumably, in the earlier period, these processing centers were more or less missionary operations by American denominations, and a reasonable assumption was that at least some of those accepted would "convert." At least efforts toward that end were not prohibited. Now they were at least limited.

In all probability, what these denominational programs were doing earlier, at their own expense, was regarded as "religious." When working in concert with the government, but still engaged in much the same activity, is it still "religious"? Answers will vary, no doubt, but a reasonable perspective on the matter is this: Religious organizations have never been *unlimited* by the state in what they could do, so the question is whether the limitations imposed by the state diminish the religious mission to the point where its religious "core" is lost. Thus Roman Catholic hospitals receive government subvention, but in exchange they cannot restrict their patients and medical staff to Catholics. Inner city churches are given tax dollars to help provide food and sleeping quarters to the homeless, but they serve all who qualify by the state's standards. A sectarian college can get financial help to construct buildings, but it must guarantee not to conduct worship in those buildings. In these examples, has the hospital, the church, or the college so compromised its reason-for-being that its core identity is lost?

This question, interestingly, is the mirror image of the question asked in "Establishment" cases. In such cases, the court asks whether an activity violates the No Establishment Clause of the Constitution's First Amendment and must answer yes or no. But just because an answer is blunt does not mean the process of arriving at that answer is clear-cut. Of the twenty-five Establishment cases heard by the Supreme Court between 1980 and 1995, only five were decided on nine–zero votes. A full 60 percent were decided on votes of five–four or six–three, indicating enormous disagreement over what is and what is not a violation of the Establishment Clause.

And so it is with the parallel question of when a religious organization sacrifices its core identity by accommodating the state's demands of neutrality in order to receive some of the state's largesse. It would seem hopeless to draw a line that will work in all cases. Just as the Court seems to waffle on where to draw the establishment line (e.g., the state may lend to parochial schools geography textbooks that contain maps of the United States, but it may not lend maps of the United States for use in geography classes), so do religious organizations seem to waffle on where to draw the compromise line. A hardline separationist such as the late Leo Pfeffer would outlaw a statue of the Virgin Mary in any Catholic hospital receiving public money, and Bob Jones University lost its tax-exempt status rather than compromise on its policy prohibiting interracial dating by its students.[15]

In asking therefore—concerning this special class of cases in which religious organizations receive government financial help—whether those are instances of religion being religious in public, we must return to the topic of this chapter's first paragraph. In accepting public tax money to support its mission, does a religious organization relinquish its authority over the activities for which the money was given? The answer is yes, meaning—in this very special sense, and only in this sense—religion is being religious in public.

ARGUMENT AND COUNTERARGUMENT

Much of the preceding material was presented orally at the annual joint meeting of the Religious Research Association and the Society for the Scientific Study of Religion in November 1997. Objections were raised along several lines. All, in my view, *sound* valid but upon analysis turn out to be specious. I conclude, therefore with some comments about these objections.

The objection most easily countered is one that asks, "If all claims of conscience are constitutionally protected, even if not couched in religious language, what is to stop anybody from doing anything in the name of conscience?" The answer is that *not* all claims of conscience are protected; what is protected is the presumption of a conscientious right *unless the state can identify a secular purpose for curtailing that right.* For this reason, judging the legitimacy of a nonreligious conscience claim is no harder than judging the legitimacy of a religious claim.

A second objection arises out of a clear misunderstanding of my argument: "that for religion to be religious in public it must drop its religious language or disguise its underlying religious motives." This simply isn't so. The public square does not rule out religious words and motives; it simply does not accord them authority until they are translated. In his *The Dissent of the Governed,* Stephen L. Carter exhibits this misunderstanding. He wonders whether the example of the *Reverend* Martin Luther King, Jr., of the Southern *Christian* Leadership Conference (his emphasis) does not show that the United States Constitution allows a religious community to "use the coercive apparatus of the state to impose its moral understandings on those in the political community who are not co-religionists."[16] I would respond that it shows religious language and motive *are* admissible in the public square, but that, although King was no doubt granted charismatic authority because of his religious eloquence, his influence came precisely from his translating the Christian gospel message into terms readily understood by non-Christians, even the nonreligious. Certainly the coercive apparatus of the state— in enforcing school desegregation, for example—was justified not by King's words but by words interpreting the United States Constitution.

A third objection parallels the misunderstanding of the second: "that constraining religion in public pushes it further in the direction of privatization." That the separation of church and state (or the constitutional interpretation of the First Amendment) leads empirically to the privatization of religion is, by now, beyond dispute. Such privatization is not *required,* however, nor is the public square *off limits* to religious persons using religious language. José Casanova puts this point nicely: "[W]hichever position . . . it takes, the church will have to justify it through open, public, rational discourse in the public sphere of civil society. . . . [Therefore, only] a religion which has incorporated as its own the central aspect of the Enlightenment critique of religion is in a position today to play a positive role in . . . the revitalization of the modern public square."[17] Qualification for religious participation, in Casanova's terms, is tantamount to acceptance of the notion that, in the public square, religion must advance its positions on empirical, rational, or logical grounds.

Another objection to my argument is that to insist on placing such a qualification on religion in the public square is to trivialize it and to imply that religion has nothing empirical, rational, or logical to say on public issues. Surely this objection is fallacious. Requiring religion to translate its positions into terms understandable to all implies that its positions may be convincing even to others not sharing the theological suppositions underlying those positions.

Finally, it has been objected that my argument ignores minority faiths and communicates a message of hostility to them. I find this objection surprising because so much of the basis of my argument, as I have explained, comes out of judicial rulings that favored the free exercise of minority, sometimes despised, faiths. Consider the conscientious objection cases: It was the Supreme Court that located the "faith" element in the consciences of Seeger and Welsh, even when they themselves denied having any orthodox faith. More important, however, the implications of this expanded understanding of the Free Exercise Clause for the Establishment Clause puts the lie to this last objection. Why? Because it turns out that, despite a long history of church–state separation, American society is still riddled with privileges extended to religion over nonreligion as well as to some religions over others. Keep in mind that people who articulate their convictions in a language other than religion are *also* required to translate their arguments based on those convictions into empirical, rational, or logical terms. Religions, then, are not being unfairly treated but simply being asked to play by the uniform rules.

CONCLUSION

This lesson is not easy to grasp. Prejudices so old as not to be recognized as prejudices are difficult to excise. I close with but one example. *Catalyst,* the Journal of the Catholic League for Religious and Civil Rights, states in its masthead that "it defends the right of Catholics—lay and cleric alike—to participate in American life without defamation or discrimination." Most of the *Catalyst* issue of May 1998 is therefore stories drawn from newspapers, Hollywood, radio and TV, and other avenues of mass communication in which Catholicism is denigrated or apologies for such denigration are reported. As the league's purpose says, Catholics should be able to participate fully in public life without discrimination. What should be made, therefore, of a contrasting *Catalyst* story, headlined "No to 'Life Partners'": "The Philadelphia/South Jersey chapter of the Catholic League . . . is supporting the efforts of the Archdiocese of Philadelphia in opposing a 'life partners' bill. The legislation seeks to put alternative lifestyles on the same legal, social and moral plane as the institution of marriage. The Philadelphia chapter placed an ad in *Catholic Standard and Times* urging Catholics to stand behind Cardinal Anthony Bevilacqua."[18] The Catholic League, it seems, not only guards *against* religious discrimination but *promotes* it as well. Justice Louis Brandeis's admonition still rings true: "The greatest dangers to liberty lurk in insidious encroachment by men of zeal, well-meaning but without understanding."[19]

Chapter 3

Public Religion Vis-à-Vis the Prophetic Role of Religion

James E. Wood, Jr.

In addressing the theme of "public religion," it is important to recall that the notion of "private" religion is a relatively modern concept and one primarily identified intellectually with the rise of modernity and historically with the American tradition of church and state. To the ancient world, and for many centuries, all of life and all of culture were viewed as sacred or religious. Conventions, customs, traditions, and taboos were all rooted in the sacred—that is, rooted in religious sanctions or prohibitions. Every important event, from birth to death, was solemnized by religious ceremonies (a pattern by no means unfamiliar in the public and state ceremonies of societies in the modern world). It is no exaggeration to say that the concept of public religion, not private religion, still prevails throughout most of the world today outside Communist countries.

From earliest history religion was a public matter—for the community as a whole and not the individual. Religion and culture were inextricably intertwined and, as religion developed from a tribal to a national stage, religious history was inseparable from what today would be called social and political history. This interdependence of all of life was expressed in the intimate and intricate relationship between kingship and priesthood.[1] Generally speaking, the religious head and political head of the community were one; the priest was a magistrate, and the magistrate was a priest. Religion was so thoroughly integrated into the nation-state as to constitute a religiopolitical system by which society was stabilized and governed. To be a king or chieftain meant that his was a sacred office, not merely one of civil or political authority, and that the office of priest was a political as well as a religious office. Consequently, distinctions between religious and civil institutions were nonexistent. The religious and the political were

fused in such a way as to be virtually inseparable. Within the structure of the nation or state was an integrated system in which ruler, clergy, political decrees,
tenets of faith, law, ethics, religious rites, and state rituals were all conjoined.
There was no place for any distinction between the sacred and the secular, between public and private religion.

In the ancient world, since the religious and political communities—the sacred
and the secular—were generally fused, or at least made to be inseparable, some
people have concluded that Israel was simply like her Near Eastern neighbors in
identifying the sacred with the secular, the religious with the political. This is,
however, to do violence to Israel's self-understanding as a nation. Although the
Israelites shared much in common with others in the ancient world in their view
of nationhood, they accomplished the integration of nationhood and the Kingdom of God in a very different way.[2] Nowhere was the unique character of the
nation of Israel more pronounced than in Israel's concept of kingship. Israelite
kings were not deified as in other parts of the ancient world, nor did they take the
part of deity in religious rituals. Indeed, the king was denied the right of priestly
functions. Nor was the faith of Israel directed toward making the genius of the
nation or the people the object of its worship. As a nation, Israel was seen by its
prophets and historians as repeatedly in rebellion against God. Far from being an
idealized tale of mythology, the historical account of Israel in Hebrew scriptures
is, in fact, a sorrowful and sordid tale of epic proportions. As has often been
noted, "Its historians and prophets told the truth about their people as have the
patriots of no other nation. The greatest heroes of Israel were at one and the same
time both sinners and heroes of faith."[3]

In a profound sense, the relationship of church and state has been historically
and theologically a problem peculiar to Christianity. The early history of Christianity was marked by conflict with the state, which came to view Christianity as
religio illicita, and so Christianity remained until the fourth century. The early
Christians were faced with an increasingly hostile state. With their resistance to
the demands of the state, Christians were repeatedly the victims of intense per-
secutions for their unwillingness to give the state their supreme allegiance and
obedience. Thus, from its roots in Judaism and the exigencies of its early history,
Christianity broke the traditional pattern of other religions, which were intimately identified with the public ceremonies and rituals of a culture, community,
or society. This traditional pattern of public religion, to be sure, also characterized much of the subsequent history of Christianity in the West, which for centuries came to be coterminous with Christendom. With the emergence of the
nation-state, some form of Christianity became the public religion of the nation,
expressed in the establishment of a state church, which came to embody the soul
of the nation and to be identified with its institutions and rulers, its society and
its people.

THE PARADOX OF AMERICA AS A SECULAR STATE AND A RELIGIOUS SOCIETY

With the founding of the United States, not only was a new pattern of church–state relations inaugurated, but the concept of the secular state also found historical expression for the first time in history. The emergence of the secular state in the formation of this republic was the inevitable result of a particular way of thinking about both the nature of the state and the nature of religion. The secular state, at least in the American experience, is one in which government is limited to the *sæculum* or temporal realm and the state is independent of ecclesiastical control—and, in turn, institutional religion is independent of state or political control. In the American experience, the state is denied jurisdiction over religious affairs, not because religious affairs are beneath the concerns of the state, but rather because, as the United States Supreme Court has affirmed, religious concerns are too high and "too holy" to be subject to popular sovereignty or the currently prevailing will of civil authorities.[4] It is a state that denies government the right to use religion for the accomplishment of political ends and denies religion the right to use government for the accomplishment of religious ends. It is a state in which there is a "benevolent neutrality" not only with respect to the various communities of faith but also between religion and irreligion, a state in which its citizens are neither advantaged nor disadvantaged because of their religion or religious beliefs. In the words of the Court, "The general principle deducible from the First Amendment and all that has been said by the Court is this: that we will not tolerate either governmentally established religion or governmental interference with religion. Short of those expressly proscribed governmental acts there is room for play in the joints productive of a benevolent neutrality which will permit religious exercise to exist without sponsorship and without interference."[5]

Because of the constitutional mandate of neutrality, the state is forbidden from consideration of religious doctrine and practice. As the Court affirmed more than 125 years ago, in what was its first major church–state case, *Watson v. Jones,* "In this country the full and free right to entertain any religious belief, to practice any religious principle, and to teach any religious doctrine which does not violate the laws of morality and property, and which does not infringe personal rights, is conceded to all. The law knows no heresy, and is committed to the support of no dogma, the establishment of no sect."[6] The adoption of the United States Constitution, with its absence of any reference to deity and only three references to religion (all negative), represented the founding of the nation as a secular state.[7]

Although the United States Supreme Court has repeatedly and forthrightly reaffirmed the *secular* character of the state (i.e., the government) and, therefore, has upheld the impermissibility of government sponsorship or support of religion, at the same time and on various occasions, it has gone out of its way to acknowledge the *religious* character of American society.[8] It is that religious character that has long been noted as a distinguishing feature of the United States. From its beginning, religion clearly played a formative role in American public life, notwithstanding the description of early America as having, according to Lyman Beecher, "the largest proportion of unchurched in Christendom."[9] Alexis de Tocqueville observed more than a century and a half ago, "There is no country in the world where the Christian religion retains a greater influence over the souls of men than in America."[10] A little less than a century later, G. K. Chesterton described America in the succinct phrase "The nation with the soul of a church," a phrase that some decades later would be used as the title of a book on religion in the United States by one of America's preeminent church historians, Sydney Mead.[11] In a recent article, Michael J. Perry appropriately observed that "the citizenry of the United States is one of the most religious—perhaps even the most religious—of the citizenries of the world's advanced industrial democracies."[12] It is this apparent paradox of America as a secular state and a religious society that has long attracted the attention of observers, both domestic and foreign, of American democracy.

Forty-five years ago, Reinhold Niebuhr wrote a perceptive analysis of the American republic to which he gave the provocative title *The Irony of American History.*[13] Nowhere is this irony more evident than in the role played by religion in a republic conceived and founded as a secular state. On the one hand, the important social and political role played by religion in American society has been widely recognized by both American and European observers throughout the nation's history. On the other hand, the United States has been frequently described as the oldest secular state and even as "the most thorough-going, if not the only truly secular state."[14] Some years after his book on American history, Niebuhr addressed this paradox in a volume of essays published under the title *Pious and Secular America,*[15] in which he argued that America was not only more secular than any other nation, but also more religious.

To almost anyone unacquainted with American history, such an observation would appear to be both incongruous and irreconcilable. Any characterization of America as a secular state would suggest to many, in the absence of any real acquaintance with American history or religion in the United States, that religion is largely limited to the private sphere and, therefore, largely isolated from the currents of American public life or the body politic: that religion is generally relegated to the essentially personal and private concerns of American citizens. Such an impression or inference, however, would be completely contrary to the reality of religion in the American experience and would most likely be held only by someone without a firsthand acquaintance with American society.

Although church–state separation, the institutional independence of church and state, has been and remains a constitutional and political reality in the United States, it would be difficult to conceive a nation in which there has been closer interpenetration of religion and society, including the involvement of organized religion in public affairs. Religion has been inextricably intertwined with America's nationhood—the formulation and enactment of its laws as well as its civil and political liberties. But the fact remains, even to this day, that any reference to a "pious and secular America" or the formative role of religion in a nation in which the concept of the secular state is constitutionally upheld would seem, at least at first glance, a contradiction in terms.

This paradox did not escape the notice of observers during the early history of this republic. Nineteenth-century visitors to America were impressed with the fact that here they found, on the one hand, a constitutional prohibition of an establishment of religion and the separation of church and state and, on the other hand, the unmistakable influence of religion on the public life of the republic. It was this paradox that prompted Alexis de Tocqueville, a French Catholic, "to inquire how it happened that the real authority of religion was increased by a state of things which diminished its apparent force." From individual members of the clergy, both Catholic and Protestant, he found that "they all attributed the peaceful dominion of religion in their country mainly to the separation of church and state." Tocqueville came to see that church–state separation also had a direct bearing on the influence of religion on American society and found that among Americans generally religion was regarded as "indispensable to the maintaining of republican institutions." Thus, "On my arrival in the United States," Tocqueville wrote,

the religious aspect of the country was the first thing that struck my attention, and the longer I stayed there, the more I perceived the great political consequences resulting from this new state of things. In France, I had almost always seen the spirit of religion and the spirit of freedom marching in opposite directions. But in America I found that they were intimately united and that they reigned in common over the country.

The paradox of a secular state and a religious society was expressed succinctly by Tocqueville as follows: "Religion in America takes no part in the government of society, but it must be regarded as the first of its political institutions."[16]

Writing in 1837, Francis Grund, a Bohemian, observed the pervasiveness of public religion in the life of the republic: "The religious habits of the Americans form not only the basis of their private and public morals, but have become so interwoven with their whole course of legislation that it would be impossible to change them without affecting the very essence of their government." Like Tocqueville, Grund found that to Americans religion was indissolubly linked with the life of the nation. "Religion presides over the councils," Grund wrote, "aids in the execution of the laws, and adds to the dignity of the judges."[17]

The fact that religion has had and continues to have a major influence on American society ought not to be viewed as incompatible with the concept of America as a secular state. As for more than a hundred years, the Establishment Clause has been repeatedly declared by the United States Supreme Court to mean the separation of church and state, America has been marked throughout its history by the closest interpenetration of religion and society. In the colonial period, the churches have been described as being "up to their steeples" in politics. Religion in America has never been confined to the private sphere or limited to its institutional expression (i.e., churches and synagogues), but is enshrined in the public life of the nation—its social reforms, its institutions, and even its laws—thus the phrase "the nation with the soul of a church."

One of the Supreme Court's most ardent church–state separationists, the late Associate Justice William O. Douglas, in a famous church–state case, declared, "We are a religious people whose institutions presuppose a Supreme Being. . . . Government may not finance religious groups nor undertake religious instruction nor blend secular and sectarian education nor use secular institutions to force one or some religion on any person. But we find no constitutional requirement which makes it necessary for government to be hostile to religion and throw its weight against efforts to widen the effective scope of religious influence."[18]

In the American experience, a secular government and a religious society are not contradictions. Rather, as one observer of American society very aptly expressed it: "It is basic to the American creed that a society can only be religious if religion and the state are radically separated, and that the state can only be free if society is basically a religious society."[19]

THE VISION OF A CHRISTIAN AMERICA AND A RELIGIOUS PUBLIC SQUARE

The vision of America as a Christian state, even without legal standing or majority support, has been tenaciously held throughout this nation's history, even to this day.[20] Although by no means new, the recent trend to denigrate the concept of America as a secular state and to deplore, in the words of Richard John Neuhaus, "the naked public square," results from a failure to distinguish between a secular state and a secular society, quite aside from the argument of a "naked" public square in America at the time of the book's publication in 1984, when the public square was permeated with religion.[21] As two scholars have recently written, "The truth of the historical matter is that religion is far more evident in public life today than it was at any time during the nineteenth century"; prior to the middle of the twentieth century, by and large, "the Supreme Court didn't have to consider possible violations of the establishment Clause, because the issue didn't come up. Cases arise now not because religion has been marginalized but because it is ubiquitous."[22] *The Naked Public Square* would have been a more appropriate title for the publication of a book in the last few decades of the nineteenth century, which constituted the high-water mark of the separation of church and state in America, rather than during the period of the Cold War, during which time the nation became more officially identified with God and witnessed a growing pattern of endorsement and sponsorship of religion from the White House on down to city hall. More than a decade later, the oft-repeated charge today of "the naked public square" is contrary to all empirical data available and, therefore, may be viewed as demonstrably false.

More than 120 religious offices or lobbies are to be found in Washington, D.C., to influence governmental policies at all levels, and similar offices in most state capitals to influence state legislatures; chaplains are provided to all branches of the armed forces, many state legislatures, the United States Congress, and many cities. Religious services are held at presidential and most gubernatorial inaugurals, and the Red Mass is held at the commencement of the Supreme Court's fall term. Approximately 99 percent of the members of Congress are identified with some community of faith. According to Americans for Religious Liberty, there are more than 1,840 Christian radio and television stations, more than 3,400 religious bookstores, more than 900 religious periodicals, and more than 200 reporters across the nation who are assigned to cover religious news—in addition to an extensive network of thousands of religious educational, social, and welfare institutions and programs carried by a wide range of America's religious denominations. A religious component has become a widely accepted part of America's public and political rituals. With respect to religion, America's public square is far from "naked."

In the 1950s, presidential prayer breakfasts were introduced; they gradually became an established practice not only for American presidents, but also for state governors and city mayors throughout the country. In 1954, Congress added the words "under God" to the pledge of allegiance, reasoning that "this would serve to deny the atheistic and materialistic concepts of communism with its attendant subservience of the individual."[23] In 1956, Congress established "In God We Trust" as the national motto, which passed both houses without a veto.[24] One author described the resurgence of religion in the officialdom of the nation's capital during the 1950s in a volume titled *Piety Along the Potomac*.[25] Religion became so prominent a part of America's political life and the public square as to produce a spate of books on the subject.[26] Meanwhile, Neuhaus's argument that the official doctrine of American church–state jurisprudence is that "there is no moral consensus in American life, that ours is a secular society," belies the language of the Court in numerous major church–state cases.[27] Although the Court has consistently and forthrightly identified this nation's government as secular, and therefore has held to the impermissibility of government sponsorship or sup-

port of religion, it has repeatedly gone out of its way to acknowledge the important role of religion in American society.

Nonetheless, the clamor for a public religion, theistic and reflective in some
sense of the hybrid usually identified with "Judeo-Christianity," has persisted
throughout American history.[28] Concurrently, unease over the concept of America as a secular state and the denial of any form of religious establishment or
religious identity for the state have been met with strong utterances of denuncia-
tion from the beginning of the nation's founding. After the adoption of the Constitution, many citizens found it to be profoundly disappointing, among other
reasons, because of its absence of any reference to deity, to God, or to Divine
Providence, let alone to Jesus Christ.[29] Within a few months of its adoption and
more than a year and a half before its ratification, it was proposed at a meeting
of Congregationalists "that some suitable Testimony might be borne against the
sinful omission in the late Federal Constitution in not looking to God for direction and of omitting the mention of the name of God in the Constitution.[30] The
Reverend John M. Mason of New York bemoaned that the Constitution made no
reference to God and did not even claim a religious foundation for the new nation. "Should the citizens of America be as irreligious as her Constitution," he
wrote, "we will have reason to tremble, lest the Governor of the universe, who
will not be treated with indignity, by a people any more than by individuals,
overturn from its foundations the fabric we have been rearing, and crush us to
atoms in the wreck."[31]

America's theocrats were quick to recognize the secular character accorded the
new republic by its Constitution. Indeed, the Reverend Samuel Austin declared
in 1811, the Constitution "is entirely disconnected from Christianity. It is not
founded on the Christian religion." Some, as the Reverend Samuel Taggart,
found the absence of any reference to Christ in the Constitution to be "a national
evil of great magnitude." Another minister, the Reverend Chauncey Lee,
lamented that "the Constitution has not the impress of religion upon it, not the
smallest recognition of the government['s] being of God."[32] The Reverend Jede-
diah Morse found the omission of God from the Constitution to mean that America, like Israel of old, was doomed.[33] It is "a great sin to have forgotten God in
such an important national instrument," proclaimed the Reverend George
Duffield, "and not to have acknowledged Him in that which forms the very
nerves and sinews of the political body."[34] Some, as the Reverend James Wilson,
castigated the founding fathers for reflecting "a degree of ingratitude, perhaps
without parallel," in drafting a constitution "in which there is not the slightest
hint of homage to the God of Heaven."[35]

Although most nineteenth-century theocrats, as in the twentieth century, accepted the wisdom of the separation of a particular church from the state, they
repeatedly reaffirmed their view of America as a Christian state, with a "mani-

fest destiny, divinely ordered."[36] The notion of the "secular state," or the separation of church and state, was viewed as antithetical to a "Christian" America. America's theocrats, past and present, not content with the winning of individual converts and the making of a Christian society, sought nothing less than a Christianization of the state.[37] They contended against the notion of the secular state and sought through various means to have America ruled as a "Christian state." To the theocrats, church–state separation never meant a repudiation of the concept of America as a Christian state. As Bela Bates Edwards expressed it, "Perfect religious liberty does not imply a repudiation of the concept of America as a Christian state."[38] In a famous fourth of July sermon delivered in Philadelphia in 1827, Ezra Stiles Ely expressed the hope of many theocrats. "I propose fellow citizens," said Ely, "a new sort of union, or, if you please, *a Christian party in politics.*" If Christians—Presbyterians, Methodists, Baptists, Episcopalians, and Congregationalists—would only unite at the polls, Ely declared, they "could govern every public election in our country. . . . We are a Christian nation: we have the right to demand that all our rulers in their conduct shall conform to Christian morality; and if they do not, it is the duty of Christian freemen to make a new and a better election."[39] Horace Bushnell and others throughout the nineteenth century expressed the hope that "at some fit time" an acknowledgment of God's sovereignty would be added to the Preamble of the Constitution.[40]

In 1863, in an effort to channel the concerns of many over the secular character of the Constitution and its omission of any reference to deity or to Christ, the National Reform Association was organized with representatives from eleven Protestant denominations. One of the Association's stated purposes was "to secure such an amendment to the Constitution of the United States as will declare the nation's allegiance to Jesus Christ and its acceptance of the moral laws of the Christian religion, and so indicate that this is a Christian nation, and place all the Christian laws, institutions, and usages of our government on an undeniable legal basis in the fundamental law of the land."[41]

The Association also petitioned the Congress to amend the preamble of the Constitution to begin with the words "We, the people of the United States, humbly acknowledging Almighty God as the source of all authority and power in civil government, the Lord Jesus Christ as the Ruler among the nations, His revealed will as the supreme law of the land, in order to constitute a Christian government."[42] The House Judiciary Committee in 1874 voted on the proposed amendment and recommended its rejection. A fundamental argument of the National Reform Association was based on the proposition of the "impossibility of State neutrality in religion and morals," an argument often used today in support of closer government cooperation with and accommodation of religion in public life. The dissolution of the Association did not occur until 1945, only to be succeeded by the establishment of a similar organization, known as the Christian

Amendment Movement, founded in 1946. The "amendment," supported by various evangelical conservative Protestants and introduced to the United States Senate in 1951, affirmed that "this nation devoutly recognizes the authority and law of Jesus Christ, Savior and Ruler of nations, through whom are bestowed the blessings of Almighty God."[43] On 28 October 1997, the House Judiciary Committee's Subcommittee on the Constitution approved a Freedom Amendment, which would insert for the first time a reference to "God" in the Constitution. Beginning with the words "To secure the people's right to acknowledge God according to the dictates of conscience," the amendment aims at allowing for government-endorsed religious speech, public school–sponsored prayer, and permitting of school vouchers and other public funds to religious groups that would otherwise be barred by the First Amendment's Establishment Clause.[44] The continued vision of America as a Christian state is largely based upon the premise that early America was Christian, a view not generally shared by historians. As one respected church historian, Franklin H. Littell, has written, "The whole image of early America as a 'Christian nation'. . . is a lie that must be struck down. . . . [I]n her early years as a nation she was overwhelmingly unchurched and heathen, regardless of pretensions and public claims."[45]

The presumption that a religious public square will in some way ameliorate many of America's moral and social ills and advance religion and morality in society is clearly not borne out in history. Rather, the pattern of the religious public square has generally served to symbolize, if not give credence to, an alliance between the religion and the state at the risk of profaning religion and sanctifying the state. Clearly the history of Christianity shows that, by and large, the culpability of the church has not lain primarily in its isolation from the public square, but rather in its intimate and repeated associations with power structures incompatible with the gospel. For centuries, whenever and wherever the church was allied with institutions of power, it became a conservative voice in defense of the status quo and an opponent of change and dissent. When allied with institutions of economic and political power, the church has almost always resisted social change and consequently has all too often been on the wrong side of economic, political, and social issues in human history. It was the church, when allied with the state, that for centuries opposed freedom of speech, freedom of press, freedom of religion, and a democratic government. When identified with the public square, public religion runs the risk of becoming a handmaiden of the state.

THE SECULAR STATE AND PUBLIC RELIGION

As indicated earlier, for many the very concept of the secular state and public religion would, at first glance, appear to be irreconcilable. Indeed, the secular state and public religion would be incompatible if by a secular state is meant not a state limited to the *sæculum* or temporal affairs, but a state committed to secularism, that is, a state that denies the reality of the nonphysical world and is hostile to all forms of religious faith and practice. At the same time, public religion that receives the endorsement and support of the state or maintains a formal alliance with the state is also irreconcilable with the secular state. Public religion has, in fact, been far more characteristic of the phenomenon of religion than private religion. In the light of the history of Christianity, a strong argument may be made that accommodation to the public square has been a far more dominant pattern and a far greater scandal in the history of the church than the privatization of religion and withdrawal from the world. In its explication of the Establishment Clause, the Supreme Court has declared that "its first and most immediate purpose rested on the belief that a union of government and religion tends to destroy government and to degrade religion. The history of governmentally established religion . . . showed that whenever government had allied itself with one particular form of religion, the inevitable result had been that it had incurred the hatred, disrespect and even contempt of those who held contrary beliefs."[46] The Court has repeatedly declared that the Establishment Clause means nothing less than the separation of church and state.[47] The Establishment Clause belongs conjointly to freedom of conscience and religion. This view was well expressed by Justice Sandra Day O'Connor, as follows:

The Establishment Clause prohibits government from making adherence to a religion relevant in any way to a person's standing in the political community. . . . [M]ore direct infringement is government endorsement or disapproval of religion. Endorsement sends a message to nonadherents that they are outsiders, not full members of the political community, and an accompanying message to adherents that they are insiders, favored members of the political community.[48]

Nevertheless, the question continues to arise: Does not "no establishment of religion" somehow restrict the role of religion in American public life? Even during the past decade, which has witnessed a resurgence of the involvement of religion in the body politic, nationwide polls conducted by the media have revealed that most Americans feel that religious leaders should stay out of politics entirely even if they feel strongly about certain political issues. It is not without significance that in church–state relations both religion clauses of the Constitution explicitly place prohibitions on government and none on religion: "Congress shall make no law respecting an establishment of religion or prohibiting the free exercise thereof." Religion is constitutionally free to engage in public affairs, in public political debates, and in the body politic. As Douglas Laycock has expressed it, "There is no conflict between free exercise and disestablishment. You have a right to freely exercise your own religion; [but] you have no right to use the organs of government in that exercise."[49] To put it another way, the Establishment

Clause prohibits endorsement and/or support of religion, and the Free Exercise Clause prohibits any coercion of religion.

Notwithstanding the Court's interpretation of the Establishment Clause to mean the separation of church and state, the courts have never denied the right of religion to be involved in public affairs or to engage in political speech.[50] Stephen Carter's plea for "a public square that does not restrict its access to citizens willing to speak in a purely secular language, but instead is equally open to religious and nonreligious argument" not only is plausible but has also been constitutionally upheld by the Supreme Court.[51] As one constitutional scholar recently wrote, "In a society that, like the United States, is overwhelmingly religious, it would not be acceptable to deprivilege religious arguments relative to atheistic ones."[52] He could have, perhaps, more appropriately said of the United States that it would not be acceptable to deprivilege religious arguments relative to *nonreligious* ones.

To do so would be in clear violation of the Free Exercise Clause, which is not a guarantee relative to belief, since no government can control or regulate, or even monitor, belief, but is a guarantee relative to religious *activity.* For example, the right "to petition the government," which in the most fundamental sense includes church lobbying, found explicit expression in the American Bill of Rights, along with the "free exercise of religion," "freedom of speech," "freedom of press," and "freedom of assembly." The right of petition is, of course, a fundamental tenet of democratic government. More than a century ago, the Court declared, "The very idea of government, republican in form, implies a right on the part of its citizens to meet peaceably for consultation in respect of public affairs and to petition for a redress of grievances." It is a right, the Court affirmed, that "existed long before the adoption of the Constitution of the United States."[53] As Chief Justice Charles Evans Hughes wrote in *Stromberg v. California,* "The maintenance of the opportunity for free political discussions to the end that government may be responsive to the will of the people and that changes may be obtained by lawful means, an opportunity essential to the security of the Republic, is a *fundamental* [italics added] principle of our Constitutional system."[54]

Public religion has thus been a part of the American experience from its beginning, long before the founding of this republic.[55] Efforts of religious leaders and religious communities even to influence legislation and public policy have been, in fact, a major feature of American political life. The American tradition of church and state has never meant the exclusion of religion from public life or the body politic. In addressing the subject of religion and the public square more than a decade ago, the *Williamsburg Charter,* signed by a broad representation of the nation's religious and public leaders, declared that in America there is to be "neither a naked public square where all religion is excluded, nor a sacred public square with any religion established or semi-established . . . [rather it] is a civil public square in which citizens of all religious faiths, or none, engage one another in continuing democratic dialogue."[56] Indeed, it may be persuasively argued that, so far as the American Constitution is concerned, religion is constitutionally protected to engage freely in American public life and to exercise the role of advocacy in public affairs. At least it may be said that the courts have never denied the right of the churches to participate actively in public life. Rather, without even questioning the constitutionality of the advocacy role of religion in public affairs, the Supreme Court unequivocally and explicitly affirmed this right in 1970, in *Walz v. Tax Commission of the City of New York.* In an eight-to-one decision, the Court declared: "Adherents of particular faiths and individual churches frequently take strong positions on public issues including, as this case reveals in the several brief *amici,* vigorous advocacy of legal or constitutional positions. *Of course* [italics added], churches as much as secular bodies and private citizens have that right."[57] Certainly, religious communities have claimed this right throughout the history of America, from the colonial period on down to the present. Eight years later, in *McDaniel v. Paty,* when the Court unanimously declared unconstitutional a Tennessee law barring clergy from state office, Justice William F. Brennan wrote:

The mere fact that a purpose of the Establishment Clause is to reduce or eliminate religious divisiveness or strife, does not place religious discussion, association, or political participation in a statute less preferred than rights of discussion, association and political participation generally. . . . The State's goal of preventing sectarian bickering and strife may not be accomplished by regulating religious speech and political association. . . . Religionists no less than members of any other group enjoy the full measure of protection offered speech, association and political activity generally. The Establishment Clause, properly understood, is a shield against any attempt by government to inhibit religion. . . . It may not be used as a sword to justify repression of religion or its adherents from *any aspect of public life* [italics added].[58]

The right of religion to enter the public square and the body politic has, of course, by no means gone unchallenged. The American philosopher Richard Rorty, for example, has written disapprovingly of public religion and the political role of religion in American life; Rorty advocates "privatizing religion— keeping it out of . . . 'the public square'" and maintains that "claims of religion need, if anything, to be pushed back still further, and . . . religious believers have no business asking for more public respect than they now receive."[59] Admittedly, the right of religion to engage in public affairs and to make political pronouncements has been, and continues to be, challenged by those within and without the communities of faith, but the fact remains that religion has been and remains an important part of American public life.[60]

Although the Court has declared that the First Amendment protects both religion and speech, it does so, the Court has said, "by quite different mechanisms. . . .

Speech is protected by insuring its full expression even when the government participates. . . . The method for protecting freedom of worship is quite the reverse. In religious debate or expression the government is not a prime participant. . . . [T]he Establishment Clause is a specific prohibition on forms of state intervention in religious affairs with no precise counterpart in the speech provisions."[61] For this reason, the Establishment Clause does place restraint on the use of religious speech by the state in the formulation of public policy and public law. There is, of course, always the question, particularly in the United States, with a secular government and a religiously pluralistic society, of the *appropriateness* and *political effectiveness* of using *religious* arguments in political speech. On numerous occasions, the Supreme Court has mandated that the Establishment Clause requires a "secular purpose." In a recent publication, *Religion in Politics: Constitutional and Moral Perspectives,* Michael Perry aptly states this test as follows: "Government may not make a political choice about the morality of human conduct unless a plausible secular rationale supports the choice."[62] For this reason, it has been argued that although the right of religion to engage in political speech and debate is undeniable, it is inappropriate for legislators and other government officials to present religious arguments in public political debates.[63] This is in no way, however, to call into question the constitutionality, at least for private citizens and religious communities, of the use of religious arguments in public political debates, including even the organizing of political movements or political parties.[64]

To be sure, religious arguments in political debate, especially when they are offered in supporting a nation's proclaimed "national interests," in advocating the diminution of the civil and religious rights of any of its citizens in deference to the sovereignty of the state, and in blindly justifying the nation's actions in time of war, easily run the risk of the subservience of religion to the state. Unfortunately, recent history is replete with examples of the conscription and capitulation of religion to serve national interests. In Japan, public religion, in the form of state Shinto, essentially became a cult of loyalty to the nation and its national institutions. It functioned primarily to serve the national interests of the nation. At present, the five public religions of China are all "Patriotic Associations," a phrase by which each is officially identified. Recently in France, a putative "liberal democracy," a 60 percent tax was levied on individual donations made by Jehovah's Witnesses because the tax administration ruled that the association is no longer to be recognized as a "worship association" because it "refuses to defend the nation, to take part in *public* life, to give blood transfusions to their minor children and that it . . . can disturb public order."[65]

"The Platform of German Christians" in 1932 provided explicit acknowledgment of the church's mission to serve the nation, but nowhere gave any expression to its mission to the world. Years later, in lamenting the loss of a prophetic voice by those German churches that used religious political speech to justify the national interests of a diabolical regime, Klaus Scholder wrote poignantly, "Truth may be painful for the church, but untruth is more so."[66] In the United States, it may well be argued that the growing alliance between the Religious Right and the political Right does not bode well for either religion or the body politic.

THE PROPHETIC ROLE OF PUBLIC RELIGION

Although public religion may serve a political purpose, namely, to sanctify the nation–state and its "national interests," a much greater purpose may be found in the prophetic role of religion—one far closer to the heart of authentic religion. To be sure, religion has served, and continues to serve, a prophetic role in American public life. Robin Lovin has recently emphasized that both Roman Catholic social teaching and Social Gospel traditions of Protestant Christianity have understood social involvement as essential to their faith.[67] Unfortunately, for many citizens the notion persists that the secular state with its corollary of the separation of church and state inevitably requires the privatization of religion and a denial of its prophetic role in society. Just how this link is made is difficult to comprehend, since the prophetic role of religion in society is rooted in an authentic and free exercise of religion that necessarily arises independently of government jurisdiction or popular sovereignty.

All too frequently it is assumed that to be a separationist in church–state relations is to be opposed to the role of religion in public affairs—that separation of church and state necessarily means the privatization of religion. Separationists are often charged with holding the view that religion should concern itself with only one's personal and private life. Some American writers have contributed to this confusion by falsely identifying the separation of church and state with the separation of religion from society and public affairs.

The truth is quite to the contrary, since separation of church and state makes possible a genuinely prophetic role of religion by freeing the church of any institutional dependence on or subservience to the state that might modify or mute its prophetic voice. In America, the institutional independence of church and state has been a natural ally of the prophetic role of religion in society and, therefore, has contributed enormously to the interpenetration of religion and society. It may well be argued that the institutional separation of church and state, as found in the Establishment Clause, provides constitutional protection for the prophetic role of religion in society. The vast array of social and welfare departments maintained by the churches and synagogues of America and the large network of church offices on public affairs in state capitals and the nation's capital are uniquely American phenomena and constitute a substantial involvement of religion in American public life.[68]

Nevertheless, there is a popular assumption that to subscribe to the separation of church and state is to embrace the view of religion's noninvolvement in public affairs and the body politic. The Baptist Joint Committee on Public Affairs, the United Methodist Church, the United Church of Christ, the Unitarian-Universalist Association, and the Union of American Hebrew Congregations, for example, all stand as a refutation of this assumption. Although most American Jewry has long strongly supported church–state separation in the United States, recent studies have continued to show that the Jewish community and Jewish organizations are perhaps the most involved of all major communities of faith on matters of political affairs and public policy.

The church that is relatively free of institutional alliances and entanglements with the state is one that is most favored to be able to carry out the prophetic role of religion in society through a free and authentic witness. Far from being a contradiction, the institutional separation of church and state makes genuine interaction between communities of faith and political society a living reality. To the degree that a church is allied with the institutions of the state—economic, political, or social—to that degree it is in bondage and its prophetic role is imperiled.

The prophetic role of religion requires a public religion, one that dares to stand with the secular. Gayraud S. Wilmore has perceptively stated the case by declaring that the church "has nowhere to stand except with the secular. It refuses to make an idol of religion. It makes common cause with the authentically secular without being permanently wedded to it. It believes in the secular not only as an instrument of divine providence and judgment but also as a partner with the church in the work of reconciliation . . . with man, the civil order and the structures of secular society."[69] Prophetic religion requires that religion be on the side of the oppressed, the dispossessed, the disinherited, and the discriminated.[70] Prophetic religion refuses to be a captive of any given culture, society, or socioeconomic class. It refuses to identify wealth and poverty in terms of moral superiority and inferiority. Prophetic religion seeks to advance justice and human rights for all members of society, even when in conflict with long established social patterns and traditions that run counter to these goals.

This prophetic role of religion enjoys its greatest legal protection where there is an institutional separation of religion and the state. As Ronald J. McAllister has written, "It is a mistake to assume that the separation of church and state will or should imply the separation of church and society."[71] To be sure, the prophetic role of religion in society means far more than mere involvement of religion in society. Furthermore, the church is called to be not a sectarian but a *public* witness to the Gospel.[72] "To be effective in the public square, religion need not and should not be sectarian in nature."[73] The prophetic role of religion necessarily calls into question the status of society as it is or sees itself to be. The prophetic role is necessarily to be about the business of questioning the established order, refusing to sanctify traditions not in harmony with the norms of one's faith, advancing justice, and promoting the general welfare of society. The prophetic role of religion is not to be found in the advocacy of class conflict, economic elitism, nuclear arms buildup, and American nationalism. To make religion a tool of social privilege and power, a widespread feature of religion in America, is a denial of the prophetic role of religion in society.

It must be remembered that religion is almost always accorded some recognition and even the blessing of the state, albeit the totalitarian state, as long as religion is subservient to and supports the national interests and public policies of that state. The point being made here is that religion may be tolerated and even patronized in the totalitarian state or any nation-state as long as it assumes a subservient role, one that is supportive of the declared national interests and stated policies. It is only when the prophetic role of religion is exercised, calling into question the declared national interests and policies of the state, that the right of communities of faith to be involved in society is most likely to be challenged and even denounced by the state, whether totalitarian or democratic. The simple truth is that the separation of church and state is the means by which the prophetic role of religion may be constitutionally protected and upheld.

The prophetic role of religion today is often threatened, even in the most liberal democracies, by what is most often called the state's "national interests." The notion of national interests has widely become the supreme value in the formulation of both domestic and foreign policy. Religion itself is readily exploited, wherever possible, to serve whatever the nation's leaders deem to be those interests, even on occasions when they may be clearly in conflict with the very tenets of the religious traditions themselves. The compromise of religion to serve political ends may be coerced as the price to be paid for social acceptance or for certain financial or political favors from the state. The accommodation may also be the result of the manipulation of religion to aid in the accomplishment of national goals and priorities, to which any national socially established church is particularly vulnerable. In any case, the consequence is the subordination of religion to the self-interests of the state, an all too familiar phenomenon in the history of religion and in the contemporary world.

Admittedly, the proclivity of virtually all modern nation-states, even the most democratic ones, is to seek the support of religion for their policies in both national and international affairs, on behalf of war and of peace, according to the self-interests of the state. In the case of authoritarian and totalitarian governments, religion's obedience to the state is generally demanded and its right of dissent is expressly denied, depending on the degree to which the government assumes absolute and complete control. All governments, of whatever type, encourage and readily welcome the church's support. Following his detailed study of the churches and the Third Reich, Scholder observed that "the important thing is . . . to recognize not so much the goals of a political movement as how it de-scribes its opponents."[74] In both politics and religion, the right to dissent is the right to be free.

Even in those countries where the churches are by law prohibited from speaking out on social and political issues, the law does not apply when the churches speak out in support of government policy or the state's "national interests." The constitution of the Soviet Union, for example, expressly forbade the involvement of the churches in addressing social or political concerns. Nevertheless, the churches' pronouncements and sponsorship of public rallies on peace, when favored by the Kremlin, were warmly welcomed by the government, and even encouraged. The lesson is clear: Governments welcome the support of religion, but view with concern, if not alarm, those expressions of involvement in opposition to government policy in national or international affairs.

For the churches to dissent from what the nation's leaders declare to be the "national interests" is for the churches to risk political disfavor, even reprisals, and to have their right to speak out on public affairs challenged as inappropriate and even unpatriotic. Assaults on the churches' claim of their catholicity and their divine obligation to speak out on national and international affairs when in conflict with the stated "national interests" of the United States, for example, are ominous signs of an assumed superiority of national sovereignty over the churches.

This is not to suggest that the church has a blueprint for the ordering of national and international affairs, but that for the church to be the church it cannot withdraw from the world or be under the control of the state.[75] At the same time, for the state to be the state it cannot make absolute claims in the political arena as to its sovereignty. All political decisions are, at best, approximate and provisional. Nor can the church define its task in such purely theological terms that it ignores crucial issues facing all humanity—freedom and justice, oppression and poverty, peace and war, and human rights and human worth.

In 1945, Karl Barth, who more than a decade earlier had been largely responsible for the wording of the Barmen Declaration, in which he denied in general theological terms that the church could allow its message to be determined by the state, wrote a letter to the German theologians who were prisoners of war, as follows: "I want to confess to all of you that if I reproach myself for anything in connection with the years that I spent in Germany it is that . . . I concentrated purely on my task in theology and the church. . . . I should have warned not only implicitly, but explicitly; not only privately, but also publicly."[76]

Separation of church and state or institutional independence between church and state must not mean that the churches leave the state to itself and its national interests, or ignore the state's claim of final authority or absolute sovereignty over human affairs. Unfortunately, in many countries in both the East and the

West, it is assumed that for the church to be an authentic participant in society, the church must be loyal and pliant to putative national interests. To do so, the church fails to be the church and thereby surrenders its real mission in the world. By being faithful to its mission and inclusive in its witness, the public church stands to make a substantial contribution to public life. In the final analysis, the public church in its work and witness must, however, take responsibility for its actions and decisions in public affairs, as to both their aims and their consequences, and hold itself accountable in fulfilling its public vocation in the world on behalf of freedom, justice, peace, and human rights for all.

Is There a Common American Culture? Diversity, Identity, and Morality in American Public Life

Robert N. Bellah

This chapter is a revised and expanded version of a talk I gave at the American Academy of Religion annual meeting in the fall of 1997; the title "Is There a Common American Culture?" was assigned to me by the convener of the session. I began by asking the question, not whether there is a common American culture, but rather how is it that a plenary session of the American Academy of Religion is devoted to this question in a society with so powerful and monolithic a common culture as ours? The answer, I said, is obvious: It has become part of the common culture to ask whether there is a common culture in America.

Martin Marty has already referred to K. Anthony Appiah, Professor of Afro-American Studies and Philosophy at Harvard; in his review of Nathan Glazer's *We Are All Multiculturalists Now* (whose very title makes the point), Appiah quotes Glazer as saying, "The Nexis data base of major newspapers shows no reference to multiculturalism as late as 1988, a mere 33 items in 1989, and only after that a rapid rise—more than 100 items in 1990, more than 600 in 1991, almost 900 in 1992, 1200 in 1993, and 1500 in 1994."[1] Appiah adds, "When it comes to diversity it seems we all march to the beat of a single drummer."[2] There is something very congenial to multiculturalism in common American culture, but such congeniality is not to be assumed as natural or shared in all societies today. It is worth looking at the contrasting case of France. Rodney Benson, a graduate student in sociology at Berkeley, is writing a most interesting dissertation, which, among other things, compares the fate of multiculturalism in France and the United States. Benson describes a nascent French multiculturalism of the late 1970s and early 1980s as ultimately being rejected by virtually the entire ideological spectrum in favor of a universalistic republicanism in the late 1980s, just when multiculturalism in the United States was taking off. Why American culture has been so singularly receptive to multiculturalism as an ideology is a point to which I will return.

But first, a sociological point about why there not only is but has to be a common culture in America: Culture does not float free of institutions. A powerful institutional order will carry a powerful common culture. An example of just how important this relation between culture and institutions is comes from the recent reunification of Germany. In the last days of the German Democratic Republic the protesters chanted, *Wir sind ein Volk,* and the chant stirred euphoria among West Germans as well. But the painful and unexpected experience of living together, as made vivid to me by an outstanding 1997 Harvard doctoral dissertation by Andreas Glaeser, using the integration of East and West German police officers into a unified police force in Berlin as a microcosm, showed that they were not, after all "ein Volk," but indeed *zwei.* It wasn't just that the *Ossies* and the *Wessies* had different views on common problems; they had different and to some degree mutually unintelligible ways of thinking about the world altogether. Forty-five years of radically different institutional orders had created two cultures, which to this day are very far from united, although the experience of a unified institutional order will, almost certainly, though not without time and pain, ultimately reunite them.[3]

The United States, surely, has an exceptionally powerful institutional order. The state in America, even though it is multileveled and, to a degree, decentralized, has an enormous impact on all our lives. For example, the shift in marriage law in the late 1960s and early 1970s toward "no-fault divorce" was a response to but also an impetus for the emergence of "divorce culture" in America as a serious competitor to "marriage culture." The state is even responsible to a degree for the construction of multiculturalism through the little boxes that must be checked on myriad forms. Haven't you ever been tempted to check them all or to leave them all empty? If the state intrudes in our lives in a thousand ways, the market is even more intrusive. There is very little that Americans need that we can produce for ourselves anymore. We are dependent on the market not only for goods but for many kinds of service. Our cultural understanding of the world is shaped every time we enter a supermarket or a mall. I taught a senior seminar of about twenty students in the spring of 1997, roughly divided into one-fourth Asian American, one-fourth Hispanic, one-fourth African American, and one-fourth Anglo. What was remarkable was how easily they talked because of how much they shared. Beyond the ever-present state and market, they shared the immediate experience of coping with a vast state university, with its demands and its incoherence.

Education, which is linked largely though not exclusively to the state, and television (and increasingly the Internet), linked to the market, are enormously powerful purveyors of common culture, socializers not only of children but of all of us most of our lives. Not only are we exposed from infancy to a monoculture, we are exposed to it monolingually. The cultural power of American English is overwhelming, and no language, except under the most unusual circumstances, has ever been able to withstand it, and that is what makes the English Only movement such a joke. As Appiah notes, 90 percent of California-born Hispanic children of immigrant parents have native fluency in English, and in the next generation only 50 percent of them still speak Spanish. One more generation and you can forget about Spanish. When third-generation Asian Americans come to college they have to learn Chinese or Japanese in language classes just like anyone else—they don't bring those languages with them. Appiah contrasts our society with his own experience growing up in Ghana, where there were three languages spoken in the household: English, Twi, and Navrongo. "Ghana," he writes, "with a population smaller than that of New York State, has several dozen languages in active daily use and no one language that is spoken at home—or even fluently understood—by a majority of the population."[4] Ghana is multilingual and therefore multicultural, in a way that we, except first-generation immigrants, have never been. When language, which is the heart of culture, goes, then so, in any deep sense, does cultural difference. I don't say identity, which is something I will come back to, but *culture*. Serious multicultural education would begin by teaching native English speakers a second language, but that, unlike in most of the rest of the world, almost never happens in the United States. The halfhearted effort to teach Spanish in California public schools produces very few native English speakers with a secondary fluency in Spanish. Why don't most Americans speak another language? Because we don't have to—everyone in the world speaks English, or so we think. Tell me about multiculturalism. (The truth is that American culture and American English are putting their stamp on every other culture in the world today.)

There are exceptions, though they are statistically small, but I had better talk about them. Enclaves of genuine cultural difference, centered on a language different from English, can persist, or even emerge, under special conditions: where socioeconomic status is low and residential segregation is effective. A particularly poignant example is the emergence among one of the oldest groups of English speakers in America, African Americans, of enclaves of Black English dialects in a few inner cities in the northeastern United States that are mutually unintelligible with standard American English. This can happen under conditions of hypersegregation where opportunities to participate in the larger society are almost completely denied. Native American languages survive on a few reservations, though many are dying out, even with strenuous efforts to maintain them. Since there is much less hypersegregation of Hispanics or Asians than of Blacks, enclaves of Spanish, or Korean, or other Asian languages have the generational transience of, say, Polish or Italian a hundred years ago.

If I am right, there is an enormously powerful common culture in America, and it is carried predominantly by the market and the state and by their agencies of socialization: television and education. What institutions might withstand that pressure and sustain genuine cultural difference? In simpler societies kinship and religious communities might do so, but in our society families and churches or synagogues are too colonized by the market and the state to provide much of a buffer. They may give a nuance, an inflection, to the common culture, but families and even religious communities are almost always too fragile to provide a radical alternative. Nevertheless such nuances and inflections are important, not only in their own right, but also because they can provide the wedge through which criticism of the common culture, and the possibility of altering it, can occur.

What, then, is the content of this common culture? If we realize that the market and the state in America are not and have never been antithetical, and that the state has had the primary function, for conservatives and liberals alike, of maximizing market opportunities, I believe I can safely borrow terminology from *Habits of the Heart* and say that a dominant element of the common culture is what we called utilitarian individualism. In terms of historical roots, this orientation can be traced to a powerful Anglo-American utilitarian tradition going back at least as far as Hobbes and Locke, although it operates today quite autonomously, without any necessary reference to intellectual history. Utilitarian individualism has always been moderated by what we called expressive individualism, which has its roots in Anglo-American Romanticism, but which has picked up many influences along the way from European ethnic, African American, Hispanic, and Asian influences. Here, too, the bland presentism of contemporary American culture obliterates its own history. Our Anglo students do not come to college with a deep knowledge of Jane Austen or Nathaniel Hawthorne any more than our Japanese American students bring a knowledge of Lady Murasaki or Natsume Soseki. What they bring, they bring in common: *Oprah Winfrey, ER, Seinfeld,* Nike, Microsoft, the NBA, and the NFL. If the common culture is predominantly Euro-American or, more accurately, Anglo-American, in its roots, the enormous pressure of the market economy and the mass media and mass education oriented to it obliterates the genuine heritage of Anglo-American, European, African, and Asian culture with equal thoroughness.

And yet, and yet, nestled in the very core of utilitarian and expressive individualism is something very deep, very genuine, very old, very American, something we did not quite see or say in *Habits*. And the core of that something is religious. In *Habits* we quoted a famous passage in Tocqueville's *Democracy in America:* "I think I can see the whole destiny of America contained in the first Puritan who landed on those shores."[5] Then we went on to name John Winthrop, following Tocqueville's own predilection, as the likeliest candidate for being that first Puritan. Now I am ready to admit, although regretfully, that we, and Tocqueville, were probably wrong. That first Puritan who contained our whole destiny might have been, as we also half intimated in *Habits,* Anne Hutchinson, but the stronger candidate, because we know so much more about him, is Roger Williams.

THE SECTARIAN ROOTS OF AMERICAN MULTICULTURALISM

Roger Williams, banished from the Massachusetts Bay Colony by John Winthrop, founder of Providence and of the Rhode Island Colony, was, as everyone knows, a Baptist. The Baptists in seventeenth-century New England were a distinct minority, but they went on to become, together with other sectarian Protestants, a majority in American religious culture from the early nineteenth century. As Seymour Martin Lipset has recently pointed out, we are the only North Atlantic society whose predominant religious tradition is sectarian rather than that of an established church.[6] I think this is something enormously important about our culture and that it has, believe it or not, a great deal to do with why our society is so hospitable to the ideology, if not the reality, of multiculturalism.

What was so important about the Baptists, and other sectarians such as the Quakers, was the absolute centrality of religious freedom, of the sacredness of individual conscience in matters of religious belief. We generally think of religious freedom as one of many kinds of freedom, many kinds of human rights, first voiced in the European Enlightenment and echoing around the world ever since. But Georg Jellinek, Max Weber's friend, and, on these matters, his teacher, published a book in 1895, *Die Erklärung der Menschen- und Bürgerrechte,* translated into English in 1901 as *The Declaration of the Rights of Man and of Citizens,* which argued that the ultimate source of all modern notions of human rights is to be found in the radical sects of the Protestant Reformation, particularly the Quakers and Baptists. Of this development Weber writes:

Thus the consistent sect gives rise to an inalienable personal right of the governed as against any power, whether political, hierocratic or patriarchal. Such freedom of conscience may be the oldest Right of Man—as Jellinek has argued convincingly, at any rate it is the most basic Right of Man because it comprises all ethically conditioned action and guarantees freedom from compulsion, especially from the power of the state. In this sense the concept was as unknown to antiquity and the Middle Ages as it was to Rousseau.[7]

Weber then goes on to say that the other Rights of Man were later joined to this basic right, "especially the right to pursue one's own economic interests, which includes the inviolability of individual property, the freedom of contract, and vocational choice."[8] I will have to return to the link to economic freedom, but first I want to talk about the relation between the sectarian notion of the sacredness of conscience and what we mean by multiculturalism today, starting with the Baptist Roger Williams.

It is worth remembering that one of the sources of Williams's problems was his unhappiness with John Winthrop's assertion that the Massachusetts Bay colonists were building "a city upon a hill," because, in Williams's view, it was *somebody else's hill!* The hill belonged to the Native Americans, and if the other Puritans were inclined to overlook that, Roger Williams was not.

When Williams was banished from Massachusetts Bay in January 1636, he probably would not have survived the winter in Rhode Island without the "courtesy" of the Indians, with whom he had, not surprisingly, an excellent relationship. Of this courtesy he wrote, in his charming doggerel:

> The courteous pagan shall condemn
>   Uncourteous Englishmen,
> Who live like foxes, bears and wolves,
>   Or lion in his den.
>
> Let none sing blessings to their souls,
>   For that they courteous are:
> The wild barbarians with no more
>   Than nature go so far.
>
> If nature's sons both wild and tame
>   Humane and courteous be,
> How ill becomes it sons of God
>   To want humanity.[9]

Williams would have nothing to do with the idea that Europeans were superior to Indians. He wrote, "Nature knows no difference between Europe and Americans [that is, Native Americans] in blood, birth, bodies, God having of one blood made all mankind (Acts 17) and all by nature being children of wrath (Ephesians 2)."[10] And he admonished his fellow Englishmen:

> Boast not, proud English, of thy birth and blood,
>   Thy brother Indian is by birth as good.
> Of one blood God made him and thee and all,
>   As wise, as fair, as strong, as personal.
>
> By nature, wrath's his portion, thine no more,
>   Till grace his soul and thine restore.
> Make sure thy second birth, else thou shalt see
>   Heaven ope to Indians wild, but shut to thee.[11]

We know that the passage of the Virginia act for religious freedom and of the First Amendment to the Constitution (and it was no accident, following Jellinek and Weber, that it was indeed the *First* Amendment), of which I will have more to say in a moment, depended on an alliance of Enlightenment Deists like Jefferson and Madison, and sectarians, largely Baptists. The fundamental Baptist position on the sacredness of conscience relative to government action is brought out in a passage in Lipset's *The First New Nation.* The idea must seem quaint to us today, but in 1810 Congress passed a law decreeing that mail should be delivered on Sundays. In 1830 a Senate committee reported negatively on a bill to abolish Sunday mail delivery. The report, written by Richard Johnson, a Kentucky senator and an active Baptist leader, argued that laws prohibiting the government from providing service on Sunday would be an injustice to irreligious people or non-Christians and would constitute a special favor to Christians. The report spelled out these principles:

> The constitution regards the conscience of the Jew as sacred as that of the Christian, and gives no more authority to adopt a measure affecting the conscience of a solitary individual than that of a whole community. . . . If Congress shall declare the first day of the week holy, it will not satisfy the Jew nor the Sabbatarian. It will dissatisfy both and, consequently, convert neither. . . . It must be recollected that, in the earliest settlement of this country, the spirit of persecution, which drove the pilgrims from their native homes, was brought with them to their new habitations; and that some Christians were scourged and others put to death for no other crime than dissenting from the dogmas of their rulers. . . .
>
> If a solemn act of legislation shall in *one* point define the God or point out to the citizen one religious duty, it may with equal propriety define *every* part of divine revelation and enforce *every* religious obligation, even to the forms and ceremonies of worship; the endowment of the church, and the support of the clergy. . . .
>
> It is the duty of this government to affirm to *all*—to the Jew or Gentile, Pagan, or Christian—the protection and advantages of our benignant institutions on *Sunday,* as well as every day of the week.[12]

Phillip E. Hammond's remarkable book *With Liberty for All: Freedom of Religion in the United States* details the vicissitudes of this sectarian Protestant concern for the sacredness of the individual conscience as it was embodied in the First Amendment to the Constitution and has been given ever wider meaning by the judicial system, especially the Supreme Court, ever since. For Hammond, the key move was to extend the sacredness of conscience from religious belief to any seriously held conviction whatever. A key moment in this transformation was the Court's decision to extend the right of conscientious objection to military service to those whose beliefs were not in any traditional sense religious, but were fervently held nonetheless. Individual conviction and conscience have become the standards relative to which even long-established practices can be overturned. Hammond argues that *Roe v. Wade* is an example of the extension of this principle, and that its logic will ultimately lead to the legitimation of gay marriage. In the course of the extension of the sacredness of individual conscience from religion to the entire range of belief, Hammond argues, the sacred core of the *conscience collective,* the very sacred center of our society, what might even be called our civil religion, has moved from the churches to the judiciary. Whether we need to go that far with Hammond could be argued, but he has surely uncovered something very important about our society, something deeper than utilitarian or expressive individualism, the sacredness of the individual conscience, the individual person. And I might add as an aside that today, in a city like San Francisco, where you can probably do almost anything within reason and still not raise an eyebrow, it is all ultimately thanks to the Baptists, even though some Baptists today find it rather upsetting!

MISUNDERSTANDING CULTURE

It is with this background in mind that I think we can understand why multiculturalism as an ideology is so appealing to Americans today, but why the emphasis on culture is so misleading. A common culture does not mean that we are all the same. Common cultures are normally riven with argument, controversy, and conflict. Those who imagine that in *Habits of the Heart* we were arguing for homogeneous "communities" languishing in bland consensus could hardly have gotten us more wrong. Difference between communities (and we must also remember that there are differences within communities, starting with the family, which someone recently defined as "the place we go to fight"), even when the cultural differences between them are remarkably thin, can give rise to significant differences in identity. I might point out that the "racial conflict" that was recently most violent at Berkeley High School and in many other schools in California was not between Asian Americans and African Americans or whites and Hispanics but between American-born Hispanics and Hispanic immigrants. The ideology of multiculturalism tells us that their "culture" is the same: The reality of violence tells us that their identity isn't. Identity is not the same thing as culture, but it can be just as important. Remember Bosnia, where Serbs, Croats, and Muslims share a common language and probably 99 percent of their culture, but where the memory of ancestral religion, in a highly secularized society, has led to murderous conflicts of quite recently constructed political identities.

It is worth pursuing this issue a bit as it is played out in our society. There is a great confusion in both language and thought that arises when we use culture and identity interchangeably, and sometimes add race to the same explosive mix. I would like to give some examples of current confusions of what I believe should be carefully distinguished. William Finnegan in a fascinating 1997 article describes the hunger for identity but the shallowness of cultural resources for it in Antelope

Valley, a recently developed suburb of Los Angeles. For example, he mentions a girl named Mindy who became a Mormon but before that had "wanted to become Jewish. But that had turned out to be too much work. Becoming a Mormon was relatively easy. All this was before Mindy got addicted to crystal methamphetamine and became a Nazi, in the ninth grade."[13] Finnegan's article concludes:

Martha Wengert, a sociologist at Antelope Valley College, said, "This area has grown so fast that neighborhoods are not yet communities. Kids are left with this intense longing for identification." Gangs, race nationalism, and all manner of "beliefs" arise from this longing. I thought of Debbie Turner's inability to comprehend Mindy's enthusiasm for the likes of Charles Manson and Adolph Hitler. "The kids reach out to these historical figures," Dr. Wengert said. "But it's through TV, through comic books, through word-of-mouth. There are no books at home, no ideas, no sense of history."[14]

These identities that lack any cultural depth are nonetheless powerful enough to be literally matters of life and death for the young people involved. My point is that though Mindy's identity swung between would-be Jewish, to Mormon, to Nazi, and that these identities could be very important to her and indeed to her fate, her *culture,* in any meaningful sense of the word, was suburban Los Angeles.

Another example that suggests just how confusing these issues can be comes to me from a Chinese American graduate student in the sociology department at Berkeley. This student lives in a housing project in inner city Oakland, partly because he has been a volunteer in the social outreach program at a nearby church, a housing project largely inhabited by immigrants from Cambodia. In a paper he wrote about his observation of the young people living in the project, he found that these youths of Cambodian descent dressed and spoke like African Americans, were quite accomplished in black music and dance, and had, in general, assimilated into what could locally be called "black culture." Since the Oakland School District has a majority of African American students, this was not terribly surprising: What the children of immigrants have always done in America is to assimilate to American culture, and in this case the available American culture was black. On the other hand, my student found that the attitude of these young people to traditional Cambodian culture was distinctly ambivalent, with a lot of hostility thrown in, again as has so often been the case with immigrant children. They had little interest in traditional Cambodian ceremonies, which they didn't understand, having little fluency in the language. And they vigorously resisted some of the assumptions of their elders: for example, that young women should marry early, with older men chosen by their parents. Nothing in the culture into which they were assimilating justified that. To add to the complexity, their African American and white peers referred to these young people as "Chinese," on the basis of a superficial judgment of their looks. Now, one thing Cambodians are not is Chinese. Neither in language nor in culture is there a link to China; Cambodian culture is overwhelmingly linked to that of India. Nevertheless, in their distinct minority situation, with gangs often organized along racial lines, these Cambodian youth were ready to make alliances with Chinese Americans or any other groups of Asian descent that would add to their own strength, and in so doing, though they could not think of themselves as Chinese, they could think of themselves as "Asian Americans." And finally, the public school, in an effort to respect cultural diversity, taught that the Cambodian culture that these students were presumed to have had to be respected by others. The confusion of culture, genes, and identity, all of which in fact were varying independently, could hardly be more total.

Finally, a personal anecdote: In 1970 at the time of the Third World strike at Berkeley demanding the establishment of an Ethnic Studies department, I was teaching a course on Japanese society when, near the end of a lecture, some students burst into the back of the classroom and started shouting at me. I recognized the most vocal of them as a graduate student in my own department. He yelled at me, "You shouldn't be teaching this course. This is a course in yellow studies, and you should be teaching white studies." He turned to an undergraduate student of obvious Asian extraction sitting in my class and said, "He should be teaching this class, not you." I spoke to the undergraduate, who I had no reason to think was Japanese American, since I knew there were at least as many Chinese American students in the class as Japanese Americans, and asked him, "Do you speak Japanese?" His answer was "No." "Do you know Japanese history?" Again, "No." "Do you know Japanese literature?" "No." So I asked the graduate student, "Why do you think this student should teach the course?" He turned and left the room. Now, I am old enough to have lived through World War II and I knew a good bit about Nazi race theory, and I had just gotten a taste of it from this self-styled Berkeley Leftist. Fortunately the term "yellow studies" never caught on, and this experience has given me an indelible dislike of the idea of "white studies," which I gather has a flickering half-life at present.

Let me say parenthetically that the widespread use of the word *race* in current American discourse is highly problematic. In the popular mind the term has an inevitable biological meaning: Think of the widespread response to the book *The Bell Curve.* Yet as a biological term it has been completely exploded. Russell Stevens in a recent review of a book on the African origins of modern humanity notes its "vehement assertion that the classical concept of race in humans is no longer tolerable, and that, to the contrary, the entire species is remarkably alike."[15] Biologically, race doesn't matter. As a cultural construct, or, better yet, as a focus of identity, race does matter. Where such distinctions are not made, the use of the word *race* can easily become, whether from the Right or the Left, racist.

To make sense of all this and to see how the issues of diversity and identity relate to morality I would like to turn to one of my few living heroes, Vaclav Havel. In a speech he gave to the Czech Parliament on December 9, 1997, he said:

We often talk about the identity of a state or a nation or a society and more than one opponent of European integration has ranted on about national identity and tried to engender
fear of its loss. Most who speak this way subconsciously understand identity as something
predestined, something genetic, almost an identity of blood—that is, something over which
we have no influence or control. This notion of identity is thoroughly discredited. Identity
is, above all, an accomplishment, a particular work, a particular act. Identity is not something separate from responsibility, but on the contrary, is its very expression.[16]

I don't think Havel's words should be read as simply advocating what is called
"social constructivism" these days. Havel knows that fate and blood are among
the things we have to work with in the act of identity. Culture, however, which is
deeply plural, is not a matter of fate or blood, but our deepest resource for the responsible accomplishment of identity. In other words, in the modern world multiculturalism is inevitably within each of us, not just between us. What that
Berkeley graduate student didn't realize is that in my study of East Asian culture
I had internalized aspects of Confucianism and Mahayana Buddhism, made them
part of my identity. It was James Peacock who, in his review of *Habits of the
Heart,* pointed out that it was a book that could have been written only by someone with a deep exposure to East Asian culture—and he perhaps didn't realize
that another of my coauthors, Richard Madsen, was a longtime China specialist.
Although Bellah is a Scottish name and I was reared in the Presbyterian church,
my deepest identity as a Christian came not from genes or upbringing, but from
a long struggle as an adult to understand what Christianity could possibly mean
in today's world, something with which my early Sunday School experience
didn't give me a lot of help. To let one's identity be decided by alleged friends or
alleged foes, though that is hard to resist in situations of internecine conflict like
Bosnia's, is finally morally irresponsible. In America to let one's identity be decided by being placed in one of five and only five boxes is irresponsible indeed.
That is to turn "multiculturalism" into something that is finally not cultural at all,
but a pure form of identity politics.

INDIVIDUALISM

And yet in America the rise of identity politics on a local or a national scale
probably signifies something else, something much closer to the core of what I
am arguing is our real common culture. Again, Anthony Appiah has put it well:

But if we explore these moments of tension [between groups in contemporary Amer-
ica] we discover an interesting paradox. The growing salience of race and gender as social
irritants, which may seem to reflect the call of collective identities, is a reflection, as
much as anything else, of the individual's concern for dignity and respect. As our society
slouches on toward a fuller realization of its ideal of social equality, everyone wants to be
taken seriously—to be respected, not "dissed." Because on many occasions disrespect still

flows from racism, sexism, and homophobia, we respond, in the name of all black people, all women, all gays, as the case may be. . . . But the truth is that what mostly irritates us in these moments is that we, as individuals, feel diminished.

And the trouble with appeal to cultural difference is that it obscures rather than diminishes this situation. It is not black culture that the racist disdains, but blacks. There is no conflict of visions between black and white cultures that is the source of racial discord. No amount of knowledge of the architectural achievements of Nubia or Kush guarantees respect for African-Americans. No African-American is entitled to greater concern because he is descended from a people who created jazz or produced Toni Morrison. Culture is not the problem, and it is not the solution.[17]

If the problem is disrespect for the dignity of the person, then the solution is to go back to that deepest core of our tradition, the sacredness of the conscience and person of every individual. And that is what a great deal of the ideology of multiculturalism is really saying: We are all different. We are all unique. Respect that.

But there is another problem, a very big problem, and its solution is hard to envision. Just when we are moving to an ever greater validation of the sacredness of the individual person, our capacity to imagine a social fabric that would hold individuals together is vanishing. This is in part because of the fact that the religious individualism that I have been describing is linked to an economic individualism that, ironically, knows nothing of the sacredness of the individual. Its only standard is money, and the only thing more sacred than money is more money. What economic individualism destroys, and what our kind of religious individualism cannot restore, is solidarity, a sense of being members of the same body. In most other North Atlantic societies a tradition of an established church, however secularized, provides some notion that we are in this thing together, that we need each other, that our precious and unique selves aren't going to make it all alone. That is a tradition singularly weak in our country, though Catholics and some high church Protestants have tried to provide it. The trouble is, as Chesterton put it, in America even the Catholics are Protestants. And we also lack a tradition of social democracy such as most European nations possess, not unrelated to the established church tradition, in which there is some notion of a government that bears responsibility for its people. But here it was not Washington and Hamilton who won but Jefferson and Madison who, with their rabid hatred of the state, carried the day.

Roger Williams was a moral genius, but he was a sociological catastrophe. After he founded the First Baptist church he left it for a smaller and purer one. That, too, he found inadequate, so he founded a church that consisted of only him, his wife, and one other person. One wonders how he stood even those two. Since Williams ignored secular society, money took over in Rhode Island in a way that would not be true in Massachusetts or Connecticut for a long time. Rhode Island under Williams gives us an early and local example of what happens when the sacredness of the individual is not balanced by any sense of the whole or concern for the common good. In *Habits of the Heart* we spoke of the second languages that must complement our language of individualism if we are not to slip into total incoherence. I was not very optimistic then; I am even less so today. Almost the only time this society has ever gotten itself together has been in time of war, and I am sure that my understanding of America is deeply formed by experiencing the Depression as a child and World War II as an adolescent. It is not easy to hear those second languages today, and some of those who are too young to have shared my experiences seem hardly able to recognize them even when they hear them. But the poignant reality is that, without a minimal degree of solidarity, the project of ever greater recognition of individual dignity will collapse in on itself. Under the ideological facade of individual freedom, the reality will be, is already becoming, a society in which wealth, ever more concentrated in a small minority, is the only access to real freedom. "The market" will determine the lives of everyone else. So, much as we owe the Baptists, and I would be the first to affirm it, we cannot look to them for a way out. All you have to do is look at the two Baptists in the White House to see that. And yes, I know Hillary is a Methodist—I mean Clinton and Gore.

But, if I can pull myself back from the abyss, which sometimes in my Jeremiah mood is almost the only thing I can see, I can describe even now resources and possibilities for a different outcome than the one toward which we seem to be heading. By the time we came to publish the 1996 edition of *Habits of the Heart* we realized that even the biblical and civic republican traditions, which we had called "second languages," had made their own contribution to the kind of individualism that we had largely blamed on utilitarianism and expressivism in the first edition. This does not mean, however, that the second languages haven't still much to teach us, even if what we have to learn from them must pass through the fires of self-criticism from within these traditions themselves. Our situation is curiously similar to that of post-Communist Eastern Europe in at least one respect. Vaclav Havel and others have opposed an effort to distinguish too sharply between the guilty and the innocent in the former Communist regimes, since it was the very nature of those regimes to draw almost everyone into some kind of complicity. The line between guilt and innocence ran through rather than between individuals, it was argued. I think of the banner in an East German church shortly after the fall of the Berlin Wall that read, "We are Cain *and* Abel." With respect to our American individualism, even in its most destructive forms, it is useless to try to sort out the good guys from the bad guys. We are all complicit, yet change is never impossible. And the deepest resource for change is the genuine diversity of the world's cultures, available to us as never before in human history, not the ideology of multiculturalism, which turns out to be only one more version of American individualism.

UNCOMMON CULTURE

So let me sum up my argument. There is indeed a common culture in America. It is a common culture dominated by the market and the state and disseminated through the mass media, the laws, and public education. I am not here to celebrate that common culture. I have spent my life criticizing it. But I have argued that beneath the surface glitter of American culture, which is making an impact all over the world—just look at the figures of the offshore response to *Titanic*—there is a deep inner core, which, I have argued, is ultimately religious: the sacredness of the conscience of every single individual. Even toward that I am very ambivalent. It is responsible for the best in our culture, but, by the very weakness of any idea of human solidarity associated with it, it opens the door to the worst in our culture. Because there is a Christian core to our culture, and even a core that derives from a type of Christianity for which my friend Stanley Hauerwas has a special sympathy, I cannot agree with him that Christians in America can be or ought to be "resident aliens." How can we be resident aliens in a culture we are so largely responsible for creating, and wouldn't the effort to be resident aliens only leave the larger society to its own worst devices? Rather, I believe Christians must take the responsibility of radical citizenship in the effort to save our culture from its excesses and to reconstruct forms of social solidarity that are currently so gravely weakened.

Conversely, I would argue for a considerable moderation of the language of multiculturalism, and that for several reasons, but above all because it makes us think we are more diverse than we really are. The negative consequences of this false consciousness are evident to me on both the Left and the Right.

On the Left it weakens the critique of our common culture by blaming its defects on one particular group rather than facing how pervasive it is in all groups. To the extent that it exacerbates identity politics it diverts attention from the reform of American society to the competitive struggle to see which middle-class groups will get the goodies. It effectively abandons the truly deprived, who are unable to enter the struggle of identity politics in the first place.

On the Right the consequences are even worse. By repeating the mantra "We're all so different, we're all so diverse, how can you expect this society to do anything effective?"—and how often have I heard that mantra—it essentially abandons the effort to face our problems together. It effectively obscures the deepest divide in our society, the divide of class, the widening gap between wealth and poverty. It is one of the oldest stories in American history that it leaves the less privileged members of our society to squabble among themselves over issues of diversity and multiculturalism rather than to unite in the demand for a greater realization of social justice.

So where does that leave us? Here I would like to return to the reference to nuances and inflections in our common culture that I made early in this chapter.

Recognizing that we are all, of whatever race and gender, tempted to exalt our own imperial ego above all else, we can still find those social contexts and those traditions of interpretation that can moderate that egoism and offer a different understanding of personal fulfillment. Every church and synagogue that reminds us that it is through love of God and neighbor that we will find ourselves helps to mitigate our isolation. Every time we engage in activities that help to feed the hungry, cloth the naked, give shelter to the homeless, we are becoming more connected to the world. Every time we act politically to keep the profit principle out of spheres where it ought not to set the norms of action we help to preserve what Jürgen Habermas calls the lifeworld and, incidentally, to prevent the market from destroying the moral foundations that make it possible.[18] It must be obvious from the example of recent history that without the legal and ethical culture of public morality a market economy turns into Mafia gangsterism. We still have more of what has come to be called "social capital" than many other nations, but it cannot be taken for granted. It survives only when we in our religious and civic groups work strenuously to conserve and increase it.

Perhaps even yet there are other resources in our common culture, such as those to which William Dean has pointed in his *The Religious Critic in American Culture,* from which we can draw.[19] I still believe that there are places in the churches, and other religious and civic organizations, and even nooks and crannies in the universities, to which we might look. But the hour is late and the problems mount. In this hour of need in our strange republic, it is up to us to teach the truth as we discern it, and that is what I have attempted to do here.[20]

Why Study About Religion? The Contribution of the Study of Religion to American Public Life

Jacob Neusner, with William Scott Green*

Religion makes a difference in the life of nations, peoples, communities, and individuals. It is public, shared, social—though some prefer to treat religion as personal and idiosyncratic. When people talk about their beliefs, they provide information. But when we study about religion, we take up what can be studied and analyzed, not merely reported about.

WHAT IS AT STAKE IN THE STUDY OF RELIGION?

When we study about religion, we ask how it matters in the everyday life of ordinary people and in the present-tense affairs of the communities where we live. Religion makes a difference in the social order and for many Americans forms a primary fact of life. One important purpose of studying religion is to ask how religion matters: So what? Perhaps no question provokes, annoys, and unnerves scholars more than this one. But it is the key question in learning about any subject, including religion: If I know this, what else do I know? How much better do I understand things, and what further learning or insight should I then seek?

Two approaches serve to answer these questions. One way is to describe a religious tradition or system: its way of life, worldview, and account of the social entity formed by the faithful. In a book that I edited, *World Religions in America,*[1] experts on the main religions of the world today that are well represented in America answered three questions: What is this religion? How does it find a home in America? In what ways has America changed, and been changed by, that

*The first half of this chapter is jointly composed; the second half is by Jacob Neusner.

religion? The strength of that work flows from the passion of its writers, scholars who care deeply about their subject. This is one part of the task. The other part—set forth in a companion work[2]—concerns the ways in which various religions matter in concrete and immediate terms, not framed as "Christianity teaches. . . ," and "Islam maintains. . . ," but as, How do Christians struggle with these problems? How do Muslims work out their place in the social order in those ways? From the data that answer theoretical questions in this equally necessary approach, we can then move to the human meaning of religion. The former approach tends to characterize scholarship in the humanities; the latter, the domain of social scientific scholarship. But in both readings of the data of religion, the question is the same: What difference does religion make? The premise of analysis is that religion may constitute an independent variable—not that it does or ought to, but that it may turn out to explain, not only to be explained by, other factors in the social order.

Other subjects do not demand that people ask, "So what?" In the humanities, the text or artifact is treated as a given, self-evidently illuminating and worthy of close study. In science and in some social sciences—the problem-solving ones—the "So what?" usually is evident in a well-crafted experiment that makes plain in its problem and procedures how it is giving a new, better, or definitive answer to an established question or how it is posing a new question on the basis of new information. But religion straddles the border between the social sciences and the humanities, and much that we learn about religion comes to us through the media of humanistic learning: texts and artifacts that are the products of culture and have been around for a long time. When we speak of sacrifice, we do not go out and buy a lamb and kill it and flick the blood on an altar; we read the book of Leviticus and learn about the rite in the arid language of a "book about." The upshot is that when we want to know about religion, we get our learning from books, rather than from direct observation of how things are in real life. We can readily lose sight of the fact that in everyday ways religion is not a matter of description at all, but of confrontation and engagement.

So the "So what?" of our work is not always so plain. The things we study when we study about religion—the texts and artifacts in art, literature, classics, philosophy and theology, music, religion, and occasionally history and anthropology—take on a life of their own. We examine what people have made because they are religious, but we do sometimes fail to find our way back from the result of religion—the way in which, in making these texts and artifacts, religion matters to that person or group—to the experienced reality of religion. We may focus on the products of religion, without remembering the human reality that the products represent and convey. It is as though, in genetics, we could trace the genes that cause this and that, but took no interest in how our learning helps us understand matters and even improve them.

Yet this is not the only reason for our conviction that learning about religion requires us to learn how religion matters. There is the matter of difference: the otherness of all religions but our own, if we have one, or of religion as a social fact, viewed in its entirety. Someone else's religion may seem quite remote from our own experience. Much that we learn about religion focuses on abstract questions: belief, ritual, history, theory. But religion makes a difference in the here and now, and that is why the *theory* of these things illuminates. If we learn how to see the religion of the other as an effort to work out a human dilemma or to confront a critical issue of the social order, the religion of the other takes on a shared humanity, a common sensibility. The details of a particular religion, bizarre and exotic as they are, point to what we too address; our capacity for empathy, for seeing the common humanity in the other, accords us the power to make sense of nonsense. And that is the reward we seek in pursuing the question in these pages about how religion matters. From the answers given by religions that appear alien to our immediate experience, we work our way back to the questions that confront us all.

Some fields of learning lose sight of the human value of what is learned. With that loss we abandon all hope that learning makes a difference. As an example, a leading journal of academic life, *Lingua Franca,* recently published an article entitled "Can Classics Die?" that chronicled the depressing decline and efforts at survival of a subject that once was central to all humanistic learning in the West.[3] Other fields, such as English and history, have lost half of their majors in the last decade. Professors who cannot answer urgent questions students bring to class make themselves irrelevant. Professors of English who cannot say what literature is or is not, professors of history with no story to tell but only opinions taken out of today's world and imposed in judgment upon times past—these have lost their students. That is because they have lost sight of their subject and why people should want to learn that subject. In urgently pursuing the issue of how religion matters, we mean to focus attention on the main point. Learning, yes—but for the purpose of understanding. We do not want the study of religion to lose touch with its subject in the way in which learning in literature and history and classics has.

That is why when we study about religion, we seek to build a bridge between humanities and the social sciences, between the study of religion as a matter of theory and the confrontation of the reality of religion in the social order and in the unfolding of human lives. Religion matters because it infuses the life of the community that takes shape around religious beliefs and practices; because it defines the right and wrong, the meaning and the goal of personal lives; and because in the public life of this country, religious convictions spill over into people's aspirations for political action. Whether on the Left, with its conviction that support for the weak and poor forms God's highest demand of us, or on the

Right, with its belief that the unborn child has the right to life, religion forms a primary source of political activity, as much as personal attitude. Out of religion come definitions of virtue and ethical behavior. Out of religion emerge visions of the good and just society. Out of religion people derive the strength to live through disappointment, suffering, and sorrow, as well as the purpose to form lives of hope and renewal.

No one maintains that religion brings about only what is good and constructive in the world; the headlines in the daily paper would mark us as naive if we thought so. In spelling out some of the many ways in which religion makes a difference in practical matters of everyday intimacy, scholars of religion mean to open up areas for further reflection upon the here and now of religion. In a field in which the then and there of texts, history, and theory predominate, introducing important learning about the workaday world and the immediate present can only restore and renew our work.

In the study of religion few advocate religion or religiosity, but rather the position that religion does make a difference in the world. Scholars in the subject are neither naive nor romantic about religion, and they paint a picture of religion that is not uniformly complimentary or positive. Their descriptive concreteness and specificity help us to see religion's capacity for partisanship and pettiness as well as its power to uplift and transform. Not only so, but religion does not always dominate the lives of its practitioners. Rather, it often is in competition with other sets of values and duties and can create as much tension as it can resolve. Indeed, in some cases, we see religion seemingly at odds with itself, as different components of a religious tradition appear to make conflicting claims on its adherents.

The question "So what?" has a special relevance to religion because of the widespread misconception that it deals with fantasy and belief rather than reality and knowledge. But social science research has shown the vitality of religion—both constructive and destructive—in the thoughts, actions, and lives of the everyday. As the study of religion has grown in American universities, it has experienced a strong tendency to treat religion systematically, in terms of histories, doctrines, texts, and artifacts. All these are important, and without them we would be poorer analysts of the living traditions than we are. But the living traditions—or religion lived—also are part of our study, and we hope this work can help lived religion find its proper way into, and place in, the discourse of the study of religion.

What is at stake for the world beyond the classroom? A focus on the concrete is not merely an academic matter. It affects the broader public as well. In the spring semester of 1995, under the direction of William Green and Nancy Woodhull, a founding editor of *USA Today,* thirty-seven senior religion majors at the University of Rochester classified every reference to religion—from story to allusion—in seven national newspapers for one month (February 6 to March 5). The papers were the *Seattle Times, Los Angeles Times, Dallas Morning News, Atlanta Journal and Constitution, Washington Post, New York Times,* and *Chicago Tribune.* By tracking the images of religion that appear in the press day by day, the study achieved a unique national perspective on the public perception of religion in America. The results of the study were stunning and help to explain the rationale for the academic study of religion: The world cannot do its business any other way.

First, in the newspapers examined, religion was everywhere and nowhere. Religion was mentioned nearly 2.5 times more often than it was the focus of a story on its own. The news media assume that religion is an essential part of the background of the news, and stories refer to religion frequently. But the media have trouble telling religion's story.

Second, stories about religion very often miss the point. Just 25 percent of all news stories, and only 21 percent on the religion page, were about beliefs and values, the core of the religions themselves. Other themes were political and legal issues (37 percent), illegality (19 percent), and internal organization (17 percent). Overall, these figures suggest that the media tend to apply the news criteria of politics to stories about religion or seek out sensational stories to grab attention.

Third, when the media do focus on the beliefs, values, and practices of a religion, the stories are often inaccurate and misleading.

The news media are not hostile to religion, but reporters are uncertain about how to cover it. Ironically, the First Amendment itself may make us gun-shy of religion. Because religion is not studied in most public schools, Americans assume that it is merely and only a matter of private opinion rather than public conversation. Because we never learn how to think or talk with our neighbors about religious difference—in stark contrast to politics and economics—we suppose religion is primarily about feelings. We thereby unwittingly ignore or trivialize what is central in many of our neighbors' lives. The American public reflects those assumptions and treats religion as faith, not fact. But faith is a very visible fact of American life. To nurture our pluralism we need to know why and how the beliefs and values of religious people translate into behavior. To do so we need to see religion in practice as well as in theory, and we need to include in our study the places in which religion matters.

WHAT DO WE NOT KNOW, IF WE KNOW NOTHING ABOUT RELIGION?

What do we not know, if we know nothing about religion?[4] We do not know what people do because they are religious, and that is a great deal: why they do much that they do at home and in public, what holds together large numbers of people and gives them a definition of their group, how to explain public policy and individual behavior over much of the globe. That is to say, people study religion for the same reason that they study politics, history, and economics: because they want to find ways of understanding public life and conduct. But they also study religion for the same reason that they study literature, art, music, poetry, and philosophy: because they want to explore the intellectual life that humanity has shaped for itself. The academic study of religion straddles the frontier between the social sciences and the humanities, because of the very character of religion. Religion finds its home in the deepest layers of private consciousness and experience. But religion also shapes the social order, introducing into public policy considerations of a supernatural character and lending to society a transcendent importance.

Note that we now turn to speak of religion, not only religions. That is to say, when we study politics, we deal with cases but search for useful generalizations; economic data point to consequences in the shaping of economic theory; history in its golden era made judgments about matters of wisdom and even stated laws of historical explanation: the causes of this war, the results of that one. The study of literature gives us the power to appreciate fiction and poetry, not only a specific novel or poem. The study of art and music tells us how art makes its statement, how music works its wonders, and a particular picture or sculpture or sonata exemplifies what we may expect, how we may encounter, other pictures or works of sculpture or music. In learning to sing our first song, we learn to sing songs, and so for religion. The study of religion is a generalizing field of learning.

But in three important ways religion stands by itself.

First, the study of religion requires comparison and contrast. That means when we study religion, we have always to ask ourselves what we are doing and why we are doing it. The study of religion always involves considerations of method, why this, not that. By contrast, literature, art, or politics may or may not seek an opening outward for purposes of comparison and contrast. We study American literature on its own, or German politics as a free-standing subject. But religion can be studied only through a labor of comparison and contrast: "Who knows only one religion understands no religion at all," the founders of the study of religion in the academy maintained, and time has proved them right. The reason is that without comparison and contrast, we have no perspective on the religion we are examining; we find ourselves describing, but if we cannot consider choices and options, we do not understand why a given religion does things this way, not that way.

Second, if by its nature the study of religion requires comparisons, then by its essence the study of religion embodies, realizes the ideals of, multiculturalism. By multiculturalism I don't mean what you and I despise—favoritism for one

group over another. I mean what America has always meant: an intelligent interest in difference, a willingness to deal with what is unfamiliar. This country is
more hospitable to difference than any other society now or ever, and that defines the task of universities too: to teach about what we find unfamiliar, and to
do so with an inquiring spirit.

Now, as soon as we try to generalize about religion—moving from different
religions to questions of what they have in common, for instance, or asking for a
single explanation of the same behavior in diverse circumstances—we must not
only compare but introduce unfamiliar cases. By that I mean that religion en-
compasses the cultures of nearly all of humanity, turning for its data to Africa as
much as Europe, Asia as much as North America. So far as multiculturalism
aims at inclusion, the study of religion by its very character shares that goal.
Putting the matter differently, we cannot do our work at all if we exclude any sizable corpus of data, any religion, anywhere. Not only so, but cases drawn from
Asia and Africa and Latin America have as high a priority in the work of comparison and contrast as cases drawn from Western Europe or the United States.

The third important way in which religion stands out within the liberal arts
curriculum—besides the comparative method, on the one side, and the outreach
to diverse cultures, on the other—carries us to the matter of relevance. The study
of religion should always bear within itself an explanation of its relevance: Why
does it matter? Why here, why now, why me? Whether or not we can understand
the world in which we live if we do not grasp what people do who write poetry
or if we do not know much about the past, we surely cannot read this morning's
headlines if we do not know what people do when they practice religion, if we
cannot say how religion affects society and changes people. For much that we
read in the newspapers requires us to know two things. First, we have to have
some concrete knowledge of specific religions, Christianity in the United States,
for one example, or Islam in the Middle East, Central Asia, South Asia, and
much of Africa, on the other. What sense can we make of the Balkans, if we
think that Protestant Christianity tells the whole story and know nothing of Orthodox Christianity (for Serbia) or Roman Catholic Christianity (for Croatia),
not to mention Islam for part of Bosnia.

Religion may stand as an independent variable, but no one claims that religion
is the sole important variable. Hence to say that religion is essential to making
sense of the Balkan conflict is not to suggest that religion explains everything we
need to know to understand the stakes in the Balkan conflict. And any conception that the Middle Eastern crisis of the past half-century stands for a religious
war between Judaism and Islam certainly distorts what is going on. But knowing
how Islam has encountered the West, from Islam's own mighty conquests of
Christianity in the Middle East, North Africa, and Spain, and how the West has
responded, from the Crusades forward, and how Judaism interpreted its own his-

tory and imposed its reconstruction upon the consciousness of the Jews—knowing Islam, Christianity, and Judaism in the Middle Eastern setting surely forms the first step toward understanding today's papers. And that is what I mean when I claim that, of all the subjects in the curriculum, the study of religion competes for the prize for acute relevance.

Why does the study of religion claim a central position in the liberal arts curriculum? It is because religion has formed a principal medium of human expression. We need not practice or even admire religion or a particular religion to acknowledge that religion can make a vast difference in the lives of individuals, social groups, and entire nations or peoples. Indeed, the academy, populated as it is by numbers of people who regard religion with contempt and dislike, pays its compliment to the importance of religion: It is a force in human affairs to be reckoned with, even for the most hostile reasons. For good or for ill (one can make the case on both sides) religion bears the burden of humanity's vision of itself in relationship to the world, both the tangible world and the world of imagination and hope; religion provides a key to understanding the works of humanity: the civilization we have made, the politics we define to mediate power, the economics we formulate rationally to dispose of scarce resources, the philosophy we frame to dictate the character of sense and logic, and the arts that we frame to embody sensibility. Concrete examples, both in the world today and through the entire history of civilization, abound. Indeed, if I had to make the case for the study of religion, I could do no better than ask for a concrete example of why knowing about a religion and also having some ideas about religion in general afford understanding of how things are.

My concrete case is local: All religion is local and particular. When I need to show how to understand a given territory, its life and culture, religion enters in, and I also have claimed that we cannot understand religions—the examples—without some broader theory of what we mean by religion—the model. Since these words were first written to be spoken in Wyoming, the listeners and I were located in the intermountain West, so let me point to a single local case. To understand the life of Idaho, Utah, Arizona, parts of California and Nevada and Wyoming, we have to come to grips with the Mormons. The life of this region, not only its origins and history within the framework of European settlement of America, requires that we see the Mormons as a critical component of the immediate social order. This none can understand without some concrete knowledge of the religion of the Church of Jesus Christ of Latter Day Saints, the literature of the Book of Mormon and related writings, the history of the Mormon people: from their beginnings in New York and Ohio, their wanderings and sufferings in Missouri and Illinois, their hegira to the Great Basin, and their odyssey as they transformed a very distinctive and particularly American experience into the foundation of a world religion and a vision for human civilization.

We need not believe in the Mormon religion, let alone contemplate adopting it, to concur that we cannot understand a vast territory if we know nothing of that particular religion. The Mormons have played, and continue to play, so central a role in the life of the intermountain West that we may say simply: You may like them, you may not like them, but you cannot ignore them, and you had best try to understand their religion, which makes them what they are—by their own word. If that religion makes so critical a difference in the intermountain West, then draw your own conclusions about why you have to know something about Judaism to make sense of the State of Israel; Catholicism to understand the life of much of Europe, Latin America, parts of Canada, and important cities and states in the United States; and living Protestantism in all its variations to interpret what happens in much of the American South and Midwest. If I then mention the words Islam, Buddhism, Hinduism, the point registers. The case illustrates the generalization: Much of the world takes shape in response to religion; since we live in that world, we had best try to understand what people do when they practice a religion.

Do we then have to learn every detail about every religion? Ideally, we should, but in reality, we cannot, any more than to practice ichthyology we must exhaust the list of fish. Rather, we seek generalization: terms and rules that pertain to all the data, a way of organizing, classifying, and understanding the whole. Without some study of religion as a set of generalizations, without thinking about relations between religion and politics, religion and the social order, religion and culture, and religion and psychology, we can make no sense of the religions we see. There has to be a theory of the whole, guiding us to make sense of the details. Note that I used the word "hegira," forced evacuation, as the critical moment in the birth of the faith—so borrowing an analogy from Islam. I spoke of the centrality of a book, borrowing an analogy from classical Christianity and the Bible. I referred to the history of a people, its wanderings and sufferings, by analogy to ancient Israel. Once we speak of a single religion, we find ourselves resorting to categories supplied by other religions, or by religion as a set of generalizations and encompassing definitions. And, it goes without saying, from the case of the Mormons to the generalizations about religion a road forms that leads in both directions. Studying about religions in general, people do well to test their generalizations against the case of the Mormons. And what I have said about the case exemplifies many other cases and possibilities.

Since I lay such stress on an important religion of the intermountain West, the Mormons, you must wonder whether I am a secret practitioner of the Latter-day Saints (LDS) religion, and that brings us to the larger question: Do I have to believe in order to study, or, if I do believe, can I study at all? The question addresses all of the humanities with which people identify, women's studies, black studies, and the like: Do I have to be the thing I study to conduct studies of that thing? Framed in this way, the question dictates two answers. The insider learns in one way, the outsider in another; and to all religions but our own, if we practice any religion at all, we are outsiders. And that fits well with the task of the university, which is to teach us about what we are not, and so to give us perspective on what we are. So when religion is the field in which to do our work, we must always see things as outsiders do: as strange and fresh. And that is the gift of the study of religion even to the practitioner of a particular religion: to make the familiar something new and interesting again. I remember first reading the work of Mircea Eliade on religion, work in which my religion, Judaism, rarely played a role, and wondering how he had learned so much about the interior structure of Judaism. His insights into religion, for that day and age, illuminated matters of which at that point in his work he was only casually informed at best—and Eliade is only one among the great figures in the study of religion who have done their best work in the United States.

If I had to point to the country in which the study of religion flourishes most abundantly—and I stress, the academic study of religion, not only religions but religion, not only theology and its equivalent for the uses of church, synagogue, or mosque but religion for the uses of the academy—if I had to say where it is done the most and the best, it is in the United States. That is a statement not merely of pride and American patriotism but of fact. It is proved by the simple fact that every year the national meetings of the principal academic societies for the study of religion in the United States, the American Academy of Religion and the Society of Biblical Literature, attract large numbers of overseas scholars, who come from Europe, the South Pacific, and nearly everywhere in between. People come to the American meetings because this is where the intellectual events take place. The academic study of religion flourishes here, not only because the Supreme Court in *Abington Township School District v. Schempp* (1963) said that although in publicly supported schools and colleges we may not engage in the practice of religion, we most certainly may, and indeed should, engage in study about religion. The Court decision said we may do it. But the conditions of our society dictate that we must do it.

The diversity of American society makes it urgent for our citizens to introduce themselves to one another. The Texaco executives having trouble with Hanukkah and Kwanzaa at Christmastime cost their company a big bundle of money. But they also illustrate why a country where nearly every religion in the world finds practitioners—in numbers—requires its citizens to learn about one another. If we must find a politics that draws us together, an economics that endows us all with the same rationality, we have to formulate a theory of religion that all of us can accept. For just as politics and economics motivate, so religion motivates, as I already have argued. What that means is that in the academy we have to teach ourselves about the other. The special promise of the academic study of religion is to nurture this country's resources of tolerance for difference, our capacity to learn from the other and to respect the other. What can the academic study of religion contribute to the cartography of religious toleration within the geography of religion—the search for the elusive passage? Specifically, how do I propose that, within the academic study of religion, we begin to reshape the way in which people perceive religious difference and learn to understand, respect, and accept that difference for what it is: in proportion and in balance? The best is the enemy of the good: Let me make three concrete suggestions of how to proceed. Scholarship, teaching, and the shape of future learning define the categories of these simple proposals, which flow from what I already have said.

Scholarship

All study of religion must find its task in comparison and contrast, so that difference will emerge at the very foundations of learning about religion. The stake that we who study religion have in interfaith dialogue proves formidable, for in the end, we cannot do our work well without the encounter beyond the frontiers of our learning. What has this simple rule of serious learning to do with renewing the religious sources of toleration, one religion for another? The answer lies in a fortuitous circumstance. People tend to specialize in a religion that they love and, commonly, also practice. If, then, my work requires me to learn about Christianity in the period of my specialization, that will bring me into intimate, intellectually rigorous contact with Christians who work as seriously on problems of learning but as lovingly on the roots of their faith as I do on mine. The result is a partnership of learning among believers, which only the academic study of religion can bring about.

A personal reference may illustrate that claim. Because I work on the formative age of Rabbinic Judaism, I have long labored as a consumer, though not a producer, of scholarship on the New Testament and the Patristic age of the history of Christianity. Those rich areas of learning provide a source of comparisons, contrasts, perspective: a sense for what others in the same time and place did. As a result, I have found one conversation and dialogue partner after another, over many years, from the New Testament scholar who first taught me Greek and also an appreciation of the Gospel of Mark, to my colleague at Bard College, Bruce D. Chilton, with whom I have undertaken a vast project of comparative theology, specifically, a study of category formations in the theology of Judaism and Christianity in the formative age: how, for example, the concepts of Israel and the church compare, how Gospel and Torah contrast, and how modes of argument and types of religious authority that operate in the one religious world correspond to counterparts in the other—a sequence of books that now extend onward into the future.

That is one form of authentic religious dialogue, the form that takes place when practicing Christians and Judaists work together on shared problems of comparison and contrast. The result, for toleration, derives not only from the respect that learning should engender, but also from the mutual understanding that learning brings about—that and mutual respect. The long-held prejudices of Judaism about Christianity and Christianity about Judaism—not to mention Catholicism about Protestantism, and vice versa; not to mention (speaking as a southerner by choice) the Methodists and the Baptists—give way to serious argument about matters of common concern and even belief. Another time, another place—who can know what a difference that sharing within learning, but not only of learning, can have made!

Teaching

The classroom study of religion in our generation has to limit its agenda, explicitly excluding political topics for the time being. If I have learned through shared projects of learning to understand and respect the religion of the other, and to do so within the framework of rigorous learning about serious religious questions, then I have to ask, Can such projects of cooperative learning take place on any topic, without limit? My answer is, No, we have wisely to identify those areas that permit encounter without confrontation, and the ones that for our generation must remain closed off from encounter, because at this time learning can only precipitate new conflict. To explain what I mean, I once more draw upon my own experience as a teacher.

In my university, which serves a large and mixed population in west-central Florida, we number among students and faculty Muslims, including Palestinians. As a matter of fact, an adjunct member of our faculty succeeded to the headship of the Islamic Jihad, and his colleague is presently under federal investigation in connection with activities in support of Islamist terrorism. So ours is not a setting in which Judaic–Islamic dialogue enjoys promising prospects. Imagine, therefore, my surprise when I found in my classroom the wife of the professor who was responsible for bringing to the university the man who now heads the Islamic Jihad, as well as the Imam of the Tampa mosque. The course that they selected was Talmud, studied as a text but in the American language. They came because they wanted to learn about that part of Judaism that corresponds to Islamic piety, namely, law as a medium of religious obligation and service. I took it as a statement of confidence that they would study with me, not only a scholar but also a rabbi and, as a matter of fact, a Zionist as well. We have agreed to study together what we can share without rancor, and it turns out to encompass much that matters.

To begin the class, I said, we have much to learn from one another, but only if we agree at the outset that the Muslims will speak only of Judea, Samaria, and

Gaza, and I will speak only of Occupied Palestine. That having been gotten out of the way, we will never again refer to anything that has taken place in human history from the tenth century forward. The result was to clear the air, and issues that we could not constructively address no longer threatened our work together. The Muslim students took to the Talmud with enormous engagement, at home with its premises as to what God most values, and their papers, comparing Islamic and Talmudic law in areas of women's affairs, on the one side, and in modes of legal argument and analysis, on the other, proved remarkably illuminating. Toward the end of the course the Muslim woman asked me for a *fatwa,* a *pesaq halakhah* (a religio-moral judgment), of a supposedly theoretical character. If a Muslim woman is required by the police, in the process of being booked for arraignment, to remove her head covering for a photograph, would uncovering her head constitute a sin? I said, I am sure we both agree that God knows the difference between what we do under duress and what we do by an act of will, so I am confident that no sin can be involved in such a circumstance. She cried at the response, but I was still more deeply moved to have been asked.

I think this is possible only in America. And I am inclined to doubt that such an exchange can have taken place under any auspices but academic ones, and in any corner of the academy but the classroom, at the fringes of a shared enterprise of learning. What made the encounter plausible was the environment of reason and shared, civil discourse of the classroom. What made it possible was the agreement up front to exclude from all discussion issues that we simply cannot treat, and to lay emphasis upon those matters of mutual illumination, of sheer learning, that we can. So, the second law of generating a more tolerant climate among religions through the study of religion, is to identify areas of learning that all parties can share and rule out areas that to begin with we cannot pursue without conflict. That is to say, we can do just so much together, so let us find out what that is and do it.

The Shape of Future Learning

Without trivializing difference, the study of religion has to discover the commonalities, in the human situation and in the shared challenges of social order, that religions exhibit. Here is where monotheisms enjoy a special advantage in their shared quest for religious roots of toleration: The three religions of one and the same God concur on much, and, as I said, the very possibility of the centuries of warfare among the three emerges from their shared insistence on a common agenda. We all claim to know one God, who is the same God, and who has made himself known in ways that we insist we can pursue. Not only so, but much that the three religions of one God teach intersects, and dialogue becomes possible not only because of our differing about the same thing, but also because of our concurring upon some of the same things as well.

I stressed limiting the range of dialogue to those topics that to begin with allow civil discourse and, moreover, opening those questions upon which our minds are open to sincere argument. That means agreeing to disagree, in some areas closing discourse, in some undertaking discussion. We know wherein we differ, and we may also identify the things about which we agree. So much for how we will deal with fiercely held points of contention in the framework of the study of religion by the faithful of the several religions.

But beyond the agenda of concurrence and difference, all of the religions that aim at shaping human society, certainly including Judaism, Christianity, and Islam, because of that fact must address a common set of problems. Here is where the academic study of religion finds its most promising tasks: to ask how the several religions solve for themselves the same problems, problems of social reality that cannot be evaded and must be confronted if the several religions are to accomplish their goals, at least in theory. And this brings us to how Judaism, Christianity, and Islam address the agenda of the social order that, for theological imperatives, all three take up and make their own. Religions build worlds, hold together groups of people, give them a definition of themselves. Religions shape and define the world that they affect. And, in many (though not all) societies, it is religion that gives us a picture of the whole—religion and nothing else. Without studying religion, we can never grasp the whole of those societies; we are left with parts that do not relate. So the study of religion integrates learning, pointing us in the direction of the heart and the center of the social order that practices a given religion.

But it is not only in the shared challenges of the social order, but the commonalities in the human situation, that they meet. All three affirm God's mercy and love; all three maintain God cares about what we do and rewards and punishes us, holding us to be creatures of free will and therefore responsibility. So the ethical and moral traditions that characterize monotheisms require attention too. And still more: All three appeal to philosophy in the Classical tradition to define the religious intellect, and they concur that our minds and God's mind correspond in such a way that we may not only love God but also know something about God: God's ways, not only God's will. That, after all, defined the adventure of medieval interfaith dialogue, the intellectual exchange of Islamic, Judaic, and Christian philosophy, all within the tradition of Classical times. So in these two further aspects, ethics and philosophy, shared scholarship finds its calling: the discovery of sources of mutual esteem and respect, beginning with the examination of those shared modes of thought and analysis that render the other less alien, less of a stranger altogether—whether the Muslim to the Christian or the Judaist, the Judaist to the Muslim or the Christian, or the Christian to the Muslim or the Judaist.

These coming labors, to conclude, I conceive to be the study of religion in the academy in particular, as I said, in the setting of comparison and contrast: specifically, studying those classical dimensions that we can examine in a shared rationality, limiting our agenda in favor of mutual respect and understanding, where we can find grounds for respect and foundations for understanding; and, finally, focusing our learning upon that shared agenda imposed upon us by the American social order, its traits, its affirmations, its aspirations. Ours is a privileged field of learning, for when we devote our lives to the academic study of religion, the very nature of the documents that we examine and the ideas that we try to understand changes our work, transforming facts into insight and insight into wisdom. Into our hands is committed humanity's heritage of aspiration, its vision of itself—to use the language of Christianity and Judaism, humanity that sees itself in God's image, after God's likeness. No more remarkable hope and vision of human worth persist in the academy than such a vision as this. Ours is not only the generalizing field of learning, not only the field of learning that by its nature requires comparison, contrast, and comprehensive coverage of humanity: Ours is the field of learning that offers students a most remarkable vision of what we are and what we can become—a vision that transcends the bounds of time and space and ascends beyond the limits of this world.

As a believer I may add, religions impart, also, a vision of how God sees us.

Chapter 6

Table Manners: Sitting Around the Public Table

Peggy L. Shriver

Directly across from the United Nations building in an economically prime location of New York City stands the Churches' Center for the United Nations. In Washington, D.C., on Maryland Avenue, immediately across from the Supreme Court building, the United Methodist Church building contains the headquarters of many mainline church public advocacy offices. In both centers of power Methodists with vision, alacrity, and resources led the way. Sitting around the public table is a natural for churches with a theology in which "everything in life has to do with God."

Other religious groups, however, restrict their piety to individual salvation and transformation of society "one citizen at a time." Only in the late 1970s, after challenges to their values had been flaunted in the activism of the 1960s, did the militantly politically active Religious Right emerge, first through the now defunct Moral Majority. Today, in an industrial park in Chesapeake, Virginia, sits the headquarters of the Christian Coalition, dedicated, as the founder Pat Robertson and the former executive director Ralph Reed often announced after 1989, to "mobilizing Christians—one precinct at a time, one community at a time, one state at a time—until once again we are the head and not tail, and at the top rather than the bottom of our political system."[1]

In this chapter we shall explore the differences between the public activism of the mainline (sometimes called oldline) denominations and their counterpart in the Religious Right. We will examine contrasting agendas; compare theological visions, political views, and tactics; and then extract some "table manners" to be learned from both groups as they sit uncomfortably around the public table.

CONTRASTING AGENDAS

Max Stackhouse in a *Christian Century* article on religion and politics reminds us of the wry and succinct view that liberals "want to use government to liberate sex and control money," whereas conservatives "want to use government to liberate money and control sex."[2] A recent review of major concerns emanating from Washington offices of mainline denominations reveals the core truth in that comment.[3] Methodist "Social Principles" call for sound economic policy that limits the rights of private property, upholds collective bargaining, discourages unrestrained consumerism and gambling, addresses world poverty, reduces the concentration of wealth, and promotes the welfare of migrant workers and more meaningful, adequately paid work for everyone. Methodists have passed resolutions on rural decline, housing and homelessness, access to health care, the global debt crisis, investment ethics, and a family policy that provides guaranteed income, affordable housing and health care, and support services for the poor. Similarly, the Presbyterians, while issuing less of a broadside to the economic system, add reform of child labor, a massive public effort to end poverty and urban decay, increased political involvement and United States international aid. Episcopalians, addressing many similar issues, are especially noted for opposition to the Gulf War. The United Church of Christ's work on environmental racism and on economic justice has stature similar to the Catholic bishops' pastoral letter on the economy. American Baptists and Evangelical Lutherans also emphasize concern for the poor and the need to address structural injustices in our society—almost as elaborate in policy as the Methodists'. All of the mainline churches subscribe to a "peace with justice" agenda that adds to economic concerns a strong antimilitarism and antinuclear bias.

The role of women in church and society, the insistent desire for recognition in the church by homosexuals, and the pressures from the Religious Right on abortion and other sexual morality issues have of necessity become major concerns in mainline churches. In the long view of history, change has been rapid in relation to the role of women, and many denominational adjustments have been effectuated in response to women's demands, although more are to be anticipated. But related to other sexual morality issues, several denominations have attempted to do comprehensive studies of human sexuality to put homosexuality and sexual ethics into a broad biblical context and have found it exceedingly difficult to produce a consensus.

During these years the Moral Majority organized around issues summarized by *Newsweek* as "against abortion, ERA, gay rights, sex education, drugs, pornography, SALT II, the Department of Education and defense cuts. They are for free enterprise, a balanced budget, voluntary prayer in the public schools and a secure Israel."[4] The Family Protection Act was soon followed by the emergent Christian Coalition's family values agenda. Recent additions to this list are privatization of the arts (eliminating support for the National Endowment for the Arts), parental rights, antimulticulturalism, tuition tax credits (including tax deferral on religious school tuition), and other education issues. Evolution, crime, and secular human-ism also enrich the list. Ralph Reed indicated prior to his leaving the Christian Coalition that they should have paid more attention to poverty and racism.

Religious persecution around the world, particularly of Christians, has become an issue that, despite agreement about the basic concern, has pitted evangelicals, including the Religious Right, and the National Council of Churches of Christ in the U.S.A. (NCC) against one another on strategy. Mandated sanctions against countries that are found to persecute religious minorities are necessary to give legislation teeth, claim evangelicals and some Roman Catholic and Jewish groups. There is not enough latitude for diplomacy, argues the Council, which is also concerned that the legislation is promoted largely against Muslim countries for persecution of Christian minorities and could actually lead to additional per-secution.[5] Some compromise may be reached, but the issue highlights the prag-matic National Council of Churches approach, the "morality of results," versus the morality of principle, voiced by the National Association of Evangelicals, that such persecution must be stopped.

A few observations about these differing agendas are in order. On issues that relate to the economy, the mainline ("oldline") agenda is struggling upstream against a very strong trend to the Right. On the sexual–social issues, the Reli-gious Right is bucking the societal trend. On the other hand, the mainline is rel-atively resigned to the current trend on sexuality, and the Religious Right is quite comfortable with the growing economic conservatism of the nation's leaders. On some issues, like pornography, gambling, and the Religious Freedom Restoration Act, both religious groups seem to unite. Neither has been particularly effective in reversing the trends most important to them. Benton Johnson, in his notable Religious Research Association presidential address in 1996, observed that alco-hol and divorce are remarkably absent from both these agendas, despite the Christian Right's harping on family values. One of the historic battles over Sab-bath observance has been Sunday closing laws, which the Christian Right seems to have abandoned. Johnson also helpfully describes these two liberal and con-servative agendas as "tectonic plates that tend to slide past each other rather than to collide head-on."[6] Except, one must quickly add, when they become public legislative issues, like the Equal Rights Amendment (ERA)!

CONTRASTING THEOLOGICAL VISIONS AND POLITICAL VIEWS

In an earlier time in the United States these agendas would not have been so disparate. Robert T. Handy, in his classic historical study of religion and politics in the United States, *A Christian America: Protestant Hopes and Historical Re-*

alities, traced the move from separate colonial states with their own establishments of religion to a merged vision of "a Christian civilization preparing the way for God's kingdom." This was to be realized not through formal establishment, since pluralism made that approach quite impracticable, but "by God working through those who responded to the outpouring of his spirit."[7]

Although this predominantly Protestant religious leadership accepted the separation of church and state, it resisted any separation of religion and morals from public well-being. Voluntary societies became the means of persuasion toward a complete Christian commonwealth, a vision theologically focused by the doctrine of the kingdom of God, whose triumph would fulfill prophecy and the promise of the gospel. The goal for Protestants was a Christian civilization, a Christian America, itself an instrument for bringing all the nations into God's kingdom on earth. Church and civilization were partners. It was a time (after the Second Great Awakening) for culture and church to collaborate, and a Christianized state could count on the support of the churches. Even civil war was not able ultimately to demolish that dream. Evangelicals and liberals together entered the twentieth century with a grand missionary spirit toward the world.

But times, they were a changin': Rough robber-baron industrialism, child labor, urban squalor, and rural poverty prompted liberal Christians to see social problems as caused not only by individual sin, but by the systems and structures of society. The social gospel of the early twentieth century drew them into politics to curb big business, to enact Prohibition, to support organized labor, to crusade against crime and poverty—to reform America and move it toward God's kingdom. Although they collaborated on many of these issues, evangelicals separated from liberals over a *social* ethic, believing that the solution lay only in converting individuals, not systems.

World War I pounded Protestant idealism with cynicism and disillusionment. A spiritual decline that could no longer respond to the optimistic vision of effecting God's kingdom in America or anywhere else was further deepened by economic depression. Only after World War II did Protestants, both liberal and evangelical, regain at least part of their former vigor.

Meanwhile, the nation had become much more diverse religiously. Catholicism was stronger in many big cities than Protestantism. Immigration was quietly adding major Eastern religions to the mix. There are today more Muslims than Episcopalians in the United States, and—if growth trends continue—by the end of the millennium, there will be more Muslims than Jews.[8] Now the challenge to make one's religious faith a force in public life is significantly more complex.

The Christian Coalition wants the restoration and renewal of the cultural influence and prestige that evangelicalism once enjoyed in American society, when "Christ and culture" seemed to be partners. There is a whiff of nostalgia and a yearning for a "purer," more homogeneous nation under God in their agenda, says Justin Watson, author of *The Christian Coalition: Dreams of Restoration, Demands for Recognition.*[9] Pat Robertson can sound reasonably reassuring that Christians in politics will simply restore a moral strength to reinvigorate the greatness of America. Or he can spew out invective against Marxism, the Illuminati, the Rockefellers and Rothchilds, the Federal Reserve Board, the Council on Foreign Relations, the Trilateral Commission, the United Nations, Secular Humanism, and New Age Religion—all conspiratorial agents of Satan to bring about a godless socialist one-world government. But the Coalition also seeks recognition, says Watson, as an oppressed, victimized group that belongs at the public table, from which it feels wrongfully deposed.

Mainline churches, working now for peace and justice in a more modest version of "kingdom theology," also yearn for the recognition in the political realm that they once commanded. On October 12, 1958, when the cornerstone was laid at 475 Riverside Drive for the Interchurch Center, in which the National Council of Churches and many mainline church headquarters were to be housed, President Eisenhower arrived by helicopter to oversee the proceedings. Today many Washington politicians are only vaguely aware of the council's existence and sometimes have discounted its spokespersons as leading a very short parade. Mainline Christians feel victim of what Stephen L. Carter described in his *The Culture of Disbelief:* "In our sensible zeal to keep religion from dominating our politics, we have created a political and legal culture that presses the religiously faithful to be other than themselves, to act publicly, and sometimes privately as well, as though their faith does not matter to them."[10]

Although mainline leaders are becoming keenly aware of their marginality in the political arena, they have done little to revise their tactics. Ponderous approaches to complex political issues are important for educational purposes, but they contribute to mainline irrelevance politically. The most effective adjustments to the current situation are parachurch groups that take on a limited area of concern and may at most receive a little denominational funding, when established policy allows.

OTHER PERSPECTIVES ON PROTESTANTS

In another way of viewing them, Protestant Christians tend to divide between those who look chiefly toward the end times, Armageddon and the millennium, and Christians who live in the present and coming Kingdom of God. The first group has tended to be nonpolitical and to wait for signs that God is beginning the closing act of the human drama. The second group feels responsible to work with God toward the realization of God's Kingdom on earth until Christ comes— thus political involvement and social action may be essential responses to their theology. The second group may differ in strategy—between those, largely evangelical, who strive for an individual change of heart to change society, and those, largely liberal, who seek not only changed hearts but changed social structures and systems.

The first group also divides into differing views, time lines, and scenarios about the end times—when Jesus returns and history ends. Premillennialists believe Jesus will return, then there will be a thousand-year reign of his King-dom—but only after the earth is devastated by wars and rumors of wars. Post-millennialists (among whom most liberals would also count themselves) look toward a faithful preparation of society with justice and righteousness for Christ's return. Pat Robertson has shifted from a pre- to a postmillennialist view, thus fueling his desire to be a political force to change society. One further sub-set of Christians believes in "dominion theology"—that Christians are mandated to have dominion over the earth, including all its major institutions, such as gov-ernment. Robertson's writings are sometimes compatible with this theology, as in this passage from *The New World Order:*

There will never be world peace until God's house and God's people are given their rightful place of leadership at the top of the world. How can there be peace when drunkards, com-munists, atheists, New Age worshipers of Satan, secular humanists, oppressive dictators, greedy moneychangers, revolutionary assassins, adulterers, and homosexuals are on top?[11]

Another group of Christians, sharing many of the characteristics of evangeli-cals, are the Pentecostals, who require an immediate encounter with the Holy Spirit. Their theology is secondary to worship, which is often exuberant and ec-static. The followers of Aimee Semple McPherson and her Foursquare Gospel denomination are Pentecostals. Offshoots from this denomination, such as Cal-vary Chapel, Hope Chapel, and the Vineyard Fellowship, have expanded so rapidly and proliferated so broadly that the sociologist Donald E. Miller per-ceives them as the new form Christianity will take in the next millennium. They attract young adults (twenty-five to forty) predominantly, more men than women, and their politics are conservative (68 percent "slightly conservative" to "extremely conservative" as self-defined). Only 16 percent are Democrats, and a slim 8 percent voted for Bill Clinton in 1992.[12]

Why are these Pentecostals and Christian Coalition–type evangelical and fun-damentalist Christians so drawn to the Republican party? Because, Miller sug-gests, they also do not believe government has the answers to the problems of society. Social programs, so important to Democrats, are considered unnecessary and wrong-headed. Conversion, changed lives and hearts, is the only lasting so-lution; meanwhile the benevolent acts of fellow Christians should supply societal aid as may be needed. Young adult Pentecostals do act upon these convictions, engaging in social rehabilitation programs for others. More than a third have themselves turned away from a past life of destructive behavior.

Among other evangelicals the pattern of conservatism and Republican strength is also evident. The Pew Research Center for the People and the Press produced an extensive report in 1996.[13] It found that white evangelical Protestants, the fastest-growing group, are 28 percent Democrat, 29 percent Independent, and 41 percent Republican. Black Christians, by contrast, are 62 percent Democrat, 26 percent Independent, and 7 percent Republican. Nonevangelical whites are in between: 31 percent Democrat, 30 percent Independent, 36 percent Republican. White Catholics, once heavily Democratic, are now 32 percent Democrat, 37 percent Independent, and 29 percent Republican. "No preference" in religion is also reflected in politics—51 percent are Independent, 26 percent Democrat, 16 percent Republican.

Neither the Christian Coalition nor the mainline churches (whose average age hovers around fifty in most denominations) have been effective recruiters of young adults. In a 1996 survey she did not identify, the *New York Times* editorialist Michele Mitchell said that, although eighteen- to thirty-five-year-olds routinely poll as economic conservatives, only 6.3 percent think that "family values" is the most important issue today. She quotes Senator Warren Rudman: "The biggest mistake that the Christian Coalition—and, in turn, the Republican Party—has made is about young people. Young people might be fiscally conservative, but they are socially inclusive."[14] Many recent studies point to the disengagement of this age group from denominational ties and special interest groups. How their presence will be visible around the public table has yet to be discerned.

CONTRASTING TACTICS

The Christian Coalition, like its defunct predecessor, the Moral Majority, is not a denomination but a movement. People sign on to a preset agenda, which changes from time to time as the leadership determines. Although members carry out local level political activity with considerable effectiveness, the organization is not democratic in the decision-making process to the extent that denominations are in determining their policies. The Coalition can set its direction and move into action much more expeditiously than the mainline denominations. Contrarily, the Coalition, whose agenda and tactics have moved solidly into the Republican party, acts more like a feisty Democratic donkey. The mainline denominations, whose policies are most at home with the Democratic party, are more like a lumbering elephant! Also, an internal National Council of Churches study I conducted showed that the Republican party tends to be the party of choice within mainline *membership*—no small factor for liberal mainline leadership to consider in setting and acting upon its agenda.

The process of developing a policy statement or position in these denominations is slow and getting slower. Once a decision is finally taken to work on a particular issue, a task force or committee is set up to gather data, study, and issue a paper or report that may require several years of work. Here is a particular dilemma: The selection of committee members, if their general stance is already known, may slant the outcome and cause resistance to or suspicion of their work in the church at large. A diversity of views is essential, but very strong dichotomous views on a committee may paralyze it. Often there is insufficient time to work through diversity of views effectively. More and more requirements to consult the church with feedback from study documents add length to the effort, but they also provide excellent educational opportunities. When the report is brought to vote at a national assembly, it may be drastically revised, sent back to committee, turned into a study document instead of policy, adopted with thanks, or simply killed. Finding resources to carry out the recommendations becomes another internal political struggle. It is not surprising that Congress might pass legislation before some mainline churches settle on a position! On the positive side, once a position is voted, the Washington office staff are empowered to work on it concertedly.

The ethicist Roger Shinn, evaluating the work of the United Church of Christ in their "Economic Life and Justice" pronouncement, described the committee's vicissitudes in a magazine article in 1991. He observed, "Any open confession of divided opinions is regarded as waffling." Yet finding clichés that cover up the differences, he suggested, was the real waffling. Shinn felt the Catholic bishops, with their exclusive hierarchical authority, could consult lay specialists and also find language "to address the body politic in terms of its values as well as their own."[15] The ecumenical voice of the mainline and other member denominations in the National Council of Churches goes through a similar process, but generally with less local involvement within the churches, and its results may or may not be owned by the rank and file in mainline congregations.

LEARNING TABLE MANNERS

With all its faults of sluggish response time, temporizing, and sometimes expression of the bias of one segment of its membership, the mainline denominational approach has learned some important table manners that the Christian Coalition might well practice. The Coalition, in turn, has some vitality and freshness from which mainline Christians could surely benefit. A nine-point examination of table behavior concludes this chapter, but without any claim to comprehensiveness.

First, the public rhetoric and discourse emanating from denominations reflect the tempering of hearing from and trying to persuade many points of view. Especially in the earlier years of entry into politics, the Christian Right used, and regrettably often still uses, overkill language against those with whom they disagree. It is not by accident that the newly formed The Interfaith Alliance (TIA), a broad-based religious response to the Christian Coalition, has made pledges of civility by candidates one of its key strategies. In its interpretive brochure the Interfaith Alliance says:

It was established to ensure that extremists such as Pat Robertson and the Christian Coalition, Jerry Falwell and others are not the only faith-based voices heard in the ongoing debate regarding the direction of our nation.

TIA believes religious and political diversity is a source of strength for our nation—not a liability.

TIA confronts all who exploit religious language and symbols to further political agendas that are hostile, narrowly self-serving and intolerant.

TIA ensures that the mainstream religious community has a say in the current political dialogue, offsetting all distortions and demonization with a constructive and healing response.[16]

One might, however, raise a question whether this very statement is partly guilty of a rhetoric that it deplores in its opposition. The effective use of the term *extremist* was called into question by a People for the American Way survey conducted by the Democratic pollster Peter Hart in 1994. Hart found 61 percent of respondents replied that critics of the Religious Right were raising exaggerated fears and bias against religious people, whereas 21 percent thought critics raised legitimate concerns. In September of that same year, George Gallup asked, "Which statement comes closer to how you would describe the Christian Right?" with the following results: Sixty percent characterized them as "conservative Christians concerned about the country," whereas 34 percent responded, "extremists with narrow views." The Sojourners' Call to Renewal in 1996, in seeking "an alternative vision both to the Religious Right and to the secular Left," took a positive stance without resorting to "extremist" charges, at least in its publicity.[17]

Second, separation of church and state issues continue to plague religious political expression. The Christian Coalition has been under investigation by the Internal Revenue Service for possibly overstepping its tax-exempt status restrictions against partisan political activity. The Federal Election Commission sued the Coalition for breaking the law by improperly aiding Republican candidates. Because mainline denominational pews are occupied by persons of various political persuasions it is perhaps easier for them to recognize and appreciate the boundaries of appropriate nonpartisan behavior. They also have years of experience in these matters. They would not bombard a local congregation with partisan literature, but they would provide authorized statements by all the candidates on issues of concern. Admittedly, there is sometimes a fine line between education and advocacy, when one candidate clearly holds the view perceived to be supported by Christian faith.

The Roman Catholic bishop Walter F. Sullivan, when expressing his concern over the Christian Coalition's establishment of a "Catholic Alliance" (recently abandoned as a cost-cutting measure), was quite clear about partisan involvement. He said, "The church has both the right and the duty to promote moral values in the public forum. At the same time, the Church should not involve itself in partisan politics or attempt to tell people how to vote. To paraphrase a recent U.S. Bishops' statement, the Church must be principled without being ideological, political but not partisan, involved without being used."[18]

At the time of this writing, Religious Right leaders are themselves divided over their reliance upon the Republican party to carry out their agenda. James Dobson, the psychologist and head of the "Focus on the Family" radio show, has threatened to take his five million listeners out of the party if more progress on his agenda is not made. He is quoted as saying, "I believe a Republican meltdown is preferable to . . . the present betrayal of the moral agenda."[19] Other leaders are seeking to consolidate their forces within the Republican party to promote their concerns. "The go-along, get-along strategy is dead," said Richard Land, president of the Ethics and Religious Liberty Commission of the Southern Baptist Convention. "No more engagement. We want a wedding ring, we want a ceremony, we want a consummation of the marriage."[20] A few speculate about forming a political party with their own candidate, or at least becoming "an independent political force" to line up behind one particular presidential candidate. Whatever the outcome, the shortcomings of close party affiliation and the wisdom voiced by Bishop Sullivan and the National Council of Churches on being "political but not partisan" may begin to have some resonance.

Third, denominations recognize the convening power of churches in society. They not only "sit around the public table" but may host or convene a public table of their own around issues of the common good. They do not set the menu at such a table—it is characteristically "pot luck," as all participants bring their own views and issues to be sampled by others. Key concerns of hosting such a public table are "Who is here and who is missing?" "How is the question being posed, the issue presented?" "Who is listening?" By providing neutral space, religious institutions can facilitate public conversations that otherwise seldom take place. One of the dangers of the coalitional movement approach is that differing views may not be present, so positions become entrenched rather than explored.

An outstanding example of the church convening people in Harlem and northern Manhattan around the public table is that of the National Council of Churches' "Resources for the Civic Conversation" program, directed by Charles Rawlings. The urgent issue of public health and medical care is drawing local citizens, hospital administrators, medical practitioners, clergy, insurers, and government agencies into unprecedentedly serious and creative conversation in this setting. Whatever its outcome, many people have heard from parts of the community with whom they seldom converse, and new understanding of the urgent needs of the public and the complexities of health systems has been achieved.

One of the sad features of Christian public life, unfortunately, is how seldom the spectrum of voices, especially the ecumenical liberal and conservative evangelical, ever listen to one another face to face. Neither is eager to sit around the same public table, and consequently they speak readily, fervently, and inaccurately *about* one another, but not *with* one another. Ecumenical openness should be first to sense the hypocrisy in such a stance.

Fourth, getting a hearing in Washington or in the United Nations is difficult in the cacophony of interests. Banding together in ecumenical and interfaith witness gets some attention, but the position on issues may also lose some important nuances of faith in the composite. Sometimes, as with the Religious Freedom Restoration Act, mainline churches function just as any other interest group does. What can make them something other than another caucus or interest group is to become intelligent, compassionate advocates for people's concerns and needs and values that are not being heard or met. Churches don't have to have all the answers, but they must keep repeating the questions until appropriate answers emerge. All church groups tend to offend against the public and their own membership when leaders try to speak their own moral position as though it represented everyone. (Politicians do it all the time when they intone, "The American people think. . . .") Religious leaders must clarify to whom and for whom they speak. (The National Council of Churches claims to speak first to its constituency in its educative role. Its public voice is only that of its voting body, the General Board, which is often not carefully differentiated by them or by journalists. Then the ecumenical body sometimes gets into trouble.)

Fifth, in an effort to be democratically fair, to resist being preemptive by asserting religious values and perspectives, and to avoid offending other religious faiths, mainline denominations and their ecumenical expressions may sometimes speak too little out of religious faith convictions in public life, as Wendy Kaminer of the Radcliffe Public Policy Institute has argued at an Aspen winter symposium on religion and public policy:

We are protesting the enforcement of sectarian values—that is, the values of a *specific* religion—on a pluralistic society. But it is terribly misleading to suggest that separationists want to deprive religious people of a voice in public affairs, or that we expect people to remain uninfluenced by their faith when they enter public life. . . . The injection of religious perspectives into policy debates is unavoidable; the right to voice a religious belief about a public policy is inarguable. What is at issue are demands that government adopt and enforce sectarian religious beliefs.[21]

At Michael Learner's Washington, D.C., Summit on Ethics and Meaning in April 1996, the Roman Catholic Sister Joan Chittester warned her subgroup audience that in the liberal effort to be open we have been too neutral on religion and values. Freedom is the one affirmed value, she declared, so that we are then free to be valueless. To her comments at that same summit Harvey Cox added that the Religious Right has raised some valid questions that liberals should explore: "How much moral consensus is needed for democracy to function? What is the minimum? Does religious pluralism necessarily lead to moral relativism?"[22]

In an article on the Religious Right, Cox's Harvard associate Peter J. Gomes took this concern a step further in commending the Christian Coalition for insisting that religious values "be restored to the center of our cultural and political discourse. These religious groups have not only filled a values vacuum created by the self indulgent and coarsening materialism of the last 30 years. They have also provided the political means for civic virtue to be debated along the wide spectrum of religious belief in the United States." He further asked, "How ought men and women in search of the virtuous life and a culture that celebrates the classical trinity of the true, the good, and the beautiful to proceed in a culture that knows how to make a living, but not a life worth living? . . . The bankruptcy of secularism has forced the questions out of the closet, and religious conservatives have given them a new and strident urgency." Gomes concluded, "They have asked the right questions, but we dare not be content with their answers."[23]

Sixth, religious people all occasionally lack the table manners to resist attacking motives. Christian liberals claim the Christian Right lacks compassion for the poor. The Religious Right argues that liberals are not really religious. They accuse liberals of being unpatriotic in their stands on militarism, a strong United Nations, the Gulf War, Nicaragua, and the sanctuary movement. Liberals see the Religious Right as captive to jingoism, not really believing "Jesus is Lord," but "America is Lord." These barbs do little to advance careful and creative thinking, though they may call attention to significant theological issues.

Sometimes, of course, the question of motive may have important legal and ethical importance. After Pat Robertson met on September 13, 1997 with a group of Christian Coalition activists in Atlanta, a tape recording of his comments by Americans United for Separation of Church and State revealed a strong partisan political agenda. Robertson said, reviewing the current Democratic lineup for the presidency, "So I don't think at this time and juncture the Democrats are going to be able to take the White House unless we throw it away. But we have to get a responsible person and we have to realize some strategy." Later he commented, "I know that all these laws say that we've got to be careful, but there's nothing that says we can't have a few informal discussions among ourselves." Barry

Lynn of Americans United heard this as justification for removing the Christian Coalition's provisional tax-exempt status, because it "is nothing but a hardball Republican political machine with a thin veneer of religiousity."[24]

Eschewing attacks on motivation, the National Council of Churches was speaking at its best when its Executive Committee on September 12, 1980, issued a statement on Christian citizenship, "consistent with its thirty-year history of a biblically motivated search for justice, peace, reconciliation and the succouring of the world's poor and oppressed." Citing the obligations of Christian citizenship, the council's probably little-noticed statement is worth quoting at some length:

> The immense resources of Christ's grace supply the courage and inward renewal to undertake citizenship responsibilities today and in the age to come. The humility to see government leaders and oneself as constantly under divine judgment and mercy is a contribution to democratic political vitality and is important for opposing totalitarianism and demagoguery.
>
> Above all, Christians are to love the Lord their God and their neighbor as themselves. They are to work diligently for peace, for the survival and preservation of God's creation, and for the good of all humanity. Loving one's neighbor has no boundaries of race, class, sex, or nationality, as Christ's ministry amply demonstrates. Christians are obliged to address the needs of those who may be excluded from the benefits of society or from the political process and to whom harm is being done at home or abroad.
>
> As citizens, Christians must not abdicate their responsibility because there is no "pure" candidate, no absolutely correct and clear course of action. God's grace frees Christians to "think our way to a sober estimate based on the measure of faith that God has dealt to each of us" (Rom. 12:3). Christians may not agree on all political decisions, but they are enjoined not to hold one another in contempt, for all stand before God's tribunal. In the tempering fires of political compromise and accommodations to the needs and interests of many diverse groups, there can be discerned no exclusively "Christian vote," nor can single issue pressures serve the best interests of our total society. Through a study of Scripture, the heritage of churches struggling to be faithful, and through the experiences of life which God opens, Christians are called upon to respond to the demands of the times and the promises of God.[25]

Seventh, Christians are caught between the desire to be effective by being engaged in the specific legislative battles of the day and holding their fire for the big moment and its overarching ethical and religiously meaningful comprehensive public word. They can be used by slick political maneuvering or rendered irrelevant because they refuse to be so used. Their voice may be heard so frequently that, in our media-dominated age, they are screened out as no longer "news," since their general perspective is already known. They can become embroiled in the twists and turns of a legislative action and neglect to see the occasion for a costly significant stand arise. They can argue small details when the whole system needs to be challenged—or, by challenging the "whole enchilada," they may be ushered quietly, or perhaps kicking and screaming, out the side door. Were the "table manners" of those who opposed the Vietnam War and ended up in Canada wholly out of line? Faithful religious citizens and institutions may answer differently.

Eighth, a related question is which public table to seek to sit around at a given time and on a given issue. The Christian Coalition has demonstrated that local and state level politics offers an access that can have great effect in relation to some issues. Electing school board members can influence what kind of policies will be practiced in local schools regarding many family values issues, so the Coalition has concentrated much effort there. Similarly, at the state level, boards of education decide choice of textbooks and other key educational policy matters. Many economic issues of the mainline church agenda have some local and state relevance, but more of them are greatly influenced by national policy or even international policy. The Interfaith Alliance is paying the Christian Coalition the compliment of imitation by establishing TIA local and state networks around the country. The Call for Renewal group convened by Sojourners is also developing a national network. But, given the breadth of their concerns, the mainline churches had better hold onto the United Nations Church Center and their Washington offices too.

Finally, for this particular set of observations, one must remember that merely "sitting around the public table" is not sufficient as a goal. How one perceives one's place at the table in relation to others is critical for the functioning of democracy. Justin Watson, writing about the Christian Coalition, said that the organization wants recognition as an equal, but wants its uncompromising "Christian voice" protected and respected. It wants to restore evangelicalism to its earlier role in the nation as the chief spokesperson for moral force, even as it sits around the table with other "moral forces." Watson observed, "If the destruction of diversity is what the CC *really* wants, then it will almost certainly be destined to disappointment and political irrelevance."[26]

Mainline denominational leadership has had to adjust to its new marginality at some loss to its energy and vision. It is painfully aware that other voices, often secular, frequently override its own around the table. The mainline recognizes and respects those other voices—with the ironic exception of the Christian Right, which it perceives to be arrogant and fanatic. The danger for the mainline today is that it will mouth its carefully crafted policy positions with a sense that it is doing and saying the right things, but with little expectation that it will matter in the political tug and haul. This is a recipe for apathy. They should pay attention to the following story, frequently told in his own inimitable way by the ardent social activist Rabbi Marshall Meyer of Argentina and New York:

A midnineteenth-century rabbi was trying to teach a group of children, but they were all excited about a locomotive coming to their village for the first time. "We've got to see it, Rabbi; the whole world is talking about it." Succumbing to their entreaties, he walked them to a hill, where they could watch the tremendous machine, vomiting flames, billowing smoke, and making a deafening noise. People got on and off the cars, and the locomotive chugged away, but the rabbi stood transfixed. "Shouldn't we go back to studying Torah now?" asked the children. "Yes, but first—what have you learned?" Some children spoke about smoke, others the noise or the force. The rabbi nodded, then said: "There was one car with a fire in its belly, and all the other cars didn't have any fire. The one car with the fire carried all the other cars and all those people. When you see something unusual you must learn from it."

But no amount of "fire in the belly" will restore either the mainline or the Christian Coalition to the dominance of Protestantism in early American culture. The skills of democratic participation in today's mixture of religions and values in American public life require a new finesse. A passion for justice and righteousness that is able to acknowledge respectfully other passionate competing views of justice and virtue is a rare but increasingly necessary democratic "etiquette." Because in such a multivariate society *everyone* feels on the sidelines, there is a tendency for each group, including religious groups, to try to elbow its way to the head of the public table. Jesus had some strong, instructive words about table sitting. He urged guests to choose the lowest place at the table—"for every one who exalts himself will be humbled, and he who humbles himself will be exalted." And when you yourself give a feast, "invite to the table the poor, the maimed, the lame, and the blind" (Luke 14:11, 13).

Chapter 7

Public Religion and Economic Inequality

James D. Davidson and Ralph E. Pyle

One of the defining characteristics of the last quarter century has been the increasing concentration of wealth and income at the top of American society and the increasing impoverishment of people toward the bottom. Evidence indicating that the rich are getting richer and the poor are getting poorer is plentiful and compelling. According to Kevin Phillips, "No parallel upsurge of riches has been seen since the late nineteenth century, the era of the Vanderbilts, Morgans, and Rockefellers."[1] Phillips's book *The Politics of Rich and Poor* shows that the United States now has one of the largest gaps between rich and poor of any major Western nation. Hacker and Braun report the same pattern.[2] In 1970, the top fifth of all families earned 41 percent of the nation's income. That increased to 42 percent in 1980, 44 percent in 1990, and 47 percent in 1994. Meanwhile, the bottom fifth's share fell from 5.4 percent in 1970 to 5.3 percent in 1980, 4.6 percent in 1990, and only 4.2 percent in 1994.[3]

Two recent comparisons of chief executive officers' salaries to workers' salaries provide effective images of how unevenly income is distributed. According to Sklar, "The average CEO of a major corporation was paid as much as 40 factory workers in 1965, 60 factory workers in 1978, 122 factory workers in 1989, and 173 factory workers in 1995."[4] Kadlec points out that a nuclear power plant employee would have to work 214 years to make as much as the average CEO makes in a single year.[5]

The government's "official"—and very conservative—measure of poverty shows that the percentage of Americans in poverty has risen from 12.1 percent in 1969 to 14.5 percent in 1994. The 1994 poverty line translates into only $3.46 per person per day for food and only $6.91 per person per day for all other expenses, such as mortgage or rent, clothing, transportation, and insurance. A more realistic measure—which estimates poverty at 50 percent of the median income—shows that almost twice as many Americans are in poverty and that the poverty rate had risen from 20 percent in 1969 to 22 percent in 1994.[6] Sklar notes, "The percentage of children living in extreme poverty has . . . doubled since 1975."[7]

But income disparity itself provides only a conservative estimate of how much inequality there is in the United States. Inequalities based on wealth are even greater. The top fifth of all families possess about 84 percent of the nation's wealth. The top 40 percent have 97 percent of the wealth, whereas the bottom 60 percent have only 3 percent. Moreover, wealth inequality has increased dramatically in recent years. The top 1 percent of families increased their share of the nation's wealth from 34 percent in 1983 to 38 percent in 1989.[8] The nation's three wealthiest individuals are Bill Gates, who was worth $18.5 billion in 1996; Warren Buffett, who was worth $15 billion; and Paul Allen, who was worth $7.5 billion.[9] In the next year alone, Gates's net worth more than doubled to $39.8 billion; Buffet's net worth rose to $21 billion; and Allen's fortune jumped to $17 billion.[10] Meanwhile, people in the bottom fifth of families have negative net worth (they owe more than they make and have more debts than assets).[11]

EXPLAINING INCREASED INEQUALITY:
A CONFLICT PERSPECTIVE

Using a conflict theoretical perspective, Ryan argues that trends toward inequality are the product of two interacting forces:

One is the amount and militancy of collective activity by groups of working people and poor people; the other is the degree of repressive power being exercised by and on behalf of the wealthy minority through such mechanisms as imprisonment and other forms of confinement, restrictive practices in the area of public assistance and other segments of the social-welfare field, and the establishment of economic policies to increase unemployment, reduce wages, and increase profits. At any given time the state of inequality seems to vary with the *relative* magnitude and balance between these two sets of forces.[12]

We agree with Ryan's thesis. We share his view that economic policies favoring the wealthy and the lack of protest by working people and the poor have combined to produce the recent trend toward economic inequality. Corporate decisions relating to increased profit margins, the relocation of plants to second and third world nations, the downsizing of domestic work forces, and the widening gap between management salaries and workers' wages have been major influences. So have political decisions relating to reductions in capital gains and income taxes. Grass-roots organizations and unions have not offered effective re-sistance. Their relative lack of grass-roots militancy has contributed to the grow-ing concentration of wealth and income at the top of society and the decline in the economic well-being of people toward the bottom.

But the economic and political sectors are not the only ones affecting the un-equal distribution of wealth and income. Other spheres of life, such as family, re-ligion, and education, also play some role. In this chapter, we call special attention to religion's role in the trend toward economic inequality by addressing three sets of questions: First, what role, if any, has religion played? Has religion supported and/or challenged the wealth-producing policies favored by economic and political elites? Has it stifled and/or championed militancy among working-class and poor people? Second, under what conditions are America's religious groups most likely to perpetuate inequality or promote equality? Why are some religious groups more inclined to perpetuate inequality, and others likely to stress policies favoring equality? Finally, has religion's role changed over the course of the last thirty years? Is religion any more likely to perpetuate inequal-ity or promote equality today than it was in the 1960s?

WHAT HAS BEEN RELIGION'S ROLE?

Although religion has not had as much impact as economic and political forces have had on inequality, it has had some influence on recent economic trends. As Hart has argued, it has played a dual role. It has perpetuated inequal-ity, *and* it has promoted equality. It has sanctified inequality, *and* it has con-demned it.[13] Religion has played both roles because the religious arena consists of so many different faiths, special purpose groups, and congregations.

Imagine a continuum. At one end are groups that contribute to economic in-equality. These groups conduct worship services legitimating an unequal distrib-ution of wealth and income, have no staff persons specifically assigned to social ministries addressing the causes and consequences of inequality, allocate very little staff time to outreach programs, sponsor very few social outreach pro-grams, invest only small amounts of money in social ministry programs, and have very few members who are involved in programs oriented toward social and economic justice. These groups include special purpose groups such as the Christian Coalition and conservative congregations that support wealth-produc-ing tax cuts and oppose the efforts of grass-roots organizations representing the economic interests of working people.[14]

At the other end of the continuum are groups that promote equality. These groups conduct worship services calling for economic justice, have full-time staff persons in the area of social ministry, devote significant amounts of staff time to social outreach, sponsor numerous programs related to social concerns, make sizable expenditures in the area of social ministry, and have many lay members who are actively involved in programs oriented toward economic justice. These groups include the Campaign for Human Development, Sojourners, and many liberal congregations that oppose legislation benefiting economic elites and work vigorously to mobilize low-income and working-class people.[15]

Most religious groups fall somewhere in between. Examples include most black congregations; many of the churches in Smith's study of Presbyterian congregations; the congregations in Wood's study of Protestant churches in Indianapolis; many of the Hartford churches in Roozen, McKinney, and Carroll's study *Varieties of Religious Presence;* the various Protestant and Catholic churches in Dudley's Church and Community Project; most of the Protestant and Catholic congregations in Davidson, Mock, and Johnson's study of affluent churches; and most of the churches in Earle, Knudsen, and Shriver's book *Spindles and Spires.*[16]

The overall distribution looks something like Figure 1. There are more religious groups toward the inequality end of the continuum than there are toward the equality end. The prevailing orientation among the nation's religious groups—thus, America's "public religion"—has been more inclined to perpetuate inequality than it has been to promote equality. The dissenting voices question the legitimacy of inequality and call for a more equitable distribution of power, privilege, and prestige. In the following sections, we examine ways in which churches address issues of (in)equality.

Figure 1
Distribution of Religious Groups

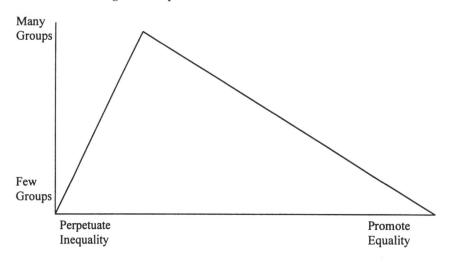

Worship Services

Worship services in most churches stress homilies and hymns celebrating God's material blessings and calling sinners to repent so they too can experience abundance. Services seldom lift a prophetic voice against economic inequality.[17] However, homilies and hymns in some congregations and special purpose groups occasionally highlight the need for economic justice.[18]

Staff Assignments and Staff Time

Most congregations have several staff people devoted to faith-oriented ministry (e.g., religious education, liturgy, choir). Very few have a full-time person working in the area of social outreach or social concern.[19] In Lafayette, Indiana, for example, only one church out of nearly 150 congregations has a full-time social minister. Some readers might argue that it is not important to have one staff person working full time in social outreach, because all church leaders have responsibility for social concerns. However, when Davidson, Mock, and Johnson examined the allocation of total staff time on social ministry, they found that on average staff people devote only about 5 percent of their time to social outreach.[20] Thus, staffing arrangements in most churches predispose churches to perpetuating inequality more than to promoting equality. Dudley's Church and Community Project showed that in those cases in which church leaders are assigned specific responsibility for social concerns, churches tend to design creative outreach programs and mobilize volunteers to participate in them.[21]

Programs

Some programs—such as Bible study, choir, and religious education for children—are inward-oriented, meaning they are mainly directed at church members. Others—such as food pantries and clothing drives—are outward-oriented; they are targeted at persons who do not belong to the church. Research shows that congregations offer their members far more inward-oriented programs than outward-oriented ones. Leege, for example, found that 93 percent of Catholic parishes have grade school level religious education programs, 84 percent have high school religious education programs, 76 percent have parish councils, and 72 percent have liturgy planning committees. However, only 52 percent offer parishioners opportunities for social service, and only 20 percent sponsor social action programs aimed at social change.[22]

Although churches generally offer their members only a couple of ways of expressing their concern for the poor and powerless, some offer members as many as a dozen different ways to pursue equality.[23] These programs invite parishioners to donate time, money, and services to helping needy individuals and families. They also provide chances to address economic and political policies.

Budgets

The conventional wisdom is that congregations spend about 80 percent of their income on their members and give 20 percent away in the form of benevolences. However, not all benevolences go to programs related to the causes and consequences of economic inequality. Once allocations to denominational agencies and missionaries are set aside, congregations typically allocate only 4 to 5 percent of their budget to activities addressing social concerns.[24]

Although churches generally spend only 4 to 5 percent, some spend much more. In Davidson, Mock, and Johnson's study of affluent congregations, one quarter of the churches were above average in allocating money to social and economic concerns; several spent as much as 12 to 13 percent. Thus, though a majority of churches invest relatively little in programs promoting equality, one in four invests more heavily in such activities.[25]

Laity's Actions

Most church members are in programs related to church administration, members' own well-being, and the well-being of their families. Very few are involved in outwardly oriented ministries related to social inequality. For example, Davidson finds that 28 percent are actively involved in administration, 25 percent are in youth programs, and 18 percent in choir. However, only 5 percent are actively involved in "local mission" and "social concerns." Our research also shows that, when it comes to charitable contributions, church members are more inclined to donate money (43 percent) than they are to donate food and material goods (29 percent) or time (17 percent).[26] Thus, although a majority of churchgoers are only marginally involved in programs and activities that might foster equality, between 10 percent and a third of members are quite active in these areas.

WHAT ACCOUNTS FOR RELIGION'S EMPHASIS ON INEQUALITY?

Why are America's religious groups more inclined to perpetuate inequality than they are to promote equality? Under what conditions are churches most likely to stress equality? We believe the answer boils down to two factors: interests and values.

By interests we mean the material self-interest of religious leaders and lay people. Studies of social stratification have shown quite clearly that the greater one's stake in an inegalitarian system, the more likely one is to support it; the smaller one's investment in such a system, the more freedom one has to critique it.[27]

Although interests explain some of the variation in religious groups' orientations toward inequality, they do not account for all of the variation. Some of it has to do with values (i.e., people's understandings of what is right and wrong; their sense of how they should and should not act). Our analysis of values includes evidence relating to religious beliefs and priorities related to social inequality.

Figure 2 shows that interests have an independent influence on religious groups' orientations toward inequality. When leaders and members stand to gain from inequality, their groups tend to favor it; when they have little or no stake in the system of inequality, their groups are more likely to promote equality. Interests also tend to shape values. When people stand to gain from inequality, they tend toward beliefs that legitimate it; when they have only a limited stake in the system, they are more likely to favor egalitarian beliefs. But values cannot be reduced solely to interests. They spring from other sources as well and have effects of their own.

Interests

Though church executives, clergy, and lay leaders are not as privileged as members of some other occupations, a majority—especially in the nation's more elite religious traditions—have advantaged social backgrounds, are responsible to affluent benefactors and economic elites who serve on church boards and commissions, and/or derive above-average income and considerable wealth from their work in the church. Thus, many religious leaders have reasons for accepting inequality; it is not in their material self-interest to challenge it.[28] Fewer religious leaders come from underprivileged families, are not accountable to persons of privilege, and/or are in low-paying ministries or take vows of poverty. These leaders are free to question inequality and are inclined to do so.[29]

Figure 2
Theoretical Framework

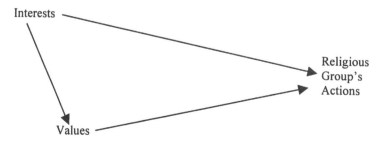

Just as some religious leaders have a greater investment in inequality than others, the same is true for lay people. Some lay people—such as business leaders, lawyers, and doctors—come from a privileged background, are closely tied to economic and political elites, and have an occupation that yields considerable wealth and income. Others—such as teachers, social workers, and many blue-collar workers—have a more humble social origin, are not as accountable to elites, and derive only modest economic rewards from their work.

Lay people in the elite denominations and other religious groups that shape the nation's public religion tend to be heavily invested in inequality. Members of these churches tend to be middle- and upper-class persons who work in the relatively lucrative private sector and blue-collar persons who are most dependent on economic elites for their well-being. Fewer members are white-collar people who belong to the "new class," employees in the public sector, and blue-collar workers who are not dependent on elites for their livelihood. Churches with a large percentage of people having a stake in the system are most inclined to perpetuate inequality; churches with the smallest percentage of such members are most likely to favor equality.[30]

Values

Religious leaders gravitate toward one of two theological orientations relating to inequality: good fortune theology or social justice theology (see Figure 3 for a summary of these "ideal types").

Good fortune theology argues that people are called to follow God's word and live according to his plan. According to this theology, those who accept the call make important contributions to the well-being of society. As a result, they are blessed by God and are entitled to the wealth and income he bestows on them. Those who do not respond to God's call fill less important roles in society and, according to this view, quite rightly receive fewer material benefits. Good fortune theology is found in Calvinist interpretations of scriptures (e.g., Prov. 12:29; Matt. 16:27; Rom. 8:33; 2 Tim. 1:12). It is similarly evident in a seminal early-twentieth-century article on wealth and morality by the Right Reverend William Lawrence, Episcopalian bishop of Massachusetts—and himself a scion of New England industrial wealth. It is a cornerstone of Norman Vincent Peale's "law of abundance," Robert Schuller's "possibility thinking," Jim Bakker's PTL ministry, Pat Robertson's televangelical messages, and Oral Roberts's ministry of miracles. It also provides the theological basis for Paul Zane Pilzer's best-selling book *God Wants You to Be Rich*. Thus, there are mainline versions of good fortune theology, as well as fundamentalist, evangelical, and pentecostal versions.[31]

Social justice theology contends that great wealth and high income are the result of social sins, such as greed and class exploitation. The poor are seen as the innocent victims of powers and principalities over which they have little or no control. Social justice theology questions inequality and calls for a more equitable distribution of economic resources. Whereas good fortune theology sanctifies inequality, social justice theology condemns it.[32] The Judeo-Christian roots of this orientation can be traced to Old Testament prophets (Isa. 10:1–2; 53:9; Jer. 5:27–29; 22:13–16; Ezek. 22:23–31; Hosea 12:2–9; Amos 2:6–7, 5:7; Micah 6:9–15) and New Testament accounts of Jesus's ministry (Matt. 19:23–24, 25:41; Luke 6:24, 16:1–31; 1 Tim. 6:9–10; James 2:14; 1 John 3:17–18). Reinhold Niebuhr, Martin Luther King, and Gustavo Gutiérrez embraced this view. Jim Wallis, Jesse Jackson, and James Cone also are exemplars of this theological orientation. Themes of economic justice are the foundation of books such as *Rich Christians in an Age of Hunger, The Just Demands of the Poor,* and *Good News to the Poor.* Thus, there are radical, liberal, and conservative versions of the social justice orientation.[33]

Leaders of America's major faiths, special purpose groups, and local congregations tend toward good fortune theology more than a theology of social justice. Good fortune theology is the heart and soul of America's public religion; social justice theology tends to be a subordinate theme in American religious culture.[34] Good fortune theology prevails in denominational constitutions, doctrines, and programmatic commitments. It prevails in both mainline Protestant groups such as the Episcopal and Presbyterian churches, and in such sectarian groups as the Church of Christ and the Church of the Nazarene.[35] The Assemblies of God's "Statement of Fundamental Truths" and its "General Christian Doctrines" are vivid expressions of good fortune theology's emphasis on the vertical dimensions of faith. Their emphasis is on such topics as the One True God, the Deity of the Lord Jesus Christ, Forgiveness and Grace, the Scripture Inspired, Baptism in the Holy Spirit, and Faith for Unanswered Prayers.

Social justice theology is a subordinate theme in both mainline and sectarian religions.[36] Among mainline groups, it is evident in places such as the Catholic church's "social teachings" and black theology. The United Methodist Church's "social principles" also include strong social justice statements about the need for a more equitable distribution of the world's resources (reducing poverty) and the need to extend social and economic benefits to all workers, including migrant workers. Social justice theology is less apparent in sectarian traditions. For example, the Assemblies of God's "Statement of Fundamental Truths" and its "General Christian Doctrines" never mention economic justice.

Special purpose groups in both mainline and sectarian traditions also are prone to good fortune theology. This seems especially true among evangelical groups such as the Moral Majority and the Christian Coalition, which have stressed individual responsibility for one's socioeconomic status, lobbied for cuts in federal income taxes and capital gains taxes, and called for a reduction in fed-

Figure 3
Good Fortune and Social Justice Theodicies

	Good Fortune	Social Justice
Human nature	Evil	Good
Social institutions	Good	Evil
Important institutions	Family Religion Education	Economics Politics
Bases of human behavior	Values	Interests
Nature of society	Order	Conflict
Origin of inequality	Society needs it for common good	Haves need it; exploit Have Nots
Is it inevitable?	Yes	No
Social dynamics	Talented (saved) earn most important positions; others (unsaved) sink to bottom	Elites (unsaved) inherit wealth; masses (saved) inherit poverty
Profile of inequality	Graduated strata	Polarized classes
Why does it persist?	Functional	Coercion
Consequences	Positive	Negative
Is it fair?	Yes	No
Social mobility	Extensive	Very little
Who is to blame?	Poor (personal sin)	Elites (social sin)
Solution	Change individuals	Change society
Religion's role	Personal salvation	Build just and equal world
Religion's emphasis	Faith (vertical)	Social concern (horizontal)

eral welfare programs—all of which benefit the wealthy more than the poor.[37] Mainline groups espousing social justice theologies include the World Council of Churches, National Council of Churches, Interfaith Alliance, Lafayette Urban Ministry, and Metropolitan Interfaith Association. Evangelical ecumenical groups with social justice orientations include Sojourners and Evangelicals for Social Action.[38]

Good fortune theology also prevails at the level of the local church: Roman Catholic parishes, mainline Protestant churches, and black congregations, as well as congregations affiliated with conservative Protestant traditions. The constitution of an independent Baptist congregation in Lafayette, Indiana, is illustrative. The section on "doctrinal belief" includes twenty tenets, all of which address the vertical dimension of faith; not one tenet addresses the causes or consequences of economic inequality. Social justice theology is a subordinate theme in most local congregations.[39]

Lay people also gravitate toward good fortune theology more than they do toward social justice theology. This pattern is evident in our previous research on vertical beliefs such as the existence of God or the divinity of Christ and horizontal beliefs such as loving one's neighbor and doing good for others. Our research and work done by others, such as Stark and Glock, indicate higher levels of consensus around vertical beliefs than horizontal beliefs. For example, Davidson found that nine out of ten parishioners in Protestant and Catholic churches strongly agree with vertical beliefs about the existence of a personal God, the divinity of Christ, and life after death. Although a similar percentage of lay people strongly agree that "faith without good works is dead," only a third strongly agree with the idea that churches ought to be involved in social and economic issues or that the way we treat others on earth affects our fate in the hereafter. Not only are the horizontal and vertical dimensions conceptually distinct, they also tend to be quite independent spheres in church members' minds. Our research shows that there is very little correlation, if any, between the two.[40]

There also have been studies of lay people's views about the structural and individual causes of poverty.[41] Overall, church members are more inclined toward a "fair play" view that inequality is inevitable and functional than they are toward a "fair shares" perspective that questions inequality and emphasizes its harmful consequences. By and large, lay people are more inclined to blame poverty on the behavioral characteristics of the poor than on structural conditions such as lack of jobs, poor wages, and racism.[42] Though a majority of churchgoers favor individualistic explanations of poverty, others favor structural explanations. These dissenting voices are quite prominent in some religious groups.[43] Similarly, a comparison of the social beliefs of church members and the unchurched indicates that church members are more likely to blame inequality on minorities and the poor and are less likely to blame it on structural conditions in society.

After examining attitudes about racial justice and women's rights, Roof and McKinney concluded that "churchgoers are generally more traditional in their attitudes than nonchurchgoers."[44]

Both Hoge and Davidson, among others, have studied the importance parishioners attach to church programs. These studies consistently show that church members place highest priority on programs relating to their own spiritual needs and/or the spiritual and moral needs of people in their families, especially their children. Parishioners do not attach nearly as much importance to social outreach, especially outreach that involves advocacy on behalf of the poor and powerless. One of Davidson's studies, for example, shows that 90 percent of church members believe that religious education for children is a high priority, 86 percent say preaching the gospel in worship is important, and 80 percent value pastoral counseling. However, only 58 percent say it is important to encourage charity toward the needy, only 31 percent say it is important that their parish support the poor and oppressed in organizing for their rights, and only 24 percent think their church ought to encourage members to support social reform. In short, a majority of church members have priorities that lend themselves to the perpetuation of inequality, but roughly one quarter to one third have views that are conducive to economic equality.[45]

HAS RELIGION'S ROLE CHANGED IN RECENT YEARS?

Our last question is whether religion's emphasis on inequality has been increasing over the course of the last thirty years. We do not have longitudinal data on all dimensions of church life, but there is considerable evidence indicating that religious groups have been pulling back from the outward-oriented, pro-equality emphasis of the 1960s and giving increased priority to an inward-oriented, pro-inequality emphasis in the 1990s.[46] Figure 4 illustrates this shift.

The 1960s was a period of social experimentation. It also was a period in which the federal government and faith groups were pouring money into programs related to the war on poverty and other social programs.[47] Religious groups—including elite denominations and other groups shaping America's public religion—participated in this period of social concern by giving increased attention to the causes and consequences of poverty. Takayama and Darnell as well as Davidson have described ecumenical urban ministries that burst onto the religious scene in the mid- to late 1960s.[48] Other writers have described local congregations that increased their involvement in social issues during this period. The literature of the time was flooded with accounts of churches' efforts to serve the needy and promote equality.[49]

The nation's social and political climate has grown increasingly conservative during the 1980s and 1990s. The federal government and faith groups have cut

Figure 4
Distribution of Religious Groups, 1960s and 1990s

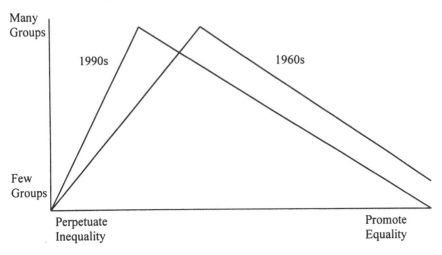

back on their investments in social programs. As a result, the number of religious groups addressing the causes and consequences of inequality has declined. Many of the ecumenical urban ministries formed in the 1960s no longer exist. Though some local churches continue to be socially involved, they have been increasingly concerned about internal matters. This shift is evident in the declining number of books on religion and economic justice, and in the increasing number that focus on topics such as the decline of mainline churches and the growth and vitality of sectarian religions. R. Stephen Warner's study *New Wine in Old Wineskins* is especially good in documenting this shift in one congregation. Warner shows how the Mendicino, California, church he studied has reduced its emphasis on social concerns and increased its commitment to the spiritual growth of its members.[50]

CONCLUSIONS

We began by documenting the trend toward greater economic inequality in American society and asking what religion's role has been in this trend. We argued that religion has had dual consequences: It has perpetuated inequality *and* it has promoted equality.

We asked, then addressed, three key questions: First, has religion been more of a force for inequality or equality? Using several types of data, we showed that the number of religious groups favoring inequality exceeds the number favoring equality. Though there is a need for additional evidence in several areas, indications are that America's public religion has endorsed the self-serving policies of wealthy elites more than it has challenged them; it also has stifled militancy more than it has promoted it.

Second, we asked why America's public religion has tended to endorse inequality more than challenge it. We argued that church leaders and members tend to have a stake in the structure of social inequality; they have little or no interest in promoting a more equitable distribution of the nation's economic resources. Also, leaders and churchgoers gravitate toward a theology of good fortune, which legitimates inequality. When religious leaders and members who are less dependent on economic elites embrace a theology of social justice, their groups are more likely to promote economic equality.

Third, we asked whether religion's support of inequality has increased over the years. Our answer was yes. Though there is a need for more evidence on this topic, it appears that the number of religious groups with outward orientations has declined while the number with inward orientations has increased. This shift in America's public religion goes hand-in-hand with the trend toward increased economic inequality in society.

We conclude with an appeal for more theory and research on religion's role in inequality. Analysts need to get past the functionalist and neofunctionalist models that tend to dominate the study of religion in general and public religion in particular. These perspectives concentrate on religion's contributions to social order but limit our appreciation of the extent to which—and the ways—religion contributes to social disorder. By contrast, sociologists of religion need to put more emphasis on conflict perspectives, which are more conducive to analyses of religion's role in fostering tensions between society's haves and have nots.

There is a need for more research on the extent to which—and the ways—religious groups pursue inequality and equality. In addition to the need for more data on worship, staff assignments and time allocations, church programs, budgets, and members' actions, there also is a great need for research on religious groups' lobbying efforts on behalf of and in opposition to legislation favoring inequality. There also is a need for more information on the conditions under which such outcomes occur. We give highest priority to the collection of data on the role of self-interests and the separate effects of good fortune and social justice theologies. Finally, there is a need for longitudinal data on the persistence of and changes in conditions leading to various outcomes. Though we have pointed to changes in the inward and outward orientations of religious groups, there is need for more longitudinal data on matters such as staff assignments and church budgets oriented toward outreach. We also need more information on changes in leaders' and church members' vested interests in inequality and changes in their religious values over time. Research along these lines will give us more complete descriptions and better explanations of stability and change in religion's role in the public arena.

Conserving Religious Identity While Doing Public Theology: On Public Churches and Common Ground

James R. Kelly

Scholars and members of American religious bodies are indebted to Martin Marty. He challenges us to examine and link the responsibilities of believer and citizen. There's no formula for such daunting projects. In his 1981 *The Public Church,* Marty asks himself, "By what right does the historian who is a participant observer of the public church step outside the reportorial role?" Six pages later—after he's defined the public church—Marty answers his own question. The historian, he says, "can serve the public church by sketching precedents for this Christian contribution to American public theology as a critical and constructive voice within public religion."[1]

The term public *church,* referring to actual churches with actual allegiances, is Marty's critical response to abstract Durkheimian-like secular-humanist hopes for a collective story, a civil *religion,* that might both integrate *and* critique American society. The public church is the opposite of the tribal or the sectarian or the abstract. Marty formulates but does not invent the public church, which he finds and points to in the increasingly ecumenically open parts of mainline Protestantism, evangelical Protestantism, and Catholicism, which, by language and actions that are *both* religious and civil, contribute their invaluable and irreplaceable resources of motivation and wisdom to the public realm in the search for justice and the common good. Public *theology,* in Marty's view, is the "effort to interpret the life of a people in the light of a transcendent reference."[2] The emergent public church is both what Marty studies and what he supports.

So do I. Marty's more recent contribution—*The One and the Many: America's Struggle for the Common Good*—gives me a fruitful lead. There Marty, following the philosophical turn to the inextricable interweaving of language and human agency, reflects on the primacy of "story" and "metaphor" for both scholarly understanding and rooted critique, the only kind that can lastingly affect the public church.[3] Marty's turn to narrative and metaphor as ways toward truth has social science precedents that have been neglected until recently. At the end of the 1960s Robert Nisbet, in his *Social Change and History,* drew attention to sociology's hidden reliance on metaphor. It's pertinent to what follows here (and elsewhere in social science) that Nisbet called early attention both to the indispensability *and* to the dangers of metaphors, especially when they are either unacknowledged or else disguised as "models." Three key sentences from that prescient book structure this chapter on the metaphor of *common ground* for the public church: (1) "To repeat, metaphor is indispensable—indispensable in language, poetry, philosophy, and even science." (2) "But clearly, metaphor is also dangerous." (3) "Metaphor allies itself well with proposals for social action."[4]

My story is about the emergence and the critics of the metaphor of common ground and its institutionalization in two domains I have studied: the abortion controversy and American Roman Catholicism. I show a relationship between the two and the significance of both for the public church. My focus here is the Catholic part of the public church, and I begin with a story about the origins and trials of the Cardinal Bernardin *Catholic Common Ground Initiative.* The story requires two flashbacks—to the Second Vatican Council, which brought Catholicism explicitly and irrevocably into the public church, and to the abortion controversy in 1989 in St. Louis, where the metaphor common ground attracted its first widespread media attention and where it received its strong seminal core meaning. Some conceptual messiness must remain. My approach is empirical and plainly cannot be the last word. Emergent terms refer to emergent practices, and both require time for scholarly judgment. I respect the fears of critics about the abuses of the common ground metaphor. Indeed, in part these fears prompt my interest in examining principled applications of the common ground metaphor. As suggested by its metaphoric cousins—such as high ground, low ground, middle ground—common ground is an analogous term leading to analogous practices. A healthy public theology will find that some promote and some impede the pursuit of the good society. I'll give examples of what helps and what impedes.

My two common ground stories—the abortion controversy and the Bernardin Catholic Common Ground Initiative—are especially important in the light of Marty's hope that the public church find translations of its traditions that are principled and pragmatic, that are faithful to religious identity, critically accessible to a wider public, and open in dialogue to all others committed to their own integrity. The core meaning of common ground suggests conflicting integrities that do not preclude a respect for the adversary's conscience and thus imply persistent, even dogged, practices of dialogue. Sociologically we can probably expect a search for common ground only when, first, adversaries' natural imperative toward *gaining ground* is seriously, if not permanently, stalemated and, second, when those risking common ground can persuade, or at least withstand, internal critics who inevitably accuse them, if not of betrayal, then of *losing ground.*[5] I cast my story in a dramatic way to raise momentary doubts about the provisionally hopeful ending I eventually give it.

BEGINNING SUSPENSEFULLY—THE TRAVAIL OF DIALOGUE

Avery Dulles, S.J., perhaps the most widely known contemporary American Catholic theologian, has been admired for his balance and capaciousness. The week before his scheduled November 19, 1996 McGinley lecture, his surprising title—"The Limits of Dialogue"—was pasted on every other post surrounding Fordham University's large commons called Edward's Parade Ground. The lecture coolly and cautiously dissected the *Called to Be Catholic: Church in a Time of Peril* statement released on August 12, 1996, as the late Joseph Cardinal Bernardin launched the Catholic Common Ground Initiative. The statement and the initiative quickly attracted a large and continuing amount of attention. The statement began, "Will the Catholic Church in the United States enter the new millennium as a church of promise? . . . Or will it become a church on the defensive, torn by dissension and weakened in its core structures? The outcome, we believe depends on . . . whether the church can reverse the polarization that inhibits discussion and cripples leadership."[6]

The *Called to Be Catholic* statement emerged from twice yearly meetings, from December 1992 to spring 1996, of men and women, clergy and laity, whose personal and professional lives were intertwined with the *reproduction of Catholicism* or, more simply, whose lives were personally defined by Catholicism and publicly committed to its vitality. The unusual support group included Bernardin, six other bishops, two heads of religious orders of nuns, eighteen lay men and women, and the Reverend Philip Murnion of the Pastoral Life Center in New York City, which now staffs the Catholic Common Ground Initiative. As church professionals and committed laity, they shared an admiration for Bernardin's ecclesial style and his understanding of the Second Vatican Council's teachings about the mission and renewal of Catholicism. Bernardin was an ecclesial visionary whose managerial approach transcended the simplifying labels of "progressive" and "conservative." In the dichotomous mode of sociological "ideal types," *community* refers to intensity at the cost of inclusion and *ecclesial* as inclusion at the cost of intensity; Bernardin's style suggested a church term of richer nuance, something like the *ecclesial community.* It attracted those, in Marty's phrase, who located themselves, for the sake of the public church, where "the right of the left and the left of the right meet."[7]

In their various ministries—bishops, chancellors, editors, superiors of religious orders—the originators of the Catholic Common Ground Initiative experienced conflicts that seemed increasingly irresolvable by appeals to authority or to a shared emergent vision of the church. They seemed unable to move backward or forward. In their jointly composed *Called to Be Catholic* statement, they wrote that many Catholic leaders "both clerical and lay, feel under siege." But while buffeted from both the Left and the Right, they shared with Bernardin a sense of Catholicism persuasively felt as deeper and richer than the currently unresolved tensions inherited from the Second Vatican Council. We might call the Bernardin legacy an effort to affirm and experience the Second Vatican Council as continuous with the past in ways that prepared Catholics for Catholicism's inevitable further revisions and adaptations. Bernardin's patent spiritual serenity and his centrist intelligence were widely acknowledged. Observers of his work as the National Conference of Catholic Bishops' first general secretary (1968–1971) and its third president (1974–1977) agreed he had "a genius for bringing about consensus."[8] But an essential dimension of the Bernardin legacy is that neither his serenity nor the consensus he promoted was purchased by evading tensions. It's highly significant that *centrist* was a self-characterization initially tried but quickly abandoned by the Bernardin Initiative.[9]

Immediately before Bernardin's August 12, 1996 announcement, the Catholic Common Ground Initiative evolved to include well-known and divergent voices in American Catholicism, such as Michael Novak, John Sweeney, Mary Ann Glendon, and Elizabeth Johnson, as well as a core of the original informal support group. Archbishop Oscar Lipscomb succeeded the late Cardinal Bernardin as its chair. The Initiative is still expanding to increase its diversity—including, for example, African Americans and more women. The Catholic Common Ground Initiative can be thought of as an attempt to institutionalize the Bernardin legacy. Through conferences and publications it seeks to model and promote common ground.[10]

Common Ground Critics

Some of the first public responses to the Initiative's call for dialogue and common ground were highly critical. Indeed, just two weeks after his press conference announcing the Catholic Common Ground Initiative, Cardinal Bernardin had to call a second conference to clarify the Initiative in the light of its "conservative" and "liberal" critics. Liberal critics tended to say either that *they* favored dialogue but that the Right did not or that the committee membership was not inclusive enough. The conservative criticisms were the more comprehensive, and since they included criticisms made by four of Bernardin's brother bishops, they received more publicity by far. Gustav Niebuhr of the *New York Times* reported,

"An unusual, public disagreement has developed among the nation's Roman Catholic cardinals, over plans by Joseph Cardinal Bernardin, Archbishop of Chicago, to lead an effort to find 'common ground' among Catholics of different opinions and try to decrease polarization in the church."[11]

In his McGinley lecture, Dulles crisply summarized and synthesized these criticisms. His final title—"The Travail of Dialogue"—was doubly surprising in that Dulles himself is a longtime contributor to several major Roman Catholic–Protestant ecumenical dialogues, and dialogue was a major theme of the Second Vatican Council. Whereas *dialogue* never appeared in Vatican I (1869–1870) documents, the word appears thirty-one times in Vatican II (1962–1965) documents. The shift in Roman Catholic self-understanding captured by that statistic cannot be overestimated. While church historians remind us that disorientation, disputes, and disunity are the predictable outcomes of all major efforts to reform Catholicism, Yves Congar reached for the dramatic term *shock* to describe the intense, even traumatic, aftershocks of the Second Vatican Council. "Vatican II," he wrote, "has been followed by socio-cultural change more extensive, radical and rapid and more cosmic in its proportions than any change at any period in man's history."[12] Ironically, dialogue came to signal both the best hopes of liberals—a more democratic church more fully present in democratic society—and the worst fears of conservatives—a loss of certainty and identity.

Dulles's opening paragraph sympathetically summarized this *dialogic turn* in Roman Catholicism:

Prior to the Second Vatican Council the Catholic Church had been polemically arrayed against other groups, including the non-Christian religions, non-Catholic Christianity, and the modern world. John XXIII deserves the credit for having seen that this posture was interfering with the mission of the Church. Following his lead, Vatican II renounced anathematization and espoused dialogue. The new stance of the Church was expressed during the Council by Paul VI's first encyclical, *Eccelsiam suam* (1964). God, he maintained, initiated a dialogue of salvation by turning to the world in love, making himself accessible through revelation, and appealing for the free response of faith. Imitating God's action in Christ, the Church must address the world in the spirit of dialogue. It should clearly proclaim the message of salvation as revealed truth, but should do so humbly, in a spirit of trust and respect for the sensitivities of the hearers. Such a Church would listen before speaking and would be alert to discover the elements of truth in the opinions of others.[13]

But after his sympathetic survey of the Catholic church's unequivocal turn to dialogue as its appropriate mode of presence, Dulles sharply turned skeptical.

"The term [dialogue]," he continued, "is often used carelessly, deceptively, and abusively to mean something else than what the Church understands by dialogue." He acknowledged that "the fault lies not with dialogue itself but with theorists who seek to evade the rigorous demand of dialogue." Dulles argued that the historic connection between dialogue and truth had been dangerously weakened in the "current atmosphere," powerfully dominated by "liberal culture," which separates the pursuit of the "right" from the "good." There is, he observed, a tendency among leading liberal intellectuals who, in the name of public peace, seek a privatization of religion, whereby to be good citizens the religiously committed must abandon any effort to urge their own religious based conceptions of the good and the true on others. Dulles mentions the influential philosophers Rawls, Rorty, and Ackerman. In terms of influential sociological theorists we might add, as still another example of the contemporary and dominant liberal assumption of the "priority of the right over the good," Habermas's communicative ethic and its implicit "consensus theory of truth."

By contrast, Dulles recalled, classical usage situates dialogue within the search for a greater grasp of truth. In this tradition, dialogue must always be civil, but civility itself is not its final purpose. Truth is—even truth that others might find objectionable. In the present context, Dulles cautioned, dialogue often becomes a substitute for authority as a search for consensus eclipses any sense of obedience owed to the magisterium or teaching authority of the church.

As did other conservative critics, Dulles singled out the term *common ground* for particular scrutiny. In the *Called to Be Catholic* statement, "The impression was given," he lamented, "that some 'common ground' other than the official doctrine of the Church was being proposed in an effort to reach out to alienated Catholics." Dulles synthesized the criticism of the metaphor of common ground made by several influential brother bishops of Bernardin, specifically Archbishop Bevilacqua and Cardinals Law, Hickey, and Maida. These prominent critics raised the important general question, *Is there a core meaning to the common ground metaphor that can effectively withstand the inevitable internal objections that common ground jeopardizes integrity?*

THE CONTEMPORARY ORIGINS OF THE PRINCIPLED COMMON GROUND METAPHOR

Paradoxically, it is the nation's most fiercely polarized and least promising debate—that about abortion—that best illuminates a distinctive emergent meaning of common ground that safeguards *and* challenges the integrity of group identity. Although it existed earlier, the common ground metaphor became common—indeed, fashionable—only after its surprising emergence in the intractable abortion controversy. Reciprocal challenge based on integrity to principle and truth characterizes its contemporary origins.[14] The contemporary life of the common ground metaphor began with a reporter's challenge to a pro-life activist, who then challenged pro-choice activists. Soon after the Supreme Court's five–four decision of July 3, 1989, in *Webster v. Reproductive Health Services* upheld some Missouri state containments on legal abortion (permitting viability tests on fetuses that might be at least twenty weeks old and allowing public hospitals to perform only abortions required for maternal health), a *St. Louis Dispatch* reporter who for decades had covered the abortion story, Martha Shirk, wearily called and asked the St. Louis pro-life attorney Andrew Puzder, "Is there anything positive about this for anyone?" *Webster* had simply deepened a dead-end polarization, and for activists' reactions from both sides, Shirk said she could skip the interviews and save time by simply changing the date of dozens of past articles she had filed years ago.

Challenged, Puzder, who had himself been a primary author of the Missouri statutes comprising *Webster,* found himself with new thoughts, which he published as "Common Ground on Abortion" in the "op-ed" section of the December 26, 1989, *Dispatch.*[15] Puzder assumed, he told his readers, that by now it was clear that neither side would definitively "win" the abortion battle: After *Roe* there would always be legal abortion, and after *Webster* legal abortion would not remain completely "pro-choice" in practice.[16] As important, although neither side could win, neither side could be expected to abandon its principles. In terms of outcome, the anti-abortion movement would fall between the prohibition and the abolitionist movements, with the former serving, by a very large margin, as the primary historical analogue. Puzder, in effect, sought a way to make principled disagreements constructive precisely when integrity precluded either victory, compromise, or withdrawal. Puzder also called attention to the fact that Missouri had both high rates of female poverty *and* of abortion, and that, in fidelity to their principles, *both* pro-life and pro-choice activists might jointly work to reduce both. "While neither side is going to make concessions on the basic underlying issue (life vs. privacy), it is difficult to see how either side would hurt its position by jointly seeking legislative aid for impoverished women and their children. . . . While the common ground may be slim, it exists. If we can put aside for a moment our simple win–lose attitudes and approach this issue sensibly and calmly, perhaps we can jointly accomplish some good for those we all seek to protect." As Puzder's common ground colleague Loretto Wagner often explained, "Neither side wants to see poor women economically compelled to have abortions."[17]

Puzder told me that the phrase *common ground* "just popped into my head."[18] But it quickly became one of the indispensable terms of the 1990s, dating from a February 17, 1992, front page *New York Times* story by Tamar Lewin about the St. Louis common ground, "In Bitter Abortion Debate, Opponents Learn to Reach for Common Ground." Among activists there is a consensus that common ground in the abortion controversy started in St. Louis.[19] It had six emergent characteristics: St. Louis Common Ground (1) began with a challenge to a pro-life activist, whose movement experience had led to the judgment that neither side could achieve its complete success and the complete failure of its adversary, who (2) in turn publicly challenged pro-choice activists to move with integrity beyond polarization to constructive joint behaviors with pro-life activists, which together they characterized as (3) *common ground* precisely to distinguish their principled cooperation from moral compromise and political accommodation; (4) as they publicly called attention to their continued respective movement loyalties while they (5) sought and promoted joint projects and policies aimed at reducing the pressures on women to abort, (6) which, in effect, challenged both pro-choice and pro-life movements in terms of their respective movement integrities jointly to explore and support ways that reduce the coercive circumstances and social policies that, at least indirectly and sometimes directly, increase the likelihood of abortion.[20]

The Common Ground of the Bernardin Initiative

It's worth noting that abortion disagreements were a source of the introduction of the term *common ground* into American Catholic religious circles and then into the Catholic Common Ground Initiative.[21] In his June 7, 1984, address to the National Right to Life Committee annual convention in Kansas City, Missouri, "Linkage and the Logic of the Abortion Debate," Bernardin told the two thousand activists, "The common ground is as yet not sufficiently explored, but there is significant potential for development in this area."[22]

Legal abortion enormously complicated Roman Catholic institutional presence in American society. The tradition, of course, had dealt with the problems of maintaining integrity in socially compromising contexts. But its traditional conceptualizations lacked the accessible moral clarity needed in a pluralistic and mass media era. I'll briefly show the relationship between contemporary pressures on Catholic institutional identity and Catholicism's increasing use of the common ground metaphor to claim integrity against the charge of compromise.

Common Ground Moral Antecedents

The classical discussion of noncompromising cooperation employed the terms *formal* and *material cooperation*. These distinctions go back to the sixteenth century and derive from situations involving conscientious individuals who found themselves inextricably involved in the immoral activities of the more powerful whom they served. The term *material* referred to the action itself and the term *formal* referred to the subordinate's intention, that is, whether he or she actually approved of the employer's immoral action; additionally, *direct* referred to the act itself and *indirect* to actions that facilitated it. The tradition taught that prudence and the common good require that material, indirect cooperation be as distinct as possible from the wrongdoer's act and that there be a proportionately good reason for risking public misunderstanding and scandal.

In the modern era these distinctions must be applied in pluralistic and institutional settings of far greater complexity. For example, alliances of Catholic hospitals with non-Catholic health care facilities are occurring all over the country. New and complex questions appear. How is institutional integrity preserved when these alliances are with hospitals that perform abortions and permit sterilizations and follow a moral code at variance with Catholic magisterial positions? How about Catholic politicians seeking office in areas with pro-choice sentiment and in states with constitutional safeguards for legal abortion?[23]

A recent study reported that in the United States there were 640 Catholic hospitals and 633 Catholic agencies within the Catholic Charities system.[24] Contemporary Catholic moral thought must pursue classical questions about material and formal cooperation, direct and indirect, in new institutional settings within modern pluralism. The term *common ground* is emerging to carry more intelligibly and quickly the subtle casuistry encoded in what, for most people, must be impossibly complex distinctions among formal, material, direct, and indirect cooperation. The term added to these rather static distinctions the dimension of noncompromising cooperation to promote the common good in dynamic and pluralistic modern societies. This trend is clearly evident in two publications produced by the Leadership Conference of Women Religious (LCWR) and the Leadership Conference of Major Superiors of Men (LCMSM), whose memberships are highly involved in Catholic charities and hospital ministries. The late Sr. Margaret Cafferty, P.B.V.M., of the Leadership Conference of Women Religious, an original member of the support group that evolved into the Bernardin Initiative, was an important contributor of the term *common ground* to the discussion. During her LCWR presidency the term did important moral work in two discussion packets—*Abortion* and *Terminal Illness and Death*—developed by the Life Issues Task Force.

Abuses of the Common Ground Metaphor

There is no fixed meaning to the term *common ground*. The *Oxford English Dictionary* does not define it. In July 19, 1994 correspondence, Alan Metcalf, the executive secretary of the American Dialect Society (founded in 1889), wrote that he did not know the origin of the term nor of any standard meaning. Often *common ground* refers simply to anything held in common despite other differences, as when the *New York Times* news summarist described a shared interest in restaurants as the "common ground" found by President Clinton and Chancellor Helmut Kohl of Germany during their first meeting.[25] In the century of the Holocaust and total war, the phrase *mere civility* is inappropriate, so describing as common ground any commonality discovered among otherwise striking differences, though trivial, should not be disparaged. I'll make no further comment about the merely trivial use of the common ground metaphor, except to say that it is widespread.

Far more significant, and equally widespread, is the metaphor's application to contexts of intense polarization where highly significant questions of principle, integrity, and identity are explicitly at stake. In these contexts, the word *compromise* causes legitimate alarm. We can place this contemporary use of the common ground metaphor in the context of classical discussions of individuals and groups seeking to preserve their principles and integrity as they find themselves confronted by variant and rival moral codes that they ought not accommodate and can neither flee nor overcome. To distinguish the principled use of the common ground metaphor from its abuse, namely, the evasion of moral responsibility, some necessarily brief analytical work is needed.

A Common Ground Continuum of Integrity

Analytically, an authentic common ground that preserves integrity has two moments: *preliminary* and *actualized*. Preliminary authentic common ground is dialogue between moral adversaries that succeeds as both sides at least partially grasp the other's moral–emotional rationale followed by a joint search for noncompromising points of agreement. Actualized authentic common ground occurs when the search for noncompromising points of agreement leads to concrete joint endeavors that result not from moral evasion but from the implied reciprocal challenge adversaries present to each other's integrity now correctly, even if not sympathetically, understood. I'll elucidate the distinction between preliminary and actualized authentic common ground later, but first I'll distinguish between forms of abuse of the common ground metaphor.

Abuses of the common ground metaphor have a weak and a strong form: A self-interested use of the term in an effort to evade the more apt word *compromise* constitutes a "weak abuse" of the common ground metaphor. Strategic subversion, that is, knowing, if not cynical, employment of the common ground metaphor as a tactic designed coercively to subvert the other's integrity, constitutes a strong abuse. These distinctions are analytic (easier to draw conceptually than confidently to find in reality), as the following examples of both broad types of abuses show. I'll begin with an example of weak abuses.

To my knowledge, Bill Clinton is the first president to use the metaphor *common ground*. He does this frequently and never in a way congruent with its seminal meaning as found in St. Louis Common Ground. *Time* captioned its report on a series of Clinton speeches during debates on welfare cuts and the balanced budget "You Too Can Be a Centrist" and despairingly characterized "common ground" as a "buzz phrase" signaling "a move to the political center." *Time* found in the Clinton speeches no principled and prudent effort to continue liberal Democratic positions on welfare assistance but only a politically driven strategy to preempt the political center that would lose the least votes.[26] When Clinton won his second term the *New York Times* headline sub-caption read, "President's Success Lay in Ability to Co-opt Republican Issues," and a *Times* columnist observed that "common ground" had become "the President's trademark phrase," a shorthand that then House Speaker Newt Gingrich claimed could create an image of being "beyond partisanship."[27]

I nominate these Clinton usages as weak abuses of the common ground metaphor. It seems far too ingenuous to criticize President Clinton, or any other political candidate, for using any metaphor—including common ground—to win elections. Besides, it's difficult to know with certainty anyone's sincerity in employing the metaphor. Here my point is simply to illustrate the dangers of common ground metaphor abuse in a weak sense.

An example from the abortion controversy can illustrate what seems to be a strong abuse of the common ground metaphor. In her op-ed report on the first conference (1996) of the Common Ground Network for Life and Choice, Katha Pollitt declared, "For pro-lifers, there is no common ground" because "'prochoicers' already occupy the common ground."[28] Pollitt's definition excludes a principled position from the dialogue and thus removes all reciprocal challenge. It works both ways, as we see when Randall Terry in an *Operation Rescue* newsletter declared that common ground between abortion opponents and those who claim to be pro-choice was as morally absurd as blacks negotiating with the Ku Klux Klan or Jews with the Nazis.[29]

But both Terry and Pollitt remind us that, in its strong sense, the search for common ground can achieve moral coherence only as a subordinate part of the search for justice and the common good. In some cases the practice of common ground might well imprudently risk justice by dialoguing past a particular point. The integrity that common ground seeks to ensure must include the possibility that moral limits can be reached,[30] but any prudential suspension of dialogue and the search for common ground should in principle be made in the hopes of achieving by other means a situation that does make dialogue possible in the future. This is close to Gandhi's rationale for civil disobedience as a tactic that is chosen as the only available means of bringing about conditions more conducive to dialogue.

It is important to thematize why many if not most custodians of Catholic, evangelical Protestant, and Orthodox religious traditions (and the majority of social movement activists) will instinctively be skeptical about the search for common ground. Initially common ground seems more natural for self-defined liberals but, at least in its strong sense, probably only at first glance. Like their secular counterparts, religious liberals emphasize, respectively, pluralism, conscience, and choice, and thus will too facilely assume that *by definition* their standpoint is neutral, as they confidently claim they *already* embrace common ground. A liberally conceived common ground in effect becomes the conservative search for the addresses of liberals. This is what Katha Pollitt did in her virtual excommunication of pro-life positions from her definition of common ground in the example given earlier.

Describing common ground simply as a nonjudgmental inclusion privileges a liberal position and misses the reciprocal challenge that has been an essential dimension of the emergent strong meaning of common ground. "Since we'll never agree about *your* traditional beliefs," the stereotypical liberal says, "let's just talk about what we share: conscience, liberty, choice," thus, in effect, defining common ground in ways that protect only one side's integrity. Apropos of the secular liberal assumption that there is an impartial, neutral standpoint underlying an appropriate public rationality that requires the marginalization of religious belief from public discourse, Michael Perry writes that in this way the liberal gets in all of his or her secular convictions while religious believers must leave out their core religious beliefs. This is like, he continues, his daughter's suggesting that since she and her parents agree only on dessert, they should simply eat desserts.[31] But a strong meaning of common ground dialogue cannot require the privatization of moral beliefs for participation. When that happens, the limits of common ground have been reached.

INSTITUTIONAL SOURCES OF COMMON GROUND INTEGRITY

In a complicated appraisal, Marty once wrote that while the organized ecumenical movement had stalled, the ecumenical spirit had flourished. As with the ecumenical spirit, it is likely that the plausibility and institutionalization of the common ground metaphor in the strong sense also depend on solidity of the organized ecumenical and interfaith movements as their official dialogues cautiously move into areas of moral disagreements. The interfaith and ecumenical movements have recently turned toward common ground endeavors. Ecumenists are now beginning to search for ways to approach contested social–ethical issues—such as abortion, euthanasia, genetic engineering, permanent married love, nuclear deterrence—in dialogues that "can offer new opportunities for the increase of mutual understanding and respect and for common witness, without compromise of a church's convictions or of Christian conscience."[32] Since it would be naive to expect that such dialogues about highly contested moral and policy positions will soon (if ever) result in a change to consensus on all disputed church moral teachings already taken and promoted, this is common ground territory, and it will become increasingly necessary to explore and map it.

Identity is at the core of fear of abuse of the common ground metaphor both in the abortion debate and in the Catholic Common Ground Initiative (which I take as emblematic of similar but more ad hoc initiatives in other religious traditions). In contemporary academic discourse, essentialist definitions are out of favor. This is understandable, to say the least. To define, for example, the essence of femininity or masculinity is to risk making the contingent the permanent. Essentialist definitions risk equating the rational with the real, the just with the presently given. This is, of course, an old issue, explicitly in philosophy and, more often, implicitly in social science.

But it is empirically clear and normatively persuasive that religious traditions especially require some notion of the essential, since their identities are rooted in past charismatic beginnings and core interpretative texts. *Organic* change is experienced as a deepening of the tradition. There are powerful sociological traditions that call attention to the necessary element of stable identity if change is to be experienced as faithful adaptation rather than disorientation and identity loss. We can briefly refer to Talcott Parsons's primacy of the *pattern maintenance* function in his AGIL paradigm and his work with Bales showing that all coherent groups (and traditions?) go through phases of *adaptation* and then pattern maintenance that restore a sense of equilibrium to members trying to assimilate the changes and tensions resulting from the cognitive and expressive tasks set by "instrumental" leaders adapting the group to external challenges.[33] More simply, as Robert Nisbet wrote in his *Social Change and History,* "The best of functionalism lies exactly in what critics have mistakenly condemned it for—its emphasis upon those processes which are involved in equilibrium and stability. For these are real processes and powerful processes in human behavior."[34]

In its past, sociological theory has not carried us far enough into the questions about identity and adaptation confronted by historical actors. This is rapidly changing—"Sociology has taken an introspective turn," Kieran Flanagan announces in his virtuoso reflection on reflexivity in *The Enchantment of Sociology*—yet the introduction of "lived experience" and reflexivity carry their own potential for moral distortion and narrow vision.[35] Sociologists interested in analyzing common ground within issues of identity, change, and integrity can find a sophisticated lens in Paul Ricoeur's "genetic phenomenology," applied admirably to key social science texts in his pertinent work *Lectures on Ideology and Utopia.* Under the influence of a false Marxian appropriation of the honorific title of *science,* he observes, we tend to think of ideology only as distortion and deformation. But at its root ideology means the core beliefs of a constitutive identity that is fiercely protected precisely because it mediates a sense of self. We might say, sympathetically, that the ideological is driven by the persistence of identity. The key Ricoeur point for my analysis is this: Ideology is integrative before it is distortive. Ricoeur strikingly writes, "An ideology is a system of resistance," which is to be restructured not by mere intellectual understanding but, as in transference, only through the mediation of the trustworthy who embody solidarity.[36]

Think of the late Bernardin one more time. In the Catholic world, spiritual guides are already referring to him as an exemplary witness to charity and unity.[37] In his reflections *The Gift of Peace* completed on November 1, 1996, just thirteen days before he died of pancreatic cancer, Bernardin explicitly recalls the Catholic Common Ground Initiative as a legacy for "the next millennium."[38] It's pertinent to note that Martin Marty titled his remembrance on the occasion of Bernardin's death "Our Joseph," and that large numbers of Catholics immediately referred to Bernardin as "saint."[39] It would be a misappraisal to think of Bernardin's common ground legacy as more style than substance, suggesting a misappropriation of the strong meaning of the common ground metaphor. Bernardin chaired the National Conference of Catholic Bishops' committee that drafted its 1983 Pastoral Letter *The Challenge of Peace,* arguably the best example of public theology of the post-Vatican era. Bernardin also gave the classic formulation to the consistent ethic of life in his 1983 Fordham Gannon Lecture, the cornerstone of the pro-life movement's contribution to common ground. A theologian who himself strives to be a voice for the public church, Richard P. McBrien, has described Bernardin's subsequent Georgetown University address on the consistent life ethic as a classic contemporary Catholic contribution to a public theology on the abortion controversy.[40] It's perhaps not premature to consider including Bernardin among Edwards, Bushnell, Gibbons, and King—earlier nominated by Marty as the "giant exemplars" pointing the way to a public church.[41]

The public church thinks of its identity in terms of mission and service. In contrast to identity-focused ideology, utopian thought breaks with the "system of self-preservation and . . . extends the boundary between the possible and the impossible in the form of rational hope."[42] By themselves, both ideological and utopian aspirations generate typical distortions. The distortion of ideology is conceiving fixity as fidelity; the distortion of utopianism is escaping from existing reality. Together, the ideological and the utopian fruitfully form the social imagination, each tendency correcting the other. To correct their respective distortive tendencies, the ideological and the utopian must be kept in conversation and creative tension. For American Roman Catholicism, this is the role played by the Bernardin common ground legacy. Although the integrative function of ideology preserves identity, it risks becoming its pejorative—a frozen, rationalizing, sheer close-minded resistance. More generally, Ricoeur writes that his conviction is that "we are always caught in this oscillation between ideology and utopia. . . . [W]e must try to cure the illnesses of utopia by what is wholesome in ideology—by its element of identity, which is once more a fundamental function of life—and try to cure the rigidity, the petrifaction of ideologies, by the utopian element."[43]

CONCLUDING HOPEFULLY

There are modest signs pointing to the institutionalization of a strong sense of the common ground metaphor in both public discourse and the public church. In the autumn of 1992 the United States Catholic Conference, the National Council of Churches, and the Synagogue Council of America announced "The Common Ground for the Common Good" project as a joint effort to help reform the United States' social welfare policies in a way that emphasized health care and the reduction of poverty—the first time the three organizations had undertaken a joint project. The participants found great agreement, but they had to put aside the issue of abortion. After representatives of the American Bishops' committees on migration and health care met with President Clinton they issued a press release explaining, "We offer cooperation and common ground wherever possible and civil and respectful disagreement when it may be necessary."[44] Finally, Avery Dulles was one of the presenters at the March 6–8, 1998, second Bernardin Common Ground Conference dealing with disputes concerning the practice of church authority.[45] His paper was "*Humanae Vitae* and *Ordinatio Sacerdotalis*: Problems of Reception." The ordination of women and the moral teaching about nonrhythm or "natural" means of contraception represent two neuralgic areas of dissent from magisterial authority in American Catholicism. For evidence of the diffusion of the common ground style, consider the following section of Dulles's paper "Divergence and Common Ground":

> The positions taken on the substantive questions reflect a mentality that potentially extends to an indefinite number of cases. The basic question is whether to accept the long-standing Catholic tradition, authoritatively confirmed by the ecclesiastical teaching office and by the pope as its supreme exponent, or to maintain a critical distance from the tradition and the magisterium and give greater weight to new perspectives that enjoy greater support in society at large. Stated somewhat too crudely, the division is between conservatives and progressives or between the sacral and the secular spirit. Since the two sides follow different principles, neither side finds the arguments of the other persuasive.
>
> In spite of the ideological cleft, *it is possible for reasonable adherents of each side to appreciate their adversaries' point of view* [emphasis added]. Few conservatives are so extreme that they deny all mutability in the tradition or question the possibility that the Church might have something to learn from developments in secular society. . . . Doctrinal conservatives should therefore be able to understand why some Catholics might regard the official teaching on the points we are considering as open to change. Conversely, any progressivist who wants to be a Christian, especially a Catholic Christian, must maintain roots in the past.[46]

Empirical attention to the reflections and practices inspired by an emergent meaning of the common ground metaphor, and the resistance inspired by fear of its abuses, seem both a worthy sociological project and a contribution to the public church, especially when they are conjoined.

Chapter 9

Religion Out of the Closet: Public Religion and Homosexuality

James K. Wellman, Jr.

One of the ironies of modern life is that just when we thought religion was in the closet for good, out pops its gnarled head, much to the chagrin of many in public life. Alan Wolfe's book *One Nation, After All,* makes it clear that most middle-class Americans at the turn of the twenty-first century believe there are problems with being *too* religious; thus he uses the phrase "quiet faith."[1] That is, most people do have faith of some sort or another, but when it comes to going public with it by judging others according to the dogmas of that faith, the vast majority of Americans refuse to do so. Thus religion remains closeted except for the comfort that it gives the individual in the space of his or her own personal sanctuary. This sentiment fits nicely into the privatization theory of contemporary religion: that is, with the modernization of contemporary life, religion goes underground, into the private lives of people's hearts. The striking fact is that around the world, and in the United States as well, religion continues to play a public role. This chapter looks at the American ambivalence toward public religion, an ambivalence exaggerated when it comes to the issue of homosexuality and more particularly in the debate in the 1990s over homosexuality within American religious denominations.

Although middle-class Americans are generally reticent about applying faith-based criteria in public, a pronounced exception to this budding toleration of public difference is homosexuality. Here, Americans prefer that gays, lesbians, and bisexuals remain closeted. This resistance to the public validation of homosexuality rests largely on traditional religious grounds. In 1993, President Clinton took a pounding when he tried to overturn the ban on homosexuals in the military. The "Don't ask, don't tell" policy of Clinton's administration is pervasive among all American attitudes toward homosexuality. Most Americans support the civil rights of homosexuals, but a similar majority resist teaching about homosexual orientation in public education, and even greater majorities believe it is morally and religiously wrong.[2] So, "Don't ask, don't tell" functions as the de facto rule in American culture. Only a generation ago it would have been uncomfortable to claim publicly that one was a Buddhist, Muslim, or Hindu in what was the American Judeo-Christian common culture. At the turn of the new millennium, few Americans care what religion you are as long as you do not force it on others. Homosexuality, however, is not okay, but it is tolerated as long as it is kept private. Nonetheless, the issue has become quite public and refuses to go away, and this is especially true with regard to religious communities.

In the 1990s, religion and homosexuality became intertwined in complex ways that reveal that there are limits to how closeted religion will remain. Moreover, the issue highlights how the lines between private and public religion have become blurred. The Religious Right has taken on the issue of homosexuality as one of its "last stands" in the battle over the heart of American public life. James Dobson, the child psychologist and president of Focus on the Family, has led the charge along with others, including Gary Bauer of the Family Research Council. In 1998 the controversy was inflamed by the Senate majority leader Trent Lott's comments that homosexuality is a sin. Lott succeeded in disallowing a Senate vote on the nomination of James Hormel to be United States ambassador to Luxembourg. Hormel would have been the first openly gay ambassador if confirmed. This campaign was joined by many conservative Christian organizations who funded national campaigns with full-page advertisements touting testimonies on how homosexuals have "changed" from their former "lifestyles" and now lead "normal" heterosexual lives. Furthermore, Dobson, who supports these efforts, condemned President Clinton's executive order of May 1998 to assure equal opportunities for gay federal employees. In response to Clinton's action, House Republicans approved a measure that would deny federal housing money to San Francisco because of its support of homosexual partners and considered a measure to refuse federal money to carry out Clinton's order regarding gay federal employees.

Dobson, the unofficial leader of this conservative movement, is heard or seen by an audience of more than 28 million people each week. In early 1998, Dobson traveled to Washington to advocate for his agenda, a laundry list of familiar issues that he feels speaks for millions of conservative religionists. It included an end to the marriage penalty tax, a guarantee of parental consent before a minor can get an abortion or buy contraception, an end to funding for the National Endowment for the Arts, and legislation that guarantees religious liberty and protection from intrusion by what he calls the "Imperial" Supreme Court. Dobson, in his *Family News* bulletin, complained bitterly about the response of the media to his insertion into the public life of Washington. He quoted various sources, all of which represent the country's media and intellectual elite, which called him a "right wing zealot, an ayatollah, intolerant, Godzilla of the Right, similar to David Duke of the Ku Klux Klan."[3]

Most Americans, and the media in particular, dislike it when religion comes out of the closet to defend and advocate for public values and principles. Should religion remain in the closet? On what basis should religion enter the public arena? I argue that religions do have the right to go public with their concerns as long as they do so within the bounds of publicly determined rules of liberal discourse, putting forth reasons that are understandable in the secular sphere. I begin with a definitional summary of private and public religion, leading into an analysis of the reasons for the American ambivalence toward religion and its public manifestations.

PATTERNS IN PRIVATE AND PUBLIC RELIGION

The distinction between private and public religion is much used and much misunderstood. In the 1998 *Encyclopedia of Religion and Society,* there is no section on private religion. There is one on public religion, but private religion has no substantive definition, other than the folk wisdom that religion is one's "private business." Indeed attempting to define private religion is similar to defining religion in general—an almost interminable task.[4] Nonetheless, the dichotomy is worth pursuing because it is so much a part of everyday discourse. The private/public distinction is often analyzed as an ideological framework either to protect behavior or to restrict boundaries. In liberal discourse, it is both. That is, privacy is the freedom of the individual to make up his or her own mind on an array of issues. Privacy is protected space. In the classic liberal tradition privacy is also an inhibiting element in that religion is restricted to the private sphere, and public space is shielded from religion's encroachment. For conservative religionists, privacy is critical for the family in order to protect it from the penetration of the state and economy. However, conservative religionists, as we will see in the homosexual debate, have gone further to advocate for their private religious standards in the public sphere.

As James Wood has already observed, for much of human history distinctions between private and public did not exist. The process of modernization, that is, the differentiation of various domains of human society, came about because of multiple historical processes. These included the Protestant Reformation (its emphasis on individual religious conscience), the formation of capitalist systems of exchange (the rationalization of the profit motive), industrialization (the separation of work from home), and the Enlightenment (the critique of religion and the rise of discursive reasoning and the scientific method). Emile Durkheim, the turn of the century French sociologist, wrote on the effects of modernization on cultural life. He was most concerned that with the loss of traditional religious moorings, chaos or anomie would cause fragmentation and deterioration of the common life of cultures. His concern was not so much for religious dogma or for the life of the institutional church, but for the moral life of the citizenry. That is, with modernization came the growing autonomy of various spheres of life, including the economy, the state, and the religious sphere, such that each was separate, causing a loss of integration in the lives of individuals.[5]

Similar concerns percolate in the thought of contemporary social scientists. Robert Bellah's well-known 1967 essay "Civil Religion in America" laid out the way in which a civil religion forms a matrix through which Americans understand their moral lives, bringing coherence and critique in times of national emergency. Bellah used various American documents as the textual and symbolic content of civil religion, including the Declaration of Independence and Abraham Lincoln's Second Inaugural Address. Civil religion is formal in that its precepts are abstract and sparse, and its institutionalization has no legal or constitutional basis. American ambivalence toward religion is implicit in its founding documents. Thus God is mentioned in the Declaration of Independence but not in the Constitution. Nonetheless, civil religion is a group of potential actuating principles nested in the founding vision of American civil culture. As Bellah argues, ideally civil religion mediates public purpose and integrity and seeds society with the republican virtues of the common good that offset the acids of self-interest that pervade what Bellah calls "liberal constitutionalism."[6]

The debate over civil religion, its reality and importance, was joined early on by a parallel analysis of the privatization of religion. Thomas Luckmann's 1967 *The Invisible Religion* outlined the ways individuals are inherently religious every time they transcend their biological rootedness through the construction of a self—or what he called a "moral universe of meaning."[7] Again, this more private form of religion functions outside the boundaries of religious institutions, yet pervades the culture as a kind of subjective latticework. This privatization of religion has been both heralded as a new internalization of meaning and condemned as one more narcissistic turn in American cultural life.[8] The vibrating axis between the private and public faces of religion has been implicit within American religion from the beginning and in a sense marks its spirit.

Historically, social scientists have interpreted the rise of privatistic religion as a response to what is called the secularization of Western societies. For many, this theory explained the dramatic declines in American participation in institutional religion in the 1960s and 1970s and the rise of New Age religion that exploited the inward turn. Peter Berger in his 1967 classic *The Sacred Canopy* asserted that secularization undermined the cultural plausibility structures of religion, leaving modern individuals without a stabilizing and ordering ideological metanarrative to interpret their life in the contemporary world.[9]

Neither the theories of secularization nor the descriptive term *privatization* expected or predicted the rise of public religions around the globe over the last twenty-five years. Religions across the world have demanded to be a part of public discourse and in many cases have led the fight for democratization of societies. Examples are multiple. The Catholic church in Poland supported and led the battle for civil rights for the Polish people; South African churches led the antiapartheid struggle; the Anglican Bishop Desmond Tutu convened the Truth and Reconciliation Commission seeking to bind the wounds of oppression in South Africa's battle-scarred land; Latin American liberation theologians have resisted the terror of their governments and demanded a voice for the poor; and, of course, the Christian Right in America in the 1980s and 1990s has embodied a very public face for religion, through organizations like the Moral Majority and the Christian Coalition, advocating a new moral agenda in American culture.

These examples are not civil religion per se in that they do not confer "a common identity and self-understanding upon a people"; rather, they are emblematic of public religion[10]: that is, religion that has used its specific religious traditions to take an intentional part in shaping civil society and the moral patterns in the common life of the citizenry. These forms of public religion are less integrative than counterhegemonic, demanding human rights, upsetting the status quo, and pushing normative narratives of their own tradition up against the cultural centers of society.

José Casanova, in his volume *Public Religions in the Modern World,* gives a concise outline of the theory of secularization, what remains true about the theory, and how it needs to be adjusted to understand the recent rise of public religion. The foundational principle of secularization is differentiation; various spheres in modern life are separated and operate with their own logic and at times in contradistinction to the norms and values of religious traditions.[11] This is the essence of what is called the secular realm, systems that function as if God did not exist. Underneath the categorical umbrella of secularization are two subthemes that are often interpreted as the consequences of the secularization process. One is the decline of religion (in belief and practice), and the second is the privatization of religion. That is, Enlightenment critics of religion predicted that in a secular environment religious belief and practice and all its superstitious variations would simply disappear. If they did not cease altogether, at least they would be privatized and thus become irrelevant to the culture's public life. On the basis of the proliferation of religious belief and practices in countries across the world, many social scientists now assert that secularization is a dead letter. In America religious belief and practice continue apace. The high percentage of those who believe in God has changed little in the century; reported weekly church attendance has experienced only minor ups and downs. For those who support what is called the "new paradigm" in the sociology of religion, secularization simply misses the continuing renewal of religion in American society.[12] Indeed, one of the progenitors of secularization theory, Peter Berger, recently disavowed the theory as an adequate explanation for religion in America, in particular, and for religion internationally as well. For Berger, the real question is no longer the exceptional religiosity of Americans but the exceptional nonreligiosity of Europeans.[13]

Casanova, aware of these recent changes, has an explanation that is subtle but more adequate than a thumbs up or thumbs down on secularization in modern societies. He asserts that the fundamental theory of differentiation in the secularization thesis is truer today than it ever was. That is, the economic domain is less tied to religious principles than ever before. The contemporary trend toward the separation of church and state has quickened. As Casanova illustrates in the example of Spain, where the church and state partnered until midcentury, established religion tends to lead to the decreasing salience of religious belief and practice. In European countries with established churches this trend toward the decline of religious participation is quite evident, exemplified by Denmark, England, Norway, Scotland, and Sweden. In countries where religion and the state are relatively autonomous, the trends point toward greater religiosity in belief and institutional involvement. In Brazil and in Latin America generally, the Catholic church has worked for democratization and has been a critic of the authoritarian ways of the state and the impingement of the capitalist economy on the lives of Latin Americans. This outsider status has led to greater loyalty to the Catholic church. Presently there are more Roman Catholics in Latin America than in Europe and North America combined. Moreover, the fastest growing Catholic churches are in Africa and Asia, countries where Catholicism is a minority religion. A similar pattern exists in the Anglican communion, as the dioceses in Africa and Asia presently outnumber those in England. Casanova argues that when religion is disestablished it tends to thrive culturally, or in what is called civil society.

The category of civil society is a concept that follows from the disestablishment of religion. In countries where there is no religious monopoly, the cultural and normative values of public life become places of contestation. These public spaces are arenas where mediating institutions, such as the church and other voluntary organizations, seek to construct and shape norms and principles for society. Nineteenth-century American evangelical Protestantism offers an ideal type of civil religion dominating American civil society. During this era American public discourse was monopolized by Protestant symbolic moral boundaries. Politically, Protestantism was disestablished (with Massachusetts, in 1833, as the last state to do so); nonetheless, culturally, Protestantism set the moral agenda of society.

Thus, the core processes of secularization have not diminished religion; rather, as religious spheres gain greater autonomy across the world stage, as Casanova describes, a process of what he calls "deprivatization" has become the trend:

By deprivatization I mean the fact that religious traditions throughout the world are re-fusing to accept the marginal and privatized role which theories of modernity as well as theories of secularization had reserved for them. Social movements have appeared which either are religious in nature or are challenging in the name of religion the legitimacy and autonomy of the primary secular spheres, the state and the market economy. Similarly, re-ligious institutions and organizations refuse to restrict themselves to the pastoral care of individual souls and continue to raise questions about the interconnections of private and public morality to challenge the claims of the subsystems, particularly states and markets, to be exempt from extraneous normative considerations.[14]

Public religion, therefore, is religion that has taken the resources of its tradi-tion and brought them into the public sphere by demanding a voice in the poli-cies and actions of the culture and the state. As I have described, the penetration of the American public sphere by religion brings much discomfort for liberals, who interpret the Free Exercise Clause of the First Amendment as a protection *from* religion. Feminists in particular have identified the ideological structures of the private/public distinction. The idea that the public realm was for the male and the private for the female was an assumption of nineteenth-century American so-ciety.[15] In the twentieth century the feminist critique asserts that "the personal is the political." It is argued that the privacy category has been used to ghettoize women and create a public sphere where male power rules the day. The continu-ing "glass ceiling" in corporations is but one example. Feminists now demand that the normative values of the public world, the reciprocal logic of equal regard, must be a part of any ethical and cultural analysis of personal lives as well as the analysis of the putatively male public realm.[16]

Thus deprivatization takes place in two ways. First, religion refuses to assimi-late the agenda of its public world and responds on the basis of its religious tra-dition. Second, religions begin to react publicly and advocate for their agenda in civil society using their tradition as a resource. Depending on the agenda of the religious organization, secular liberals respond quite differently. When religious groups advocate for the expansion of civil rights, as some do, liberals applaud. When conservative religionists organize themselves in terms of values distinct from individualistic liberal norms, there is a severely negative reaction, as in the case of Dobson. Thus public religion is on trial; it can no longer assume that in the public sphere the rules of religious authority apply. In the public domain, rules of rational discourse are the necessary tools of the trade, an accommoda-tion demanded by the underlying principles of liberal democracies, the same principles that allow religions access to the public domain.

PUBLIC RELIGION ON TRIAL

Phillip Hammond's book *With Liberty for All* (as well as in his chapter in this volume) argues on the side of greater separation of religion and the public sphere. He does so in order to contest the implicit establishment of religion and to advocate for the free exercise of individual conscience in American public culture. Hammond forcefully asserts that accommodationists often allow majority religions to exercise an implicit establishment of their normative principles that violates that conscience of minorities who do not hold these positions. For Hammond this does not push religion into the closet: "Rather, what gets pushed into the closet is the *authority* of religion, its capacity to give orders *on its own terms in public.* In private it can be authoritative as its followers allow."[17] He specifically argues that on the most contested issues of the day, the courts have frequently ruled in ways that establish the conscience of the Judeo-Christian majority in America. These rulings burden the conscience of those who do not hold these religious traditions as authoritative.

Hammond's criteria of judgment for how public religion should argue in public consist of three standards: public reasons, falsifiable arguments, and secular purposes. First, does the religion have a public reason or common good that conditions its rationale? Reasons must be understood by all and argued without reference to the authority of private experience or religious tradition; it is not enough that people claim that God told them that euthanasia is wrong. Second, are the arguments falsifiable? Evidence must be public and testable. The statement that life begins with conception cannot be falsified or proved one way or another, and thus cannot be used in public discourse. Finally, are there secular purposes for the judgment that, for example, homosexuality is wrong or that same-sex marriages should be illegal? The statement that homosexuality is sin has no standing in public secular discourse because "sin" has no legitimacy in the secular domain.

Hammond tenaciously protects the public sphere from the inroads of religion. Religion must act as any secular public advocacy group does to make its point in the public domain. Thus religion's authority is reduced to the private sphere and the homeplace of those who assent to it. The danger of Hammond's view is that the individual conscience becomes the final arbiter of the secular domain. Hammond argues that it is not that individual preferences dominate; all personal interests are adjudicated in the light of diverse interests. Nonetheless, the common good is sublimated to individual conscience. The pitfalls of this individualistic tendency, I would argue, are compensated by religion's interest in the common good. As Casanova argues, public religion is essential for

maintaining the very principle of a "common good" against individualist modern liberal theories which would reduce the common good to the aggregated sum of individual choices. As long as they respect the ultimate right and duty of the individual conscience to make moral decisions, by bringing into the public sphere issues which liberal theories have decreed to be private affairs, religions remind individuals and modern society that morality can only exist as an intersubjective normative structure and that individual choices only attain a "moral" dimension when they are guided or informed by intersubjective, interpersonal norms. Reduced to the private sphere of the individualized self, morality must necessarily dissolve into arbitrary decisionism.[18]

It must be recognized, however, that there is a deep ambivalence among Americans to public religion. The ambivalence is not only toward conservatives. Most Americans would find the liberal side of religious scholarship, such as liberation theology—particularly its demand for economic redistribution, its critique of laissez-faire capitalism, its broadside against the militarism of the state, and its advocacy of the welfare state—aberrant at best.[19] Indeed, the Christian Right condemns religious liberals as anti-American. In the 1980s, liberal Protestants were involved in the sanctuary movement, hiding and protecting illegal aliens. Few Americans, and even fewer conservative Christians, found this acceptable behavior, much less Christian. To be sure, liberal religionists have neither the same visibility nor the same grass-roots support as the Christian Right. Nonetheless, their agenda, as subversive as it might be to political conservatives, is an important voice in the public sphere that adds greater depth and integrity to contemporary political debate.

The political power of the Christian Right, on the other hand, achieved dramatic visibility with the success of Republicans in the 1994 congressional elections and the assertion of their Contract for America. Secular liberals find the Christian Right more menacing in its ability to shape American moral and political life. Indeed, the motivation of many in the Christian Right goes beyond a simple validation of a "common good." For them there is a metanarrative that focuses on America as a nation of divine destiny. Few within the Christian Right explicitly advocate the establishment of a religious state, although Christian Reconstructionists are adamant on this point.[20] Most mainstream evangelicals, such as Pat Robertson, Jerry Falwell, and James Dobson, are postmillennial in their theological outlooks; that is, they are motivated to get the country "right" with God in order to bring in the thousand-year era of righteousness, followed by the second coming of Christ. Indeed, this prevents them from receding into a privatistic type of religion as an exclusivist organization that abjures any contact with the wider culture. These groups seek a return to the era of evangelical Protestantism of the nineteenth and early twentieth centuries, which sustained a conservative Christian civil religion and dominated the discourse and moral values of American civil society. In an American society that no longer works within an explicit Protestant ethos, for many this drive toward a new Christian civil society is discordant at best and subversive at worst. Thus, the Christian Right becomes an interest group that is difficult to fight and more difficult to ignore—a fact that the leaders for gay liberation have come to understand.[21]

PUBLIC RELIGION AND HOMOSEXUALITY

From the time of the Stonewall demonstrations in 1969, the gay liberation movement has sought civil rights and antidiscrimination legislation to protect gays and lesbians as a minority group in American society. The Religious Right has resisted this movement from the beginning; it has been behind efforts in Oregon, Maine, and Colorado to withdraw civil rights from gay and lesbian individuals.[22] Polls taken in the 1990s of the American population and particular religious groups within it reflect decreasing degrees of opposition to gay rights. Indeed only 31 percent of all Americans are against gay civil rights. Among evangelical Protestants this percentage jumps to 48 percent, with similar percentages among Orthodox Jews. The percentage falls precipitously when it comes to Roman Catholics (24 percent), mainline Protestants (27 percent), and Black Protestants (31 percent).[23]

The Religious Right is far from the moral majority in the country. Nonetheless, in 1992, it won a narrow victory in Colorado with the passage of Amendment 2, which repealed local gay rights laws and prevented any similar enactments in the future. The Colorado for Family Values group, backed by the Religious Right, worked tirelessly to pass the amendment. Jim Woodall, a Christian Right activist, described it as the "the *Roe v. Wade* of the homosexual issue." This victory of conservatives was short-lived, as in May 1996, the United States Supreme Court declared the amendment unconstitutional. The claim was that Amendment 2 violated the right of equal protection guaranteed by the Fourteenth Amendment. The long-standing argument by those against gay civil rights is that homosexuals are not a minority group like African Americans and thus do not deserve a protected status. Moreover, to hold up gays as worthy of civil rights "normalizes" their behavior and paves the way for acceptance of a "gay lifestyle" in the wider American culture.[24]

Didi Herman's *The Antigay Agenda* gives a vivid description of the opposition to gay rights. She uses an investigation of the magazine *Christianity Today,* a relatively moderate magazine of Christian conservatives, to outline the changing ways gays are constructed by evangelical Christians. The position during the last forty years has gone from one that portrays gays and lesbians as sad and unhappy individuals in need of compassion and change, to a more recent depiction of gay activists with fists in the air demanding their rights. In the 1990s with this less sanguine portrait of homosexuals, the need for compassion and understanding is still a part of articles in *Christianity Today,* but there is also a clear rejection of gay rights and a call for greater support of ex-gay organizations that advertise the ability to change homosexuals into heterosexuals. The 1998 advertising campaign was a part of this agenda. Exodus International, the largest national exiting organization for homosexuals, was one of the funders of this campaign. This

moderate position is but one layer of the deep opposition to the broader acceptance of homosexuality in American culture. Voices that call for the death of gay
and lesbian people are a small minority in this conflict, but they are vocal in their
insistence on returning to Levitical laws that demand the death of homosexuals.[25]

The degree of acceptance and rejection of homosexuality varies dramatically
across American religious organizations, from an exclusivist position to one of
full acceptance that entails the ordination of what are called "practicing" homosexuals. Within each of these positions one notes the diversity of opinion on the
issue and the variations in the ways public and private religion is negotiated on
the controversial issue of homosexuality in American religious institutions.[26]

Exclusivist Position

The moderate opposition embodied in *Christianity Today* frames the position
of those religious organizations who fundamentally oppose gay rights, same-sex
unions, and the ordination of homosexuals. The Greek Orthodox church,
Lutheran Church–Missouri Synod, National Association of Evangelicals, Roman
Catholic church, and Orthodox Judaism all adopt these stands. In the 1990s the
Southern Baptist Convention has taken uncompromising positions against homosexuality, calling it an abomination in the eyes of God, and has expelled two
of its churches for allowing same-sex unions and licensing a gay candidate for
ministry. Moreover, it has gone beyond its usual policy of "freedom of conscience" for congregational decision making to a new rule requiring Southern
Baptist churches to oppose homosexuality, and subsequently asserting that biblical inerrancy is the only acceptable theory of interpretation.[27]

Public religion in this matrix comprises boundary keeping within the religious
organization and advocacy in the wider cultural domain. Religious groups know
that if public policy shifts, popular opinion will follow, putting greater pressure
on the religious group to change. The course of civil rights legislation took this
very pattern. Thus there are both greater specificity about the group's internal
boundaries and a more forceful explanation of the denomination's perspective in
the public sphere.

The Roman Catholic church embodies this twofold thrust. It fights to maintain
its hierarchic position and tradition within its own religious domain but also
moves to support public campaigns against the liberalization of societal opinions
on homosexuality. Joseph Cardinal Ratzinger's 1986 "Letter to the Bishops of
the Catholic Church on the Pastoral Care of Homosexual Persons" is the clearest
declaration of the church's exclusivist stand on homosexuality. The position is
subtle but unyielding: "Although the particular inclination of the homosexual
person is not a sin, it is a more or less strong tendency ordered toward an intrin-

sic moral evil; and thus the inclination itself must be seen as an objective disorder."[28] The statement equivocates to a degree on the sinful status of homosexuality but is forceful in condemning homosexuality on medical and moral grounds. For the Catholic church, the "complimentarity" between the sexes is a part of God's creation, and thus same-sex urges are disordered, are sinful, and tend toward evil when acted upon.

Ratzinger warns Christians who advocate for the liberalization of rules against homosexual behavior that homosexuality leads to human destruction and activists lead people down a road of evil without regard for the consequences of their actions: "The Church can never be so callous. It is true that her clear position cannot be revised by pressure from civil legislation or the trend of the moment. But she is really concerned about the many who are not represented by the pro-homosexual movement and about those who may have been tempted to believe its deceitful propaganda."[29]

These arguments are aimed at the heart of debate over the norms and principles that will rule the cultural space of American civil society. The Roman Catholic church, following Vatican II (1962–1965), made official its approval of religious liberty and freedom of religious conscience. This historic change in course was a critical element in transforming the perception of Catholicism in American culture, from an ideology whose agenda sought to establish itself as a state church to one that joined the liberal experiment of representative democracy. This position, however, in no way dislodged the Catholic church from its desire to shape the norms and values in American civil society. The Catholic church became quite active as a public church, particularly after the 1973 *Roe v. Wade* decision by the Supreme Court to legalize abortion. Indeed, in the 1980s, the American bishops presented major moral statements on nuclear disarmament and on a just economy, as well supporting and leading the pro-life movement.

Clearly, the extremes of religious conservatism, particularly in the outbreaks of virulent hatred of homosexuals, are not only illiberal but immoral.[30] At the same time, when organizations within the conservative religious camps work at changing public policy through their tenacious grass-roots campaigns, it is within the liberal democratic tradition to honor their right to advocate for their position. For most of them, creating an established religion is no longer an option, nor is it their agenda; most are driven by powerful normative principles in their tradition and an ideal of the common good that is rationalized theologically as a utopian vision of the city of God or as a way to trigger the coming of God's kingdom. It is not simply an antimodernist agenda but a theologically reasoned one with unmistakable ideological ramifications.

Yet the question remains: Should these religious traditions advocate for their deeply held theological positions in the public domain? From a legal standpoint, all have the right to free speech. But from the angle of Hammond's criteria of liberal public discourse, the assertion that homosexuality is sin is not falsifiable. These groups do, however, put forth public reasons for restricting homosexuality. They argue that it distorts the order of human relationships and corrupts the common good of heterosexual family life. To be sure, this argument is hotly debated in family studies in American culture.[31] The question comes down to whether or not the "good" of traditional family life overly burdens the rights of gays and lesbians in the exercise of their personal life. There is little doubt that the sanctions against homosexuals are burdensome to them. In the 1990s the American populace continues to support sanctions against homosexuality, and most American mainline religious denominations continue to stand against its public validation. Yet the pendulum is moving toward greater recognition of the rights of this group.

Semiexclusivist Position

In the semiexclusivist type it is not the orientation of homosexuality that is sinful but acting upon it. This position mirrors the general American population in its ambivalence toward homosexuality. Moreover, it is the position that produces the deepest conflicts in religious organizations. Indeed, in the 1990s the dialogue over the subject of homosexuality in many religious bodies has broken into side taking, in which threats of dividing the organizations are heard daily. Many who can agree on a baseline theological perspective divide over this single issue. So the assertion that the topic of homosexuality is critical for the future of American religious organizations is an understatement. Like slavery before it, this single issue could divide several denominations and lead to fundamental fissures in American religious culture.[32] The religious organizations that come under this heading include the United Methodist Church, American Baptist Churches in the U.S.A., Disciples of Christ, Conservative Judaism, and the Presbyterian Church (U.S.A.).

As has been noted, the results of opinion polls of Americans are divided over the issue of homosexuality. A 1998 analysis shows that 73 percent of Americans support the rights of homosexuals to teach in college or universities. At the same time, 70 percent of the American public believe that sexual relations between members of the same sex are wrong. Moreover, Americans do not support same-sex marriages (65 percent against, 28 percent for).[33] There is a clear distinction between tolerance for the private behavior of homosexuality and strong condemnation of the public affirmation of homosexuality as a generally sanctioned sexual alternative. Religious traditions on a broad scale are historically unequivocal in their condemnation of homosexuality. American opinion mirrors this judgment. Yet Americans are hesitant about forcing these religious strictures on the public at large.

Nonetheless, the condemnation of homosexual activity has become the official position of several mainstream Protestant denominations. The dilemmas over the issue are aptly illustrated by the 1998 trial of the United Methodist minister Jimmy Creech. After the 1984 decision by the United Methodist General Conference to oppose the ordination of practicing homosexuals, Creech, a heterosexual married man, became an outspoken advocate for gay rights in the church. Creech became the pastor of a church in Omaha, Nebraska, in 1996. In September 1997, he told the Nebraska bishop Joel Martinez that he was going to perform what the Methodists call a "covenanting" service between two women. Creech did so against his bishop's advice. He was then suspended in November 1997 and was to be tried in a church trial in March 1998. The thirteen jurors were from the Nebraska Annual Conference. The trial verdict was eleven to two that Creech had performed a homosexual union ceremony. But more important, the jury voted eight to five that he had disobeyed the order and discipline of the church. Nine votes were needed to convict him. Creech was acquitted in March 1998 and immediately reinstated as senior pastor of First United Methodist Church of Omaha.[34]

On Creech's initial Sunday back in the church he was greeted with a standing ovation. But this reaction was mixed with strong opposition within his own congregation. After his reinstatement, some members held a "laity rally" to object to the decision and the continuing ministry of Creech at their church; three hundred signatures were gathered on a petition for Creech's removal. Many urged Bishop Martinez to end Creech's ministry. Moreover, this apparent victory for the pro-homosexual forces galvanized the organizations within the United Methodist church who oppose same-sex unions and the ordination of homosexuals. The Methodist conservative groups, the Good News and the Confessing Movement, were outraged by the decision. "We believe that this crisis is so severe that it threatens the connection and ties that bind us together in worship and ministry."[35] In response to this decision, in turn, ninety-two more Methodist ministers publicly announced their intention to perform same-sex unions. Thus the fracture is not merely cosmetic but indeed deep-set. In fact, in the months following the controversy, Creech's appointment at his church was not renewed by his bishop. The success of the efforts of the Methodist bureaucracy to staunch the controversy remains to be seen.

The core interpretative strategies of those who pursue the semiexclusive typology are best exemplified in Richard B. Hays's essay "Awaiting the Redemption of Our Bodies: The Witness of Scripture Concerning Homosexuality."[36] Hays, an ordained United Methodist minister and seminary professor, outlines the way decisions are made within the Christian tradition. The Wesleyan quadrilateral, practiced in many mainline Protestant denominations, employs four criteria for authoritative religious judgments: scripture, tradition, reason, and human experience. For Hays, the historical tradition is clear in its condemnation of homosexuality; it strengthens the biblical witness condemning homosexuality as sin. The tradition of reason and science is ambiguous. Science has not confirmed that homosexuality is genetically caused, nor is the argument about the etiology of human behavior a determinative factor in judging the righteousness of an act. The conventional ethical error of arguing from an "is" to an "ought" is asserted. Finally, the example of human experience, which lifts up homosexuals who are active in the church in exemplary ways, may point to the fact that God's grace is active in the lives of gays and lesbians, but this only further reinforces the scriptural adage "We have this treasure in earthen vessels." For Hays, the tragic and broken nature of the human community is not reason to justify behavior as good or normative.

This begs the question of the weight given the scriptural texts that censure homosexual activity, particularly when compared to the clear condemnation of divorce that Jesus makes in Mark 10:1–12. Most mainline Protestant denominations have adjusted their interpretations of the Markan passage and made their rules on divorce and remarriage more flexible.[37] By contrast, Jesus never comments on homosexual behavior. The question becomes, What is the criterion that allows change over against the words of Jesus on the normative issue of divorce, but demands inflexibility when it comes to homosexuality on the basis of the relatively scarce texts that refer to homosexual activity in Christian scripture? Sociologically the force for change on rules of divorce was precipitated in part by enormous cultural shifts, not the least of which was the early feminist movement and a male culture that saw the benefits of freedom from family obligations. There is no parallel populist movement with homosexuals that incorporates a similarly large constituency. Indeed, it is remarkable that despite the minority position of gays and lesbians, American political opinion has moved toward the expansion of their civil rights at all.

This model of semiexclusion is problematic to those outside the theological community precisely because of the paradoxical idea in Christian theology that one can be found a sinner and yet be justified at the same time. Reconciliation with God does not obliterate one's sin but redeems it and allows one to be reconciled to God. As Wolfe reflects, one may admire this ability to make strong moral judgments, but "one cannot also deny that, when they do so, they are, in effect, condemning the person and not just how he acts."[38] This paradoxical idea of "hating the sin and loving the sinner" is in part the reason why religious bodies in this model support gay civil rights and yet deny the privilege of ordination to practicing homosexuals.

From the perspective of public discourse the distinction between sin and sinner is incoherent. Liberal discourse does not uncouple the action and the person; rather it tends to validate distinct human preferences as long as they do not interfere with the rights of others. The distinction between sin and sinner reflects the profound inner conflict within the American tradition over private and public religion. For the most part, private behavior, decisions about one's health, one's political party, even one's pregnancy, are protected and validated by the state and by most American religious denominations. Yet in the area of homosexuality, the privacy barrier is breached, and gays and lesbians are found at fault for the private practice of this minority sexual orientation. Furthermore, the argument that homosexuality tends to corrupt the common good is a valid counterargument but very difficult to justify. The old canard that homosexuals are sad, lonely, and destructive people has been overturned by the counterevidence of many publicly productive homosexuals, as well as by all medical and psychological associations that assert that homosexuality is neither psychologically nor physiologically deviant, but merely an alternative sexual orientation. Thus the position of those who oppose homosexuality for secular reasons is becoming less tenable.

Semiinclusivist Position

The semiinclusive typology is less represented than any of the others, but significantly distinct and thus warrants its own category. The two religious organizations that best exemplify this category are Reform Judaism and the Episcopal church. In the case of Reform Judaism the claim is made that a heterosexual union is the ideal and the relationship that should be held up as normative for society. Nonetheless, in the 1990s the Central Conference of American Rabbis has asserted that all rabbis, regardless of sexual orientation, should be "accorded the opportunity to fulfill the sacred vocation which they have chosen." This acceptance of diversity in the rabbinical ranks goes with the warning that the public acknowledgment of homosexuality can have detrimental effects on one's vocational trajectory.[39] This ambiguity brings with it some confusion; yet it leaves the door open for homosexuals to be ordained and to exercise their duties regardless of whether or not they choose to practice this orientation. In this typology plurality is recognized, but public norms are also authorized. It is a position that again reflects an ambivalent accommodation between the liberal and religious traditions. It upholds traditional standards yet leans toward an unofficial acceptance of practicing gay and lesbian individuals.

The complexity of this position is demonstrated in the debate in the Episcopal church. The church denominationally is at once more hierarchical and yet less centralized institutionally than the Presbyterian church. The Presbyterian Church (U.S.A.) in 1997 passed an amendment to its constitution that explicitly prohibits the ordination of any individual who participates in sexual activity outside a monogamous, heterosexual marriage. With this action Presbyterians have given even less authority and flexibility to local presbyteries (governing bodies) in making decisions on the ordination of candidates. Episcopalians, although clear about proscriptions against the ordination of practicing homosexuals, have left room open at the level of polity, giving bishops pastoral discretion and dioceses greater latitude to decide who should and should not be ordained.

The revealing example of this flexibility is the case of the retired bishop Walter C. Righter. In 1995, ten Episcopal bishops initiated an action to put him on trial because he had knowingly ordained a practicing homosexual in 1990. Moreover, Righter had signed "A Statement of Koinonia," which was brought to the General Convention in 1994. The bishop of Newark, John Shelby Spong, had taken the statement to the convention, and it was signed by various bishops (including the current presiding bishop of the Episcopal church, installed in 1998). In fact, some dioceses in the Episcopal church are now in the process of approving the document as a statement that expresses the mind of the church. The accusation against Righter was that he was teaching a *doctrine* contrary to the core teaching of the Episcopal church.

In the presentment against Righter, the bishops outlined the history of the Episcopal church in relation to the status of homosexual ordination. In 1979 the House of Bishops put forward a resolution proscribing the ordination of practicing homosexuals as contrary to the teaching of the church; this proscription was reaffirmed in 1984 and 1989. In 1994, however, the General Convention put forth a broad resolution that guaranteed nondiscrimination for individuals in the ordination process.[40]

Righter was acquitted in May 1996 of all charges against him. It was found that Righter did not act contrary to any of the core doctrines of the church. That is, the resolutions concerning the prohibitions against the ordination of practicing homosexuals had the status of advisories and not doctrinal authority. Bishops thus are not bound to these resolutions and can use pastoral discretion in individual cases. In response to the Righter decision, the bishops who had brought the case claimed that the Episcopal church had abdicated the authority and the accountability of their tradition in making the acquittal. Contrariwise, the bishops writing to dismiss the charges against Righter made it clear that their intention was neither to overturn the resolutions against the ordination of gay and lesbian candidates nor to affirm committed, monogamous same-sex unions; in the end it was only to affirm the core doctrines of the church, what is necessary for salvation, and to uphold the discretion of bishops to make decisions on other matters in individual cases.

Nonetheless, the movement to include gays and lesbians is making inroads in the Episcopal church, at least in America. At the 1997 General Convention, a resolution to direct the Standing Liturgical Commission and the Theology Committee of the House of Bishops to work on rites honoring love and commitment between persons of the same sex as a part of common liturgical practice failed by only one vote in the House of Deputies. This was interpreted as progress for those who support same-sex unions, as a two-thirds vote is needed to pass this type of resolution. Many believe that the resolution will carry at the next General Convention in 2000. Moreover, at the 1997 General Convention, the church apologized to gay and lesbian men and women who have suffered abuse in society. At the same time, the 1998 Lambeth Conference, the worldwide decennial gathering of Anglican bishops, voted overwhelmingly that homosexual relations are "incompatible with Scripture." North American bishops dominated the minority position. The meeting, which drew more than seven hundred bishops, has no authority to set doctrine among the twenty-two national churches, though it is the main consultative body for the world's 70 million Anglicans. It is telling that the most vocal opposition to the liberalization of views on homosexuality came from bishops in Africa, precisely the area of the world where Anglicanism is growing fastest. Thus it remains to be seen to what extent the movement toward the public validation of homosexuality in these religious communities is simply a North American phenomenon.

Inclusivist Position

In the inclusive or more liberal stance the experience of gays and lesbians and their supporters is proffered as the main court of appeal by the various religious organizations that promote the ordination of practicing homosexuals. The following religious bodies in varying degrees support this position: Unitarian Universalist Association, Reconstructionist Judaism, numerous regional meetings of the Religious Society of Friends, the United Church of Canada, the United Church of Christ, the Metropolitan Community Church, and the Moravian churches.

As we have seen from denominations that stand against the ordination of practicing homosexuals, tradition and scripture are the fundamental planks opposing liberalization. Peter Gomes, chaplain and professor of morals at Harvard University, asserts in his *The Good Book* that the issue is in fact a hermeneutical problem in that one comes away from scripture with what one brings to it: "What is at stake is not simply the authority of Scripture, as conservative opponents to homosexual legitimization like to say, but the authority of the culture of interpretation by which these people read scripture in such a way as to lend legitimacy to their doctrinaire prejudices."[41] Human experience becomes the pivot around which issues must be interpreted and negotiated. Gomes, a homosexual African American whose conservative political and economic views are well known, extracts from scripture a perspective quite different from those in the Religious Right, at least on the issue of homosexuality. Moreover, Gomes argues from the social experience and history of oppressed groups in American culture.

He notes that in the persecution of African Americans under slavery scripture was often used to justify a history of inhumanity against this group:

The legitimization of violence against homosexuals and Jews and women and Blacks, as we have seen, comes from the view that the Bible stigmatizes these people, thereby making them fair game. If the Bible expresses such a prejudice, then it certainly cannot be wrong to act on that prejudice. This, of course, is the argument every anti-Semite and racist has used with demonstrably devastating consequences, as our social history all too vividly shows.[42]

Stanley Hauerwas, a postliberal Christian ethicist in his provocatively titled essay "Why Gays (As a Group) Are Morally Superior to Christians (As a Group)" after outlining the state of moral turpitude in American society asserts: "This moral confusion leads to a need for the illusion of certainty. If nothing is wrong with homosexuality, then it seems everything is up for grabs. Of course, everything is already up for grabs, but the condemnation of gays hides that fact from our lives. So the moral 'no' to gays becomes the necessary symbolic commitment to show that we really do believe in something."[43] Hauerwas argues that the construction of religious authority issues from a narrativist theological perspective developed in religious community. Interpreters act as the mediators of scriptural canon, event, and application of the canon to human experience. Thus the construction of religious authority is not an a priori act but is developed through interpretation and struggle with human experience in a community of interpretation. With Gomes, Hauerwas pleads for greater sensitivity to contemporary human experience. In a sense they both open up religious interpretation to an expanded public account of what they understand as ideal moral standards for the common good of both wider public life and the religious community.

This same acknowledgment of wider public experience is consistently noted by those who would open religious organizations to gays and lesbians—whether this involves the awareness of their own homosexuality or the homosexuality of friends or colleagues. The volume *Called Out With: Stories of Solidarity* is an exemplar of this genre in that it is a response from a group of heterosexuals to an earlier book, *Called Out: The Voices and Gifts of Lesbian, Gay, Bisexual, and Transgendered Presbyterians.*[44] In each of these volumes the experience of homosexual individuals—or those close to homosexual persons—who confront the issue existentially is recorded in autobiographical voice. William P. Thompson, a Presbyterian layperson and lawyer, an ordained elder, and stated clerk of the General Assembly from 1966 to 1984, expressed how his mind had changed on the ordination of homosexuals: "I felt that God was nudging me in the new direction. I am now convinced that the Presbyterian Church (U.S.A.) will ultimately recognize that, like other members, its homosexual members are eligible to be ordained to church office, because I am persuaded that this is 'the will of God.'"[45]

In the book *Coming Out While Staying In,* Leanne McCall Tigert weaves together her own story of coming out with the story of the United Church of Christ (UCC). Shortly after Stonewall in 1969, the UCC presented what they called the "Resolution on Homosexuals and the Law." The General Synod adopted the stance that homosexuality and the practice thereof should not be a bar to ordination. It encouraged UCC local associations to adopt this stance. Not all have. In the 1990s the Western North Carolina association has implemented policies that disallow gay or lesbians from being ordained or serving in their member churches.[46] Thus, as Tigert enumerates, the way is not always clear for gays or lesbians even in the UCC, where inclusion is the official norm.

Homosexual advocates condemn the proposal of any single moral norm in gender and sexual relationships as bankrupt because of the implicit scapegoating that occurs when minority groups are excluded and therefore stigmatized. Following Gomes, the concern is that majorities in society need pariah groups to ensure their own sense of superiority. The historical and sociological precedents for this pattern are hardly insignificant. Yet others argue that social norms within society demand judgments for the common good.[47] In response, liberal religionists argue that an authentic biblical and theological vision is more radical in that all are included in God's grace, and so judgment is the prerogative of God alone. God's preference is for the weak, the disenfranchised in any group. Human judgments are always liable to parochial interests and should be looked at with suspicion because someone is always going to be left out. Thus a standard for interpersonal behavior may make sense for majorities in democratic societies; within religious communities, however, the plight of minorities, as Gomes and others would argue, becomes a moral priority.[48]

POLITICS AND PUBLIC RELIGION

These arguments for the inclusion of homosexuals get at the heart of the issue over public religion. On the one hand, liberal religionists argue that minority sexual behavior should be recognized and validated, brought out of the closet as publicly appropriate activity. This is the quintessence of the personal as the political. But this argument raises objections from within both liberal political constituencies and more conservative religious traditions. Many secular liberals accept alternative sexual behavior but prefer that it be kept in the closet. Private behavior should be kept private. Similarly, conservative religionists object precisely because homosexuals want their behavior adopted as a publicly sanctioned sexual orientation. For most traditional religionists this goes against their historical and sacred scriptural tradition. Moreover, it impinges upon their children in particular by encouraging them in behavior that their tradition finds abhorrent. Thus when gay activists force the issue into the public domain, threatening the normative values of traditional religionists, the latter respond with campaigns of their own. They demand that before this public validation is given, debate must take place, so that society can set the standards for behavior and not be forced to bend to the views of minority groups.

In liberal democracies, however, minority groups are protected from the burdens put on them by the majority. It is evident that Americans in general find homosexuality objectionable. They do not want it taught to their children. This majority opinion burdens the conscience of homosexuals who want their behavior publicly validated and recognized as one more option in human relational life. Hammond argues that in the case of homosexuality the religious sanctions of the majority are established and thus are unconstitutional according to the Establishment Clause in the Constitution. I believe that this is a persuasive argument that will prevail over time. Nonetheless, as we have also seen, few American religious denominations show a willingness to liberalize rules against homosexuality. As American civil society expands the rights of gays and lesbians, it remains to be seen whether this will have similar results in American religious denominations.

To be sure, historically, the trend in American society is moving toward a more secular public domain. Secularization as differentiation shows few signs of abatement. This, however, should not be interpreted as an attempt to push religion into the closet but as a challenge to religionists to sharpen the tools of their public discourse. Religious language of sin and salvation is not the language that Americans use in public discussions. Liberal religionists have come to understand this need to accommodate their vocabulary in order to be persuasive in the public sphere. The struggle for religionists at either end of the ideological spectrum is how to maintain their religious identity as they go public. This translation of theological vocabulary is a perennial challenge for American public religion, one that needs to be addressed continually in each historical period.

It is the argument of this chapter, and this book, that public religion plays an essential role in the life of our American democracy. That is, religion has always functioned to complement the individualist strain in American polity. Religion has been recognized since at least the time of Tocqueville as critical to the health of the American democratic experiment. At the same time, it has no implicit privilege in public discussions. This decentering of American religious authority has been painful for many religionists, but for the health of American society it is a position that must be accepted and understood. All voices count in the American public domain: When any is dismissed, trouble erupts. The religious voice should not be about courting violence with the assertion of some special authority, but about reconciling and making possible the peaceful conversation of diverse interest groups. Indeed, the ability for diverse groups to argue and debate in public life with a sense of civility and respect for differences is at the heart of what the essays in this book attempt to elucidate.

Chapter 10

Public Religion and New Religions

James T. Richardson

Martin Marty and others at least since H. Richard Niebuhr have noted that new, "extraordinary" religions often become much more ordinary by the second generation. However, the process by which they do so is sometimes not a smooth one. As they develop, newer groups may receive support and encouragement from mainline faiths, but often they do not. In this chapter I will explore a series of situations to illustrate various ways that mainline groups react to nascent faiths, and to examine the possibilities of some of the newer faiths becoming part of what Marty refers to as "public religion," a term usually reserved for discussions of mainline faiths.

Marty's concept of public religion is a provocative and useful notion focusing on the role religion plays in developing and promoting mainstream culture and society. He attends insightfully to activities of the mainline faiths in America to demonstrate the power of his concept. But Marty does not offer much detail about how newer religious groups relate to the notion of public religion. Only occasionally in his delineations of public religion does Marty touch on the role (or lack thereof) of minority faiths, sometimes called "new religions" or denigrated in public discussions with the designation "cult." For example, in discussing the involvement of religious groups in presidential politics he states, "Eastern Orthodox, Occult, 'New,' New Age, and similar religious groups have not been major actors."[1] In other writings in which he defines the role of religion in modern life, Marty ignores, perhaps justifiably, any role played by "new religions" in this arena.

Marty is certainly aware of the development of the new religions in recent decades, but he assumes that they are of little consequence because they have been readily absorbed into ordinary cultural life. For instance, after writing about "extraordinary religion" involving the recent development of such phenomena as "occult explosions in astrology, cult formation, and support for Eastern religions," Marty says that "extraordinary religion acquired an ordinary cast." He summarizes this process as follows:

By the mid-1980s such extraordinary religion had established itself, although without essentially changing the map of American religion. Present in a number of thriving cults and persistent in holistic health movements, and most of all in private spiritual pursuits, most of this religion had begun to fit quietly into the larger landscape. What the public called cults no longer made news as a harbinger of the spirit that might alter consciousness and national life, bringing in a new age. Instead they were seen as only slightly less conventional denominations, studying accents among other Great Book interests, or, most of all, as merely self-preservation groups constantly fighting for legal rights and privilege—and often thus winning support of both mainline and evangelical–moralistic partisans. In other words, they made news on the familiar and ordinary church–legal front, not on the horizon of extraordinary spiritual promise.[2]

In one important sense Marty is plainly correct in his assessments. Many new religions, including some controversial ones, have attempted accommodation to the greater society through altering their values and practices in ways that make them more acceptable to the dominant culture. Thus one might say that some newer religions have made overt efforts to become a part of "public religion" in America and other Western societies. Also, as Marty seems to assume, it may be that the new religions have had little lasting impact on American society. However, one can argue that the presence of the newer high-energy groups has helped make this a more spiritual age. It is acceptable to be more openly spiritual now in part because of the major impetus given by the new religions, a not insignificant development. The very presence of so many newer religious groups in contemporary society also puts the lie to secularization theory's predictions about the diminution of religion in modern society.

NEW RELIGIONS AND THE LEGAL ARENA

Marty is correct about legal rights and privileges being a major arena of activity for newer faiths, and examining this area more closely should reveal how major faiths and newer religions relate to each other. But, I must take some issue with Marty's conclusion that the newer religions "often" win support from mainline and other religious groups in legal battles. Certainly there are examples of mainline faiths supporting the cause of newer ones in legal and political battles, but there are also many examples of newer religions being left to fight alone when governmental agencies or private entities attack them.

An example of a closing of the ranks of mainline faiths with newer religions can be found in the tax evasion trial of the Reverend Moon, founder of the Unification church, which took place in the early 1980s.[3] The Reverend Moon, leader of the controversial church, had been charged with tax evasion by the Internal Revenue Service for allegedly not paying taxes on the dividends and interest from some assets that were registered in his name. The Reverend Moon claimed that he was only the trustee of the assets, and that all proceeds were going to further the work of his organization. This defense was not accepted, however, and he was tried and found guilty by a jury in a federal court in New York. The renowned Harvard constitutional lawyer Lawrence Tribe carried the case on appeal but was unsuccessful, and the Reverend Moon ended up serving time in a federal prison.

In this particular case *amicus* briefs of religious groups representing 125 million Americans were filed in an effort to overturn the Reverend Moon's conviction when it was appealed to the United States Supreme Court. Included in those groups filing briefs were the Mormon church, the National Council of Churches, the Catholic League for Religion and Civil Rights, the Southern Christian Leadership Conference, and the National Association for Evangelicals. Those organizations realized that they had something at stake in this case, which has been called an inquisition by one critical writer.[4] Many religious groups keep their funds and other assets in the name of their leader; thus it was feared that the case might establish a very problematic precedent for other religious groups. Also, the amount of money involved was relatively small (the IRS claimed that the Reverend Moon owed about seven thousand dollars in unpaid taxes), suggesting selective prosecution of a religious group. Allowing such prosecution to go unchallenged was viewed as a serious problem by leaders of some more traditional religious groups, leading to the effort to assist through the medium of filing "friend of the court" briefs.

Another important instance of major religions coming together in a way supportive of minority faiths was the tremendous effort of many groups to pass the Religious Freedom Restoration Act (RFRA). This act was passed after a much-criticized decision of the Supreme Court in *Smith v. Employment Division of Oregon,* a case involving members of the Native American church who lost their jobs and were refused unemployment benefits because of their use of peyote in church rituals. In the *Smith* decision the Supreme Court threw out the "compelling state interest test" and adopted a "facially neutral" standard that granted no primacy to religion when governments were passing and enforcing laws. The decision raised the ire of a large number of religions organizations, including major faiths, and a coalition of over sixty religious groups was established to help push legislation to overcome the effects of the *Smith* decision. After several years of effort by this unprecedented coalition, RFRA was passed, causing much celebration—which, however, turned out to be premature.

RFRA required that governmental entities demonstrate a compelling state interest with any new law that infringed on religious freedom of individuals and groups and that those entities seek the least intrusive alternative method to accomplish the goal of the state in passing a new law. However, the huge effort notwithstanding, RFRA was declared unconstitutional in a 1996 decision involving whether a Roman Catholic church in Boerne, Texas, could renovate a building even though it was in a historical district offering special protections for older buildings.[5] The decision left all religious groups with less protection, since the demonstrated need of a church to service its parishioners was overridden by a secular law designed to preserve historical buildings.

These two well-publicized instances notwithstanding, the overall pattern seems more often to have been one of mainline groups' allowing the activities of religious minorities to be circumscribed by legal action of various kinds. It is rare that mainline religious groups that make up "public religion" go to the aid of minority faiths when they are engaged in defending their religious freedoms and even their very existence. Only when leaders of mainline faiths decide that their own interests are being jeopardized does such assistance develop. All too often they stand aside while the state attempts to exert control over smaller and more exuberant faiths, or when private entities seek self-help solutions through the courts, such as using the civil courts to promote attacks on new religions based on so-called brainwashing theories.[6] Also, minority faiths have not had much assistance from mainline churches in the many battles over ordinances governing solicitation of funds that have often been used in efforts to limit the raising of money by newer religions. Thus it seems that being a part of public religion may involve allowing such efforts at social control or even on occasion encouraging them.

Sometimes when the legal system is used for social control of smaller religions the fact that more traditional groups have something at stake is readily apparent, as in the *Smith* and *Moon* cases, but other times the potential loss is less obvious, and thus more easily ignored. For instance, the Alamo Foundation lost a Supreme Court case involving the issue of whether the Fair Labor Standards Act applied to religious groups, thus requiring the group to pay wage rates established by the federal government to Alamo's members who worked within the organization. No other religious group came to Alamo's aid when this case was being fought in the courts. The federal Labor Department won a ruling forcing the Alamo group to pay its members minimum wage rates for making clothes that were sold to support the communal group. Shortly after this ruling, the Labor Department attempted to apply the ruling to the Salvation Army's hundreds of volunteers in its soup kitchens and aid centers across America. Such a hue and cry was raised that the Labor Department withdrew the effort, clearly suggesting differential treatment of religious groups.[7]

Solicitation cases, of which there have been hundreds in the past several decades, also go unnoticed by religious organizations that raise their funds from members and investments. Indeed, an argument can even be made that the more traditional groups sometimes support efforts to limit fund-raising by newer groups that do not have the luxury of living off relatively well-heeled members or investments. When the Minnesota state legislature passed laws to regulate public solicitation that were obviously aimed at the Unification church, one legislator said, on the record, that the law was not intended to apply to the Catholic church.[8] The Unification church went to court over the issue and eventually won a close United States Supreme Court decision (five to four), but it had little help from any other group in fighting this legal battle.

So-called brainwashing cases have generally had a similar fate. Mainline religions have not been concerned about the attacks on recruitment under the guise of "brainwashing" accusations. Instead, such groups have usually stood by when newer religions have been hauled into the dock for activities that can in truth only be characterized as aggressive recruiting. The fact that such recruiting sometimes results in the loss of potential members from mainline churches is not lost on leaders of those organizations. Thus, quiet decisions have been made with some regularity to stay out of the debate about such cases and to allow the legal system to work its will with these new and often unpopular groups. There have been some efforts by mainline organizations such as the National Council of Churches to critique deprogramming, the forcible removal and resocialization of a participant from a newer religion. However, in the main, the public and popular attacks on recruitment of new religions have been unanswered by spokespersons for mainline faiths.

Thus, the best that can be said is that there are mixed findings when examining the way major religions have supported actions of minority religions in the legal area. And, perhaps as a result of this ambiguous support, there is evidence that much has been lost in terms of the impact of religion on public life as well as the idea of religious freedom in our society. In a series of court decisions about religious freedom made using minority faiths as the vehicle, there seems to have been significant change brought about in what religious freedom means.[9] Religious freedom for minority faith participants has been circumscribed in ways that might be thought to lend strength to public religions in the short term. However, an argument can be made that in the long term the role of religion in the public square has been diminished by the cumulative effect of these decisions.

DIRECT RELATIONS BETWEEN NEW RELIGIONS AND MAJOR FAITHS

There is always built-in tension between new and traditional religions. The new faiths are exuberant and aggressive as they spread their new-found truths. Often, as they attempt to spread their faith, they end up recruiting participants who might well be claimed, rightly or wrongly, by a more traditional faith. More traditional religions are concerned about the maintenance of their more dominant societal position, not to mention the retention of their parishioners. They worry about allowing new religions entrée to the society and to their own participants. Dominant faiths may take severe umbrage when newer faiths appear to encroach on their territory and membership through aggressive proselytizing or political lobbying, especially when such efforts are accompanied by strong public condemnation of the traditional faiths. The following is a discussion of some specific newer religions' relationships with representatives of more dominant religions.

The Children of God (COG)/Family and Mainline Religions

Tensions between newer and more traditional faiths can be overcome with effort, but the problems remain, and gains on the rapprochement front are often short-lived. Thus, the World Council of Churches (WCC) in Geneva had significant liaison with some of the new religions back in the 1970s. A representative of the Children of God (COG) spent several years stationed in Geneva, where he was also serving as a "local shepherd" for the COG, supervising four "colonies" or communes of this group.[10] This shepherd served as a liaison at the invitation of one particular World Council official, to work with a few WCC people willing to have such a dialogue. But this dialogue broke down with changes in personnel at the WCC and with the advent of practices by the COG that were unacceptable to WCC participant groups.

We have seen other efforts at cooperation by the COG/Family with religious organizations or interfaith groups, especially more recently. The Family, the successor group of the COG, works regularly with religious relief organizations of various kinds where it is possible. For instance, they have worked with the Salvation Army in Russia, and in the United States local Family groups have worked with African American churches on various evangelical and service projects. Family representatives have attended conferences sponsored by the Muslim community, and Family leaders express the hope of engaging in meaningful joint efforts with that group in the future.

But, although some Family leaders, particularly in recent times, have been interested in interfaith dialogue, such dialogue has been hindered through the years of COG/Family existence by the actions and perceived beliefs of the group. For instance, this group has in its past been accused of anti-Semitism, a charge they deny, but that derives in part from some of their own writings. Also, the development in the 1970s of so-called Flirty Fishing, which used sex as a recruitment tool, was upsetting to those of traditional beliefs about sexuality, including mainline Christian churches who thought the biblical justification developed for such practices was outrageous.[11]

The rampant particularism that characterized the early COG was very off-putting as well. Early in their history the COG would sometimes visit local traditional churches dressed in sackcloth and carrying large staffs. They would in unison hit their staffs on the floor and say things like "Woe unto you." These demonstrations, designed apparently to send the message that traditional churches were not presenting the proper view of biblical Christianity, were quite upsetting, of course, to the churches visited with such tactics and did little to endear the group to such organizations. These early activities, which were sometimes focused on traditional churches, contributed to animosity between this large Jesus Movement organization and the churches. Leaders of these traditional churches also sometimes felt that the COG was "stealing their children," whereas the COG defined their recruitment as making real Christianity available to interested young people. Thus, the tension was strong between this controversial group and mainline churches, especially early in the group's history.

The COG/Family have experienced a number of major events in the life of the group when assistance would have been welcome from more traditional faiths as social control efforts were made by governmental agencies around the world.[12] Many members have been deprogrammed from the COG/Family over the years, with little protest from any mainline groups. (The National Council of Churches is an important exception to the widespread silence on the issue of deprogramming.) The Family has suffered a number of raids around the world in which hundreds of Family children have been taken away by authorities seeking to have them permanently removed and made charges of the state. Mainline religions did not defend The Family in such circumstances, and some of them may have contributed to what happened, indirectly if not directly. This seems particularly the case with the Roman Catholic church in Latin America, which has not looked with favor on the aggressive recruitment activities and general life-style of groups such as The Family. Thus, although The Family has eventually won all these legal battles over control of their children, they have paid a heavy price in terms of disruption of normal life.[13] Also, some members have spent months in foreign prisons or been denied access to their children for months as the cases were being resolved.

The Unification Church and Mainline Religions

The Unification church is another of the controversial new religions that have attracted both animus and support from mainline church groups. The Unification church has engaged in overt efforts to work with other religious organizations over the years, in part because of its own theology, which moves it in the direction of inclusiveness.[14] However, it has often been rebuffed, although progress has been made on some fronts.[15]

As noted, the tax evasion trial of the Reverend Moon engendered a major ecumenical event, with all sorts of religious groups and individual leaders signing on in the effort to overturn the guilty verdict. Thus, it is clear that the Unification church has on occasion enjoyed apparently strong support from mainline religious groups and interfaith organizations.

But, as with the COG/Family, this is only part of the story. In particular the Unification church has considerable grounds to protest its treatment by some major religious organizations and by some religious groups. There is, for instance, a history of animus between some Jewish leaders and the Unification church, based in part on the perception that the church has been attracting an inordinate number of young people of Jewish descent. Some Jewish leaders have become prominent in what is sometimes called the "anti-cult movement."[16] Also, the Unification church has been the focus of repeated accusations that they "brainwash" recruits, accusations sometimes contributed to by representatives of at least some traditional churches. Solicitation methods of the Unification church have also been openly attacked, sometimes with brainwashing-based arguments—"People would not do such activities if they were not brainwashed." Such claims about recruitment and fund-raising practices of the Unification church have been made recently in Russia by representatives of the Russian Orthodox church and in Latin America by representatives of the Catholic church, as grounds for severely curtailing Unification church activities in those areas. Thus, in these instances we have seen religious leaders leading an attack against a newer faith.

Most interesting from the perspective of this chapter, with its major focus on the United States, is the saga of ongoing relations between the Unification church and the National Council of Churches (NCC), an organization with perhaps the best overall record of support for newer religions of any mainline group over the past several decades. Jonathan Wells, a theologically trained member of the Unification church who teaches at the Unification Theological Seminary in Barrytown, New York, has written two related papers concerning this lengthy history.[17] His discussions, although written from the perspective of a Unification church insider, reveal the ambivalence that mainline religious organizations can have toward controversial new religious groups.

Apparently the episode began with an overture to the National Council of Churches from the Unification church in the mid-1970s about the church's becoming a member of the NCC, which is, of course, a Christian-based organization. This overture led to the sponsorship of a review by the NCC that included preparing a "study document" to use in a "theological assessment" of the Unification church. This report, written in 1977 by a theology professor at a Southern Baptist seminary, was made public through press releases that attracted considerable attention within religious circles. The report was written, according to

Wells, without input from Unification church representatives, and he further claims that after the critical report was released the NCC rebuffed efforts to engage in dialogue about the contents of the report.[18] According to Wells, the NCC would not agree to talk with Unification church representatives or to attend seriously to considerable materials about Unification church theology that were submitted to the NCC by church representatives and others. Instead, Wells stated, the council chose to rely mainly on only one perspective on the *Divine Principle*—the Unification church's unique book of revelation, doctrine, and discipline—and gave that critical view wide publicity.

The National Council of Churches has, as one might suspect, another view of the interactions between it and the Unification church. According to one well-placed NCC source, the Unification church made a concerted effort to force itself on the Council. But the NCC felt it had a responsibility to itself and its member organizations to review any applications carefully to see whether the organization applying for membership was in fact Christian according to guidelines used by the NCC. The Unification church was eventually found wanting in this regard, and from the NCC's perspective the Unification church is now complaining about the outcome of a rather thorough review.

Whatever the truth about the process of reviewing the Unification church application for membership in the National Council of Churches, it is a fact that the widespread and continuing dissemination of this report on the Unification church has caused considerable disquiet among Unification church leadership. They seem caught in a classic "catch-22" situation, in that the report was never adopted as "official policy" by the NCC, but it was distributed under NCC letterhead. Unification church officials have been told that the report cannot be retracted or revised since it was never officially adopted. But the National Council of Churches has allowed it to be published and disseminated widely. Since 1991, according to Wells, the report has been officially circulated in Japan, Korea, Europe, the Caribbean, as well as South America.

According to Wells, in England the National Council of Churches' report was used as part of the unsuccessful effort to have the tax-exempt status of the Unification church withdrawn by the government. This battle cost the church half a million dollars in legal fees before the attempt was defeated. In South America the report has served to undergird current harsh tactics being promoted by the Roman Catholic church to limit Unification church activities, and even to attempt to drive the church out of some countries. In the United States, Unification church ministers have been denied participation in campus ministry organizations, using the National Council of Churches report as a basis. Wells also claims that some mainline religion ministers have lost their position because of their willingness to work with the Unification church, with such losses attributed to the impact of the NCC report.

This is, of course, not the place to review in depth Unification church theology or to decide whether they are truly Christian. And it is not a forum simply to condemn naively the National Council of Churches for its specific actions. The NCC was, after all, involved as an *amicus* in the tax evasion case of the Reverend Moon, and the organization has been one of the foremost opponents of deprogramming (which targeted Unification church members more than others), indicating that the NCC is not totally opposed to the Unification church. But the NCC has engaged in possibly problematic actions particularly concerning dissemination of the report. Wells has harsh words for the National Council of Churches on this issue and perhaps with some justification.

Christian Science and Battles over the Health of Their Children

Christian Science, another minority faith, but one that has been present in the United States for some time, has also had difficulties within the legal arena in recent years. The problems have arisen from some unusual doctrines concerning the meaning of health and how one should achieve good health. Christian Science is not alone in having unusual doctrines concerning health, of course, and other groups, such as Jehovah's Witnesses, also have encountered difficulties in attempting to live a life-style that includes practices such as spiritual healing or, among the Witnesses, refusal to use blood transfusions. These practices have become the focus of public attention mainly because of their potential application to children in the groups. When spiritual healing is used with children and a child dies, this attracts the attention of secular authorities and the media, especially in recent years in the United States, at a time when concern about child abuse has become a major cultural value.

Over the years the Christian Science religion had worked out an accommodation with authorities both nationally and at the state level. The accommodation often took the form of establishing by statute or regulation exceptions to laws about child abuse that preclude prosecution if a child appears to suffer (or even dies) as a result of well-meaning efforts by parents to use spiritual healing methods with the child. Thus, if a child died after the use of spiritual healing during an illness, the law excused parents in most states, and federal policy also allowed use of such methods.[19] Admittedly, this accommodation could not have been worked out without the tacit approval of people not members of the Christian Science religion. Thus, it seems probable that leaders of dominant faiths allowed the accommodations to be developed, or at least they did not protest when such accommodations were worked out. Thus, there seems to have been some support, however tacit, for Christian Science among mainline faiths, as they sought exemptions in the laws concerning child abuse.

In recent years, however, when some Christian Science parents have come under attack for use of spiritual healing in situations in which the child dies, that kind of support has not been found very readily. Christian Science parents have been "on their own" in fighting these battles, as has the church itself. A number of cases have arisen around the country of parents being charged with child neglect, child endangerment, child abuse, or even manslaughter, when their child has died after use of spiritual healing. Such cases have sometimes been resolved in favor of the parents, but some have been convicted. On appeal, courts have often overturned the convictions on due process grounds, which means that the parents could not be expected to know they were violating the law since there was usually an explicit exemption in the law for spiritual healing. What is of interest here is not the specific outcome of the cases, but the fact that other religious groups did not come to the aid of those parents in the dock or of the Christian Science religion itself in these trying circumstances. Thus, a well-known American faith, fighting to defend itself against attack in the courts by governmental officials, was left to fight virtually alone, even though what it was fighting for was integral to its doctrine and way of life. Few in the religious community seemed to notice, and if they did, they still made no effort to support Christian Science in its battles with governmental authorities.

PUBLIC RELIGION AND NEW RELIGIONS OUTSIDE THE UNITED STATES

Martin Marty was writing about religion in the United States in his discussions of public religion, as is shown by virtually all his illustrations and examples. However, it seems just as clear that the ideas involved in public religion would have application in other societies, particularly those related to the United States historically and culturally. Thus it seems useful also to examine, even if briefly, some of those other societies, with a particular focus on the relationship of newer faiths to older ones within those societies.

Currently in Western Europe, a place of considerable religious pluralism, there are examples of strained relationships between dominant faiths and newer ones. Not all such societies are experiencing problematic relations, but some are, and their circumstances warrant study.

In France great tension has developed between the dominant faith, Catholicism, and other religious groups, particularly newer ones. There is fairly open collusion between the Catholic church and the French government, so the animus that exists has some real consequences.[20] The French government has been engaged in official studies of religious groups that have led to the 1996 publication of a list of nearly two hundred groups labeled "sects" (a very negative term within France) or "cults." This labeling has had repercussions. Some groups on the list have had difficulty renting space to have meetings or getting permission to construct buildings.

Perhaps the most egregious use of the listing has been the 1998 decision by tax authorities in France to claim millions of dollars from the Jehovah's Witness organization, a group that has existed in France for many decades.[21] Specifically, as James Wood has mentioned, the taxing authority has demanded a 60 percent tax on all revenue taken in by the Witnesses over the past several years, meaning that a sum in the range of $50 million is due to be paid—and all donations made to pay off this sum will be similarly taxed. This action, indirectly sanctioned by the Catholic church by virtue of its support for the efforts that have led to the categorization of religious groups in ways amenable to such governmental actions, would destroy the Witnesses in France. Much international attention has been paid to this development, and the issue is not resolved at the time of this writing.

Similar activities concerning newer and smaller faiths are taking place in Belgium and in Germany. The Belgian government has also had a major study done of such groups and has published its own listing of suspect groups that require official attention. This has had negative repercussions in Belgium as well. Again, the point would be that such governmental action is hard to contemplate without at least the tacit approval of the traditional dominant faiths.

In Germany, the Lutheran church has been quite aggressive concerning newer faiths. The church has appointed a number of its ministers to official "cult-watching" positions, with the apparent goal of having these people monitor newer faiths and inform the citizenry about them. Official agencies of the German government are involved in these activities as well, and there seem to be quite close relationships between the government and the Lutheran church on these matters.[22] The efforts of this anticult/antisect coalition in Germany have attracted attention internationally, including from the United States government, which has expressed concern about the actions being taken toward some minority faiths in Germany.[23]

In Australia there have also been episodes that show less than full openness of dominant faiths toward minority faiths, and one such episode explicitly involved those dominant religious groups. Australia does not have a Bill of Rights like that of the United States. Indeed, it is one of only a few Western societies without such a statement as a part of its governing documents. Over the years there have been some efforts to add a Bill of Rights to the Australian Constitution, but these have always been defeated, sometimes quite handily.[24]

The major churches in Australia have always opposed the addition of a Bill of Rights to the Australian Constitution. They cite problems with American law and practice in the area of religious freedom and make all sorts of arguments that Australia should not follow America's lead on this matter. Although irrefutable evidence is hard to obtain, it seems clear to many observers that the dominant faiths do not want provisions in the Constitution that can be used by minority faiths to integrate themselves more fully and easily into Australian society.

An effort in the early 1980s to add religion to the antidiscrimination law in New South Wales (Sydney) also resulted in failure (New South Wales Anti-Discrimination Board, 1984). A strong law that protected people from racial discrimination and even from discrimination on the basis of sexual preference was not amended, in spite of the fact that the movement to add religion to the law had strong support in some quarters. The major reason given was the opposition of dominant religious organizations in New South Wales.[25]

Thus, it appears that, perhaps not surprisingly, those faiths involved in what we are calling "public religion" in some other Western societies also sometimes act toward minority faiths in a manner that is less than positive. The dominant groups seem intent on maintaining their monopolistic (or oligopolistic) position, even if it means defining some well-meaning newer and smaller groups out of that sacred fraternity.

PUBLIC RELIGION AND NEW RELIGIONS IN FORMER COMMUNIST COUNTRIES

It seems clear that Marty's ideas about public religion have some application to Western societies. It also may be useful to consider their application to former Soviet bloc countries. This may seem odd to some readers, given the decades of domination by an openly atheistic regime in that part of the world. It is now clear, however, that religion was not dead in the Soviet Union, but repressed, sometimes ruthlessly. And, particularly in Poland, religion was playing a major role even in the time of Soviet domination. Indeed, one might say that the Catholic church led the effort to overthrow communism in Poland and other countries once under Soviet rule. Catholicism in Poland was very "public" and came to be defined as the not-so-loyal opposition to the Soviets, promoting values antithetical to theirs.

Since the fall of the Soviet Union, religion and religious organizations have begun to play a role not unlike that of such entities in Western societies. Indeed, there is evidence that former Soviet bloc countries want to emulate the West in many ways, including the role of religion in society.[26] Thus, we may see former Soviet bloc societies moving rather quickly to allow and even encourage formerly dominant religious organizations to assume a major role in public life in those countries. As this happens, again the question is raised about how such formerly dominant groups act toward minority and newer faiths.

In Poland, the relationships between the Catholic church and newer faiths are strained. Although there are new laws that on their face grant equality to all religious groups, the special place of the Catholic church is apparent in both formal statutory agreements and the way non-Catholic groups are treated by state authorities. Newer religious groups especially are sometimes dealt with in a summary fashion. The closeness of the Catholic church to the government in Poland (especially in the time of Lech Walesa) makes it seem that the church is exerting considerable influence on how governmental agencies treat minority faiths. They are sometimes not allowed to register under the law that seems to allow such registration, and other strictures exist as well. Thus, in Poland it seems that the Catholic church is influencing the government to limit competition from other groups.

In Hungary the situation has been somewhat different, but not for want of trying. After the fall of communism and the passage of laws that seemed to offer considerable religious freedom, a number of new groups from the West, including some of the more controversial ones (Unification church, Hare Krishna, The Family), arrived in Hungary. Some leading Protestants led a fight against the Western "cults," a fight that, according to some reports, had the tacit approval of the Catholic church in Hungary. The effort to limit newer religions was not greeted as enthusiastically by governmental officials in Hungary as it was in Poland, however. The legal system was even used by one of the groups (Hare Krishna) to secure a libel judgment against one of the prominent Protestant ministers involved in the anticult/antisect activities. Winning such a suit is rare, however, and indicates that, although some religious leaders were seeking to limit the activities of smaller competitors, they were not able to work their will so easily in Hungary as in some other places, such as Poland and Russia, to which we now turn.

The Russian Orthodox church has reasserted itself and has rapidly achieved a position of dominance in the new Russia. As a part of the campaign to reestablish itself as the major religion in the land, Orthodoxy has sought to stifle minority faiths, and it has found many political allies in this effort. After several years of trying, the Orthodox church has finally succeeded in getting major changes made in the 1990 law in Russia that had granted freedom of religion for individuals and considerable freedom of activity for religious groups, even foreign ones from the West.[27]

The Russian Orthodox church has formed political coalitions with governmental officials and parties and has worked hard to encourage legal limitations on the actions of foreign religious groups. They have had considerable success in those efforts, as indicated by the change of law, and by other official actions, as the government now seeks enforcement of the new law against unwelcome groups.[28] Thus it seems clear that in Russia, as elsewhere, dominant religious groups will sometimes seek to solidify their position by using newer and smaller faiths as vehicles to reassert and maintain a dominant position.

CONCLUSIONS

Martin Marty's concept of public religion is a powerful one that deserves attention from all interested in the role of religion in public life. Public religion is an idea with wide application, not just in Western countries, but in others as well. Most thinking people, even in former communist countries, view the role of religion in society positively, even if they themselves are not believers. But that perspective carries with it some responsibilities and implications that need to be examined, especially as it relates to minority faiths in our society.

Mainline religions and interfaith organizations should make major efforts to be inclusive of the new faiths, even as those faiths sometimes take actions and espouse beliefs that are upsetting to the mainline faiths and when those faiths are viewed as potentially destructive of a given religious organization's position in society. Much is at stake. As has been shown, losses of court cases by minority faiths can and have impacted traditional religions and the impact they in turn may have in public affairs. Leaders of mainline faiths engaged in the public life of society should realize that they have a responsibility to define religious freedom broadly and to defend religious freedom in any forum where it is challenged, however unpopular the particular group involved. Public religion must be responsible religion, or all will suffer in the long run. Especially when newer religions make efforts to move toward a more normal role in society, they should be encouraged and assisted by those religious groups that are part of the normative establishment.

At the same time, the newer religions need to be cognizant of their own responsibilities to seek dialogue with mainline faiths and to play a role in the public life of societies in which they operate. They must learn to be good citizens acting responsibly toward others, including other religious organizations. Even when the beliefs of newer religions contain elements highly critical of traditional religions, the new groups should seek dialogue in ways that make communication possible. Newer faiths should realize that they have much in common with traditional faiths, and vice versa. Both the old and the new are needed if religion is indeed to play the kind of role envisioned by Marty's notion of public religion. If the newer groups want to find a permanent place in society, they must learn to play a part in the public religion of their society, assuming the attendant responsibilities of occupying such a position.

Chapter 11

Public Religion and Hegemony: Contesting the Language of the Common Good

Rhys H. Williams

An irony lies at the heart of the idea of the "common good" in contemporary pluralist societies. The symbols that form the notions of the common good, by definition, are meant to embody an overarching, potentially unifying system of thought and expression. They are meant to encompass the entire society, and although perhaps not benefiting every specific person within society, they represent the good of the greater whole.

But these symbols do not arise in a vacuum. They are created by a "public"—but not by "the" public. It is a fact of social life that the public expressions of a given society—the symbols that represent it—emerge out of the cultural repertoire of a particular sociocultural group. That is, they are *somebody's* culture, even as they claim to speak for a holistic public. And indeed, the public for which the "public good" stands is as often as not an abstraction, rather than a clearly definable social group. Thus, no vision of the common good is ever completely transcendent, located outside the society in which it is used. Every vision or symbol implicates the culture of some social groupings and in the process slights others. In the literature of political culture, this points to the idea of "hegemony"—the notion that the symbols forwarded by powerful societal groups are tools for maintaining their continuing privilege, even if they purport to speak for a generalized public.[1]

And yet, images of the public good—the symbolic expressions about the good society that are common in a culture—are generally not reducible to mere self-interested ideologies. Although there may be ideological functions of common good language, and self-interests are sometimes rather thinly disguised, that is not *all* they are. In part, this is due to their content. Symbols of the common good are, again by definition, attempts at defining a space that goes beyond the sectarian and the momentary. Elements of the transhistorical and translocal are central to all claims to be about a common good. The present is bound to the past and the future (at least some imagined future); generations are connected, and implicitly differences are transcended in favor of unity, or perhaps harmony, or at the least, a greater purpose.

To use the evocative words of Benedict Anderson, there are "imagined communities" that are represented by common good language.[2] One may not have the intergenerational and diverse spatial experiences that provide direct evidence that one lives in a community that stretches across time and space; in that sense, communities are imagined. But they are nonetheless "real," for they are "symbolically constructed repositories of meaning."[3] Their existence as located, geographically bounded entities is no more important—and in the modern world may be less important—than their existence as symbolically constructed cultural categories. It is through such categories that we gain personal and social identities, differentiating who we are, and what that means, from who we are not, and why.[4]

Thus the irony in the "public good": Although purporting to represent the whole, common good language is inevitably rooted in the cultural processes of particular social groupings; yet, by its very content, the particularities of the cultures producing public good language must be generalized, abstracted, and in some sense transcended. Particularities are the necessary social origins of symbolic universalisms, but the universalist aspirations of the symbols themselves pull them beyond the particular.

This has consequences for understanding the processes of political culture and the uses of common good symbolism in public life. The very notion that the symbolic products of socially privileged groups define a good for an entire society requires them to be abstracted enough that socially marginal groups can claim some stake in that common good, and thus be a part of the relevant public. Having made such a claim, groups may then challenge their marginalization. Thus, public good language is *both* a hegemonic cultural construct *and* an ideological tool for challenging that hegemony. In sum, the need to embody the parts in the whole, while making the whole at least in part irreducible, is the challenge of public culture.

This chapter examines this paradox in public culture through the interplay between public religion and hegemony. I examine each of these three concepts— public culture, public religion, hegemony—in turn and show how they form a complicated symbolic triangle in contemporary societies. My purpose theoretically is to keep a focus on the relationship between religion and public power, while undermining both the traditional Marxian view of religion as only the hegemonic tool of the privileged and the functional perspective that too often accepts claims for "the public" at face value without investigating their contributions to inequality. In contrast, I argue that each of these three symbolic forms (public culture, public religion, hegemony) has dimensions that both reinforce and contest the others, leaving the actual state of public symbolic life fluid—without implying that it is shallow or vacuous.

In order to ground some of the abstractions I engage, I draw empirical examples from recent social and political controversies in which the actors are claiming to speak for and about the "public" or "common" good. As I have argued elsewhere, American political culture has several different languages available to imagine the good society and the public good that supports it.[5] These are normative, moral claims about the social arrangements that form the good society and how that society should be achieved; that is, they are calls for pursuing and constructing the public good. The rhetorical models that compose common good language are, however, often built on very different assumptions about the relations between the individual and society, between groups within society, and between society and the sacred. This is due, in part, to the different social origins of the various cultural constructs involved—that is, they are different somebodies' cultures. As a result, though contemporary public discourse has many calling for a common good, the good being imagined is often built on opposing worldviews, increasing the distance between the desires for a truly public culture and the ability to achieve it.[6] My purpose here is to show that claims to the public good may be attempts at hegemonic cultural forms but, if successful, contain the conditions that contest and challenge them.

Although there is not room here for a lengthy discussion about the relationship between rhetoric and action, it deserves mention. My prime example of public culture in this chapter is public *language*, that is, spoken and written rhetoric used in public forums. Specifically, as I noted, I am interested in "public good" language. I focus on language for three reasons. First, I am interested in public culture, and language is a major cultural system. Second, as noted, in contemporary societies the political community must often be "imagined." Much of that imagining is done through language—indeed, I would argue that language use actually "constitutes" the public good. Visions of the good society, if they are to be acted upon, must be created in forms in which they can be widely shared and interpreted. Language is one such form—it puts ideas, beliefs, and values into an embodied structure upon which action can be taken. Third, the actions of creating and dispersing a public language have a structuring effect on the actions that follow from it. There is a "discursive structure" to public life; the ways in which normative visions are articulated shape the modes of action in which they are embodied. So, how people talk about public life contributes significantly to shaping it. In sum, far from being "only talk," public good language is essential to, and even formative of, the public cultural issues I tackle here. It is a form of public and political action and must be considered as such.

Using these considerations about the common good as an empirical base, I now consider each of the legs of my conceptual triangle in turn: religion and culture, culture and hegemony, and hegemony and public religion.

RELIGION AND PUBLIC CULTURE

In this chapter I use the terms *public good* and *common good* interchangeably. Public good language is that set of symbols that describe social arrangements or cultural values that serve as components of an ideal society. In that sense, I use the term roughly analogously to what Bellah and his colleagues mean by "the good society."[7] I do not mean public good the way an economist would use the term—to indicate a good or service that is nonrival and nondivisible, and thus in theory accessible to all members of a public. Rather, I mean the moralized language of political culture that offers normative assessments of what will benefit the entire society. Because this language is inherently normative and ordering, it has deeply entwined, and deeply complicated, relations to religion.

Society and Moral Authority

Any attempt to discuss a "transcendent" vision of society, embodied in symbolic forms, implies that public culture has a sacred quality to it. Finding societal unity in elements of "transcendence," or in a Parsonian "value generality," or in the "celebratory visions" of civil religious language clearly locates society in some type of cosmos. This paraphrases one of Durkheim's abiding legacies to our field—that society itself is a moral construct, and maintaining it is a "sacred" effort. That religion produces a *public* culture that consists of a fundamentally universalizing idea is at the heart of Durkheim's analysis of the social origins of religion.[8] Of course, in societies marked by a certain level of homogeneity, where *gemeinschaft* organization predominates, the social whole does not seem difficult to envision. Although such a society may not be the harmonic unity of romantic conservatives, it does make sense to think that the social whole is more apparent to direct experience in "traditional" settings. Where identity is relatively undifferentiated, history and destiny seem necessarily interconnected, and the idea of a unified common good appears available to commonsense empirical inspection rather than abstraction.

The unity evoked by common good language is more problematic in pluralist societies (granted that pluralism is an inherently cultural construct and can be "invented").[9] Yet even in such settings, visions of the public good are meant to have a "bridging" quality—both recognizing and ignoring heterogeneity. The common good may deny difference or it may celebrate difference, but its purpose in either case is to "generalize upward" so that differences are subsumed under more lofty and important similarities.

Political theories of interest-group pluralism, so central to the core ideologies of liberal democratic states, explicitly understand the public good as social arrangements that in some way offer connections among the partial visions of specific social groupings.[10] As long as there is a general consensus on the "rules of the game," the particular substantive version of the public good (or what is usually taken as its proxy, state policy) is a process-driven product that has room for both majority decision making and minority communities. "Procedural justice" becomes the hallmark of equality. All persons should be treated alike—in accordance with the same set of rules. An inequality of outcome is legitimate as long as the procedures that produced it were standardized and appropriate.

Clearly there is a connection between this notion of the production of the public good and the development of capitalist economics and classical liberal political theory. Just as individuals pursuing their private economic ends in the marketplace can produce a public good (a growing economy), so can contending groups in the political arena produce a decision-making system of fairness and cooperation. There are hints of this kind of societal order in Durkheim's "optimistic" writings, such as his description of "organic" solidarity or the way the "cult of the individual" may keep the sacred alive in modern societies.[11]

In such societal settings it is not unusual for the rules of the game themselves to take on a sacred quality—that is, they become thought of as ends in themselves, values and goods that need no justification beyond their existence. In American culture, phrases such as "Change through the ballot box" or "If you don't vote, don't complain" have that aura. They indicate an acceptance of the efficacy and importance of the existing rules and assume their capacity to produce just outcomes. My personal favorite in this regard is "That's unconstitutional." I hear it used to express disapproval of political or public policies, but separated from any knowledge of the Constitution itself. Rather, it is meant to express a bedrock faith in the power of fair rules. I often imagine that a century ago these same persons might have exclaimed, "That's not Scriptural." In that transition may be a cultural shift from a vision of substantive justice to one of procedural justice.

In a Durkheimian perspective that views society as religious, culture is therefore inherently "public" and necessarily moral. Indeed, there is not much conceptual distance between "religion" and "culture" in such theoretical formulations. "Public religion" becomes one expression—perhaps the central expression—of public culture. Of course, to the extent that religion is a distinct institutional field within society, the two ideas are not synonymous. But clearly there is great overlap in the symbols that can be said to be part of a society's public culture and the expressions that compose public religion. There are benefits to specific social groups in conflating the two ideas, such that public religion seems as natural, taken-for-granted, and integral as the general culture. If the religion of a particular group achieves a taken-for-granted status, the legitimacy and authority of the group itself can be beyond challenge.

A too often overlooked dimension of the understanding of the sacred aspects of society is the importance of collective moral authority in efforts to achieve social change. The anthropologist David Kertzer links the moral authority generated by societal ritual directly to the moral outrage necessary to foster change efforts (in contemporary societies, this means "social movements"). In that way he explicitly uses Durkheim's (and Victor Turner's) insight on the moral underpinnings of social groups as a way of understanding both stasis and change. Challenge groups must generate their own sacred qualities in order to bind members to the group and to its visions for change. The sense of injustice needed to motivate action, the rhetorical appeals needed to recruit members, and the ideological vision necessary to prompt unified action must all have moral dimensions.[12] Similarly, Clifford Geertz notes that religion is a crucial sense-making system in social change, whether or not change is self-consciously pursued. Both groups that want to preserve society and those who want to change it draw upon society's inherent moral authority in their efforts.[13]

"Public" Religion

Institutionally differentiated societies may have an overlapping of public culture and public religion, but they are not identical. Because a public culture is a "wider" phenomenon than public religion, the latter becomes differentially available as a way of understanding society. Some understandings of society are "religious," and some are not. Religion becomes one, often competing, way of articulating public life and a public good. In part, this is due to a disarticulation between morality and religion, but it also recognizes that religion itself is not a unified phenomenon. Religion, thus, becomes more like a "resource" that can be invoked or not invoked differently by different actors for different purposes.[14] Even as public culture and public religion are analytically distinct, public religion is not synonymous with all the religious expressions in a society. For my purposes here, public religion means two distinct, but related things.

First, public religion is the religious expressions used in public settings, intended for public consumption, by actors intentionally representing the public (however conceived). Such settings could be public ceremonies such as dedications of buildings or facilities, political rituals such as swearings-in or formal speeches, or public "interpretive" events such as the official statements made after natural disasters, human tragedies, or public milestones. Many of the religious expressions in these settings could very well fall under the rubric of "civil religion."[15] Of course, like many attractive concepts, civil religion has no precise, consensually validated meaning. Bellah's seminal formulation, for example, exempted from his civil religion the type of national, celebratory self-worship that is the essence of other definitions.[16] These shades of meaning are not central to this essay. I use the term *civil religion* to mean a set of cultural understandings that link the nation, its history, and destiny to a sense of divine purpose. Again, civil religion as a cultural form is thought to be a unifying element within a pluralistic society; sectarian differences can be encompassed and transcended by a symbolic form that is less specific and more generalized.

A second type of public religion is that used by definable societal groups when they speak to and about the public. Thus, although the origin might be in sectarian groupings, the message is intended to resonate more widely. In that sense, this is "strategic" communication meant to persuade; the negotiation between the group's ideas and beliefs and the group's assessment of the language that will resonate with others in the society is more or less explicit.[17] The public is the *target* of expression in this case, as distinguished from those expressions in which the public is the *source*. The second type of public religion is found commonly in social movements and other claims-making activities whose purpose is to propose or oppose change.

My distinction of two types of public religion is not merely a definitional matter. The alternative definitions represent two versions of the phenomenon, both of which are potentially present in the *content* of public religion itself. True, the definitions denote an analytic distinction that may well be more difficult to disentangle when actually encountered in the public religion of a society. Nonetheless, public religion is both the general societal expressions of religious content (that necessarily originate in the cultural repertoire of particular social groups) and the direct use of religious content to try to shape the public sphere (where the search for wider resonance means that many groups potentially have access to its meanings).

Put another way, the public religion that is civil religion is, at least originally, the public expression of sectarian religious commitments. For example, commentators on American civil religion have located many of its founding ideas in Puritan religious culture; America was the "New Jerusalem" that was particularly favored by God—a "city on a hill" that was to be an example to the world.[18] In that sense, many versions of civil religion are forms of, or least remnants of, Protestant—specifically Puritan—hegemony.[19]

Conversely, when public religion is conceived as the public religious pronouncements of particular sociocultural groups (the second definition), it is being used as an ideological appeal, but it is not merely ideology. Perhaps it is more accurate to say that although such pronouncements may begin with ideological intentions, they do not remain there. Symbols are multivocal and have an inherent ambiguity about them.[20] Particularly those symbols that are more widely shared across a society will concomitantly have more shades of meaning and nuances of interpretation. So even if culture producers intend their public expressions to represent their particularistic viewpoint, they cannot guarantee those expressions will be interpreted that way.

Further, the very process of "publicness" itself contributes to the diffusion of meaning. Because of the multivocality of symbols, expressions entered into the public sphere cannot be completely controlled by those who originate them.[21] Strategic rhetoric may be "launched" in the interests of particular groups, but its trajectory and ultimate destination (to push the metaphor) are indeterminate and can be altered. Competing groups may both adopt or adapt rhetorical frames, for example, the way "rights" language is used by religious groups to frame abortion politics as either a "right to life" or a "right to choose." Also, particular rhetorical expressions may not resonate with members of other groups in ways intended by the originators, thus limiting a group's ability to recruit new members or to persuade others of its cause. In any case, public religious expressions, to the extent that they do become authentically part of the public cultural repertoire, do not remain the sole symbolic property of the groups who first used them. They take on an air of the civil religious and are thus open to rival interpretations and potential transcendence in meaning.[22]

The ability of public actors to wield symbols in pursuit of their ends lends credence to the idea that ideology and language are "cultural resources" for political action. Religion's legitimacy and wide resonance with a variety of publics make it a particularly useful resource to those trying to mobilize movements for collective action.[23] But religion's special place in public culture is not just due to its usefulness, nor is it just about the sacred quality of culture. Many religious expressions have an inherent note of challenge in their content, simply because they do not take the world-as-it-is as an ultimate value. There is a transcendence built into a religious worldview that can relativize any societal arrangement. Thus, in almost any public form, religion can contain both senses of being a public religion. This observation necessarily leads to a reconsideration of the concept of hegemony, its relationship to the distribution of societal rewards, and its susceptibility to cultural challenge.

HEGEMONY AND CULTURE

Hegemony is the collection of social and cultural forces that reinforces—and even "naturalizes"—the extant organization of society.[24] Hegemony includes the dominant symbolic forms, ideologies, and cultural themes in a society and focuses on how those cultural forces reinforce inequality. Hegemony is particularly useful in understanding social stability; coercion may be effective in producing stasis, but it is not efficient. Potential sources of upheaval within society (usually organized around some type of social inequality) are better dealt with through prevention than repression. Hegemonic cultural forms present inequality as natural or taken for granted; alternately, they help defuse the potential grievances that could challenge the social order. In that sense, hegemony is a more encompassing concept than ideology. Whereas ideologies are *idea systems* that are ob-fuscatory—leaving interests veiled from public scrutiny—hegemony is the sum of the cultural forces that reinforce extant power. Thus, when I contend that public culture comprises the symbolic forms of some particular social group (at least in its origins), I imply that public culture is a component of hegemony. This necessarily means that extant cultural arrangements favor some at the expense of others.

It follows that public culture and hegemony, although not identical, are inextricably intertwined. But that relationship can be paradoxical. When public culture is the public pronouncements of a particular group concerning their views of how society should be, public culture is hegemonic; it legitimates certain cultural objects or social arrangements and marginalizes others. The ideas and symbols of groups constructing public culture—when they are successful in getting those constructions instantiated into institutional forms—contribute to reinforcing the social positions of those groups.

This legitimation is most effective when it appears to be "natural." Again, I use the example of the interest-group pluralism that is integral to the public political culture of the United States. There is an assumption that a public good can be created out of the partial visions held by contending groups. The content of the public good is unspecified, but the existence of sound procedures ensures a public life in which all groups can be partly invested but none dominate. However, interest-group pluralism necessarily assumes that there is a certain justice in the "rules of the game" themselves. When one recognizes the "mobilization of bias" inherent in the structure of the rules, it is clear that not all voices are heard equally.[25] What is thus portrayed as neutrality among contending parties in fact reinforces differential access to power.

It is not merely by choice that some social groups do not organize around their interests, whether these interests are a political campaign or pursuit of a particular religious vision. Some groups lack resources to compete in the public arena. More crucial to my argument here, the legal order itself may not recognize their interests as legitimate. For example, race and gender are special legal categories that can prompt judicial review of new legislation—a type of preemptive search for discrimination. But economic class is not so recognized. There is no particular protected legal status for the poor. In sum, the rules governing public participation are themselves tools for including some and excluding others.

Nonetheless, the paradox of the public reappears here. Openings in the political system do provide opportunities for challenge, contestation, and cultural change—witness the fact that discrimination by race and gender are relatively recent bases for organizing. What constitutes the public good is abstract enough to become a point of contention in itself—often providing the very tools that challenger groups need in the public contest. That is, if marginal social groups can claim to be a legitimate "public," they have the opportunity to question whether their good is being served by the social arrangements called "the" public good. So religious observances were removed from public schools from the early 1960s to prevent the implicit discrimination against non-Protestants. By the 1990s some evangelical Protestant groups are calling for a return to school prayer because the secular nature of public schools now implicitly discriminates against religious persons. The very abstractness of the hegemonic component—its existence as *procedures* rather than as a substantive *outcome*—provides an opportunity for rival interpretations and cultural contestation. Liberal proceduralism is simultaneously hegemonic—in that it hides the reinforcement of privilege behind a "naturalized" set of political arrangements and "neutral" rules—and counterhegemonic in that it provides interpretive room for contested understandings.

Because public culture has the implication that whatever its origins it has a self-transcending quality, the symbolic objects that public culture comprises must develop meanings that transcend their sectarian origins to reach to a variety of populations. Thus, the cultural forms produced by dominant social groups, that are intended as public culture, are pressed by their own logic to transcend the narrower group-specific interests of their creators. This is a case of the "autonomy" of cultural forms; cultural objects have a logic of their own, which is due to their aspiration to be public culture. Their putative universalism means that they can "get away" from the dominant group and in time be used against the particular interests of their creators.

Another way of thinking about hegemony is through the lens of David Laitin's "two faces of culture."[26] The first face is made up of the interpersonal ties and relational networks in which people are embedded. This could also be thought of as a definition of social structure, but because these relationships and networks have content—they happen in particular places and have particular forms and meanings—it is also a way of thinking about culture (perhaps a little more as anthropologists use the idea than as sociologists do). The second face of culture includes the symbols, language, and ideas people use to interpret the social worlds in which they are embedded. Hegemony clearly implies that the second face of culture reinforces the strengths and weaknesses—the dominant or subordinate situations—of those people connected in the first face of culture.

But understanding the "autonomy" of culture means that these two faces need not be parallel or coterminous. The second face of culture can be dissociated from those people who create it; alternatively, it can become so thoroughly ingrained in the social order that it turns and the creation constrains the creator. It may have been a public expression of the interests of the "first face," that is, the social networks that particular societal groups comprise. But the inherent multivocality of the symbols themselves keeps the meanings potentially indeterminant. Different people, different contexts, and different eras produce different plausible readings and multiple meanings. This is, following my earlier argument, particularly true when cultural objects are introduced to the *public* sphere, where by definition a variety of social groups can have access to them. Thus, the entry of a symbol into the public culture is a double-edged sword: It can be a tool for shaping social life to the benefit of the interests of the group using the symbol, but the symbol can simultaneously (or consequently) become less controlled by its originators—as different social groups can use it, reinterpret it, and perhaps challenge the original meanings and interests.

Daniel Rodgers offers a useful example of this process (though put to use for a different theoretical purpose) in his analysis of the idea of "natural rights" in American political thinking.[27] Originally, the idea that "rights" accrued to individuals as a result of their status as citizens and that they were a form of individual property that could not be abridged by the state was revolutionary.[28] In the English, American, and French revolutions, this notion was put at the service of rising commercial classes and political challengers. "Rights" theorists such as Locke and Paine presented individual rights as a natural part of the created order and thus in accord with Divine Will. But this idea clearly supported the interests of middle classes who were chafing at the economic controls of feudal society and the political privileges of the aristocratic state.

However, the paradox of public culture meant that the very notion of unabridgeable rights would later support various groups of disenfranchised people as they began to challenge the social arrangements of the states created by those commercial classes. From nonowners of property, to religious dissenters, to women, to racial and ethnic minorities, various groups have successfully obtained a degree of political empowerment by constructing themselves as "citizens" and members of the "public," whose rights were being unjustifiably constrained. This construction has come only through political struggle, of course. But once it was accepted that, for example, women had rights, it was an effective wedge into conventional political power and social mobility.

The example of women's rights is a particularly good illustration of the double-edged nature of public culture. Although women used a connection between "public" and "rights" as a way of gaining access to societal rewards previously denied them, that connection has then served to bind them to particular courses of action. Women gained rights and access to public life by arguing for their status as a public—in essence, by arguing their equivalence to men. As noted, that proved to be a difficult challenge for the political system to resist, and it opened. However, there are ways in which women and men are not the same, and pretending they are disadvantages women. But gaining recognition for policies that would adjust gender-equivalence thinking has met serious resistance. In effect, many opposed to feminist policies that would provide for women's roles in motherhood, and the like, call any recognition of difference "special privileges."[29]

Thus, the power of the rights construction opened up paths into public life and now constrains alternative readings of how that public life should be realized.

The power of language and the autonomy of culture in hegemonic contests over participation in public life are revealed by an old cartoon. Seated around a table at the Constitutional Convention are the nation's founders. Benjamin Franklin, pen in hand, is reading aloud from a document draft—"We, the white, male, Protestant, landowners . . . no, no, too wordy. . . ." The rhetorical switch is significant for more than its commitment to good editing. The Framers conceived of themselves as speaking for "the People," but it is clear they thought of themselves as embodying the people, and thought of the people as white, male, and Protestant. And yet their particular reading of who constitutes "the People" could be and has changed over time. Disenfranchised groups have laid claim to membership among the people as a way of forcing the political order to accommodate them. In sum, the universalism of natural rights language, so useful in legitimating one social group's rise to political power, provided cultural resources to groups that would eventually challenge them. Public culture was by turns ideology, hegemony, and counterhegemony.

Identification and Discursive Politics

The crux of my argument to this point is that all social groups involved with public life must contend with the autonomy—and potential universality—of public symbolism. This is true even for those social groups that have provided the substantive moral content for public culture. Both culturally central and culturally marginal groups are faced with certain boundaries governing what can and cannot be expressed publicly. And what "can be expressed" has two components: intelligibility (Can this even be understood by nonmembers of our group?) and legitimacy (Will this have the moral authority to be persuasive or even binding?). This means that every attempt at expressing a public religion (the second definition of the term) contains a degree of accommodation to the public, an implicit acknowledgment that symbols must resonate with audiences that reach beyond the subculture of origin. And, in turn, groups who do not control much public space—that is, groups for whom the dominant public symbols are not part of "their" culture—must step outside their "home" language in order to communicate publicly.

This process is, in essence, hegemonic. It is a cultural process in which some groups are forced to use expressions that originated with their rivals in order to achieve a place at the table of public politics. For example, consider the "right to life" language of the anti-abortion movement. The phrase "right to life" is evocative and effective, at least in part because it calls upon the deep American commitment to individual rights in the pursuit of "life, liberty and . . . happiness."

However, for major portions of the anti-abortion movement, their actual ideological commitments are antithetical to the type of society and political philosophy that originated the notion of "rights."[30] Indeed, many activists are concerned with creating a society that emphasizes the *duties* that individuals have to the collective—a society in which collective moral health allows individual discretion and preferences to be curtailed.[31] The variance between the logic of their rhetoric and the grounding assumptions of their worldview presents problems both for the public presentation of their arguments and for the practical political compromises they can make. They are often forced into a "liberalism" with which they fundamentally disagree.

However, it would be wrong to overstate the extent to which individuals and groups identify with the substantive moral message that their discursive symbols evoke. The multivocality of symbols provides for a number of possible readings of any given symbol, and subcultural processes of meaning creation make many particular readings plausible. I am not making a charge of hypocrisy or cynicism (although that may happen), nor am I maintaining that symbols are totally arbitrary and thus are only plastic masks over material interests. Rather, I note that public actors may participate in the discursive structure of a hegemonic public culture without identifying with the substantive content with which the culture was traditionally imbued. There are a distinction and a potential disarticulation between the substantive content and discursive structure of public politics. This presents a challenge to both established and challenger groups when they encounter and try to influence a pluralist public.

AMERICAN PUBLIC RELIGION AND HEGEMONY

For most of the United States' history, of course, its public religion has been decidedly Protestant—"evangelical" through the nineteenth century, and "liberal" from the 1920s to the 1980s. Most of the nation's political leaders have been Protestant and have used a "protestantized" civil religious language when addressing public concerns.[32] Concomitantly, the major religious denominations of the Reformed tradition (Presbyterians and Congregationalists), along with Episcopalians and Methodists, have long taken active roles in speaking out on public issues, helped to formulate public policy, and considered the state of the *society's* moral health as much a part of their purview as the state of their members' souls.

American Catholics have experienced a transformation in the status of their religion's "public" status. From a marginal status that was an identity marker for discrimination, American Catholicism developed into a "denomination" in the religious mainstream. The National Conference of Catholic Bishops now speaks to a national audience on issues from abortion to the economy to national defense policy. Importantly, the bishops do not speak only on behalf of their religious constituents. They speak *to* the public and on *behalf of* the greater society—enunciating a vision of a good society and how that society should embody moral and religious principles.

The story of mainline Protestant dominance and Catholic emergence is one oft told and the basis upon which some see public religion as hegemony. What are *public* visions of morality came out of these particular confessional traditions. Since the late 1970s the contest over the content of American public religion has become quite visible. If it is not strictly true that the 1950s was a period of harmony and consensus (its status in recent nostalgia), it does seem unequivocal that religion is currently a consistent object of public contention. Specifically, the resurgent public stance of evangelical Protestantism in the last two decades, and the call for a renewed public presence for religion generally, have been greeted with suspicion by many non-Protestants—they sense a "restorationist" bent, a continuing search for a "Christian America."[33]

The involvement of religion in American politics is not a new story, of course. But what makes much of the language of contemporary conservative religion and politics interesting is its disavowal of sectarian intent or origins—that is, its self-conscious attempt to be "public" within a pluralistic setting. Rather than assume a homogeneous public for which a moral content is easily discerned, there is a search for a putative "common ground" as well as arguments built on generic "social health" rather than sectarian revealed truth.

There have been incidents of sectarian exclusionist sentiment, as when a prominent Southern Baptist pastor declared at a national forum, "God himself does not hear the prayers of the Jew." And indeed, religious particularism among evangelicals and fundamentalists is often credited with the failure of the first wave of Christian Right mobilizing, as conservative Protestants could not overcome their theological differences in order to cooperate politically.[34] But these expressions of sectarian belief have been controversial and often disavowed by evangelicals themselves. Nonetheless, these types of partisan rhetoric in portions of the politicized Christian Right, and a history of social tensions, make a certain wariness about their intentions seem reasonable; the language of "culture war" often used to mobilize activists undermines the consensual dimensions usually considered essential for public religion.[35]

However, it is also the case that much of that rhetoric has moderated. A de facto distinction has developed between the evangelizing rhetoric of conversion—in which sectarian particularism is important—and the language used to call for changes in public policy and politics. Many activists on the Right continually stress the ecumenism of their coalitions and their goals. And there is good evidence of ecumenical and interfaith cooperation along political and ideological lines, at least on certain highly salient issues.[36] Even more important, the more general thrust of politicized religion currently calls for an advance of what might be called "religion in general."[37] Although some still call for explicitly supporting sectarian beliefs by using government to enforce their own values, many others from the Christian Right speak more generally about "freedom of religion." They claim that conflict over values is not about any particular creedal positions, but about the rights of all religious persons—"people of faith," as Ralph Reed puts it—to be unfettered from the values of "secular humanism."[38] In this claim, all religious people share a common interest in being able to live without having hostile values imposed upon them. All religious commitments are implicitly equalized, and all are put on the same side of the discriminatory line.

Given the contours of my argument to this point, it should be clear that there is a hegemonic component in this form of public religion. The call for religion in general hides the particular interests of one group, mostly conservative Protestants, behind a veil of ecumenism and shared victimhood. Whereas apart from abortion-related issues, conservative Protestants, Catholics, and Jews have relatively little else in common—and share even less with increasing numbers of Muslims, Buddhists, and Hindus—the rhetoric glosses these differences to create a single "people of faith." However, when positions on particular issues are analyzed, the "religious values" being espoused in such general terms appear very close to particular social forms that are held dear by evangelical Protestants. For example, although calls for "family values" or "pro-family" policies are supported in general terms, the content of such policies consistently enforces a normative ideal of a nuclear family with clearly gendered divisions of labor and internal hierarchy.

The ideological dimensions of such claims become even more clear when "school prayer" is offered as an antidote to problems in the public school. There is, of course, a constitutional battle over whether school prayer is permissible at all in public schools. On one hand, there are the historic American practice of imagining all education as a form of moral education and the very real tradition of American public schools emphasizing a "common" culture to the children immigrants. On the other hand, there is the recognition that the "common" culture offered was Protestant, and it was often coercive. Whether that is appropriate in a pluralist society that values freedom of religion, and where citizenship is distinct from religious status, is the heart of the issue.

Beyond whether prayer should occur, the content of such prayer becomes an issue. Overtly sectarian prayers are too controversial to be explicitly offered as the official prayer. Even political leaders clearly identified with the politicized Christian Right, such as Senator Jesse Helms of North Carolina, do not suggest that. As a result, two alternatives are often used as substitutes. One is a completely neutral, generic prayer. This satisfies no one, as it seems to be completely form without substance, and the most ardent supporters of the efficacy of prayer do not claim that the act alone, devoid of content, is all that matters. The other alternative is to decide on prayer content by majority rule in the school district. Not surprisingly, this is a popular answer among those prayer supporters that live in regions and communities where majority votes would institutionalize their own religious commitments.[39] In short, a religious solution to a public problem—a solution offered as an example of public religion—has the potential impact of reinforcing, with the power of the state, one religious group's values and beliefs at the expense of others.

And yet, within the hegemonic construct of "school prayer" there are potential tools for other challenges—both to the status quo and to the interests of the politicized Christian Right groups pushing their own solutions. For example, an appeal to recognize "religion in general" opens the door to public legitimacy for so-called New Age beliefs or to marginally "deviant" traditions such as Wicca. Or, as Muslims or Buddhists become sizable populations in some districts, their religious values or styles of prayer could become part of the public order. Not only is there the very real possibility that school districts in many of the nation's cities could institutionalize non-Christian forms of religious observance, the situation of rival groups competing to control the religious content of public institutions seems exactly what the Constitution's framers wanted to prevent. There is some recognition of this potential, particularly among fundamentalist Protestants; warnings against New Age paganism and the need to keep the nation "Christian" are regular features on much Christian talk radio, for example.

This dilemma between, on one hand, a hegemonic place in formulating public religion and, on the other hand, an opening of public culture to "unacceptable" alternatives repeats the long-standing tension in American religion between uncompromised purity and influence in the world. To be efficacious in a liberal polity, one must on occasion compromise the values that provide the moral authority that legitimates public engagement in the first place. That is, success in liberal politics—particularly for numerical minorities—means forging coalitions among groups with only partially overlapping agendas. Some compromise is inevitable as an entire agenda cannot be realized. That compromise, necessary for efficacy, can also lead to charges of "playing politics"; if morality is uncompromising (a theme in American pietist religion), and a social group has mobilized its supporters and made its public claims on the basis of its moral purity and authority, then compromise, practical politics, seems out of the question. There lies another irony of contemporary politics—the factors that help mobilize social movements can also prevent them from working effectively in institutionalized politics.[40] This dilemma is common enough for many religious movements that they find a balance through a type of "separate spheres" argument; they demarcate private "religion" from public "morality." Another common response is a separatism that protects a totalizing worldview but only for the community of believers.[41]

But to the extent that participation in public politics forces this type of accommodation—or to the extent that religious groups join noncoreligionists to press a broader public agenda—they engage in a de facto ratification of the liberal, pluralist project. They make a place for themselves in the public sphere by using the tools of liberal pluralism. That those tools are then also available to other social and religious groups ends up being a price of trying to establish a hegemonic place through *public* expression. In this regard, conservative religion repeats a dilemma now familiar to liberal religious traditions. Liberal religion discovered that to institutionalize its values of tolerance and pluralism, it also had to learn to tolerate religious expressions that are both intolerant and hostile to liberalism itself. The hegemonic dimensions of public religion, once accepted as embodying some of the universalism that makes them truly public, help create the very tools that rival groups may use in contrary ways. Concomitantly, although challenge groups may use such tools in contrary ways, they often must act like "liberals" in order to be effective. The "master's tools" it seems, are often useful when challenging the foundations of the master's house; whether they can actually dismantle the house is a different question.

CONCLUSIONS: CULTURAL AND RELIGIOUS POLITICS

I have examined the relationships among three symbolic forms—public culture, public religion, and hegemony—with the aim of disentangling how they function in the public politics of modern pluralist society. Religion, no longer the central component of culture as it once was in Durkheim's scheme, nonetheless retains a special place as a cultural resource for public action. Public culture, as an integral component in creating a taken-for-granted naturalness for societal arrangements, is hegemonic to the extent that it reinforces order and inequality. And religion has had and continues to have a role in social hegemony by providing a substantive content for the entire society from the cultural repertoire of a particular religious tradition. And yet, because of the public nature and universalist tendencies of public religion, it also forms a critical dimension to the attempts by marginal groups to gain social access and societal standing. Civil religion, to use one example, both celebrates and challenges.

If we think of culture as the "realm of the possible," public culture expands that realm because it provides tools to groups who were previously without them. To return to my consistent example, public good language is a set of resources in the public arena, legitimating political and social speech and legitimating the status of the speaker as a participant in the public. It is a repertoire that is public precisely because it resonates widely and can be used by many actors. Even if public good language is intended to be ideological—intended as the "power tools," so to speak, of particular groups used to justify their privilege and normalizing their status—it does not remain that way.

Public culture can be ideology; it can be obfuscatory, leaving something veiled. Indeed, by definitions I have used before, public good language can be seen as the prototypical ideological language—hiding power and veiling the favorable arrangements of societal institutions with a universalizing and normalizing discourse.[42] However, as a result of its *content*—its aspirations to universalism in a pluralist society—public culture can potentially bind its society's dominant groups as it does its subordinate groups. Thus public culture can, through its aspiration to universalism, undermine its own function as a power tool in the reproduction of inequality.[43]

Chapter 12

The Public and the Pubic: Is Nothing Private Anymore?

William H. Swatos, Jr.

Amid the moral and spiritual pluralism that pervades our time, religious persons are wont to cry, "Is nothing sacred anymore?" How far the bounds extend may be open to debate—the National Endowment for the Arts may ultimately have been crucified by Andres Serrano's *Piss Christ*—but there is no question that in the United States generally one person's eschatological hope may be another's scatological humor. But there will be those who point to "underground" currents in popular culture that have persisted for centuries and tell us these have always been so. Well they may have been. The sacred has always had a counterside in blasphemy—which is still a crime in England, though the statute has not been enforced in over a hundred years. (This was part of the uproar by British Muslims over Salman Rushdie's *Satanic Verses* that Americans generally failed to understand, since we have no corresponding statute.) As Max Weber has pointed out, religion has had multiple layers of encounter with the larger society, including not only politics and economics, but also the erotic and the artistic.[1] There has likewise been a continuing dynamic encounter between "the sacred and the subversive," though in different cultures at different times it has correspondingly played itself out in different modes.

Our own time and place in the United States at the turn of the twenty-first century present a historically unique configuration that is characterized by dramatic globalization at all levels of the social system combined with systems of communication that allow almost unlimited access for the publicization of information.[2] The concept of a "hurtful truth," if it ever had any standing legally or morally, has gone the way of the horse and buggy. Whereas the arena of personal conduct once allowed wide discretion for the suppression of information, current codes recognize only the most narrowly circumscribed arenas for the control of information. Some states, for example, do not allow the AIDS status of murder victims or suicides to enter the public record from an autopsy, or protect the identity of a molestation victim—though a similar protection is seldom allowed the alleged perpetrator, and the alleged details are normally fully public.

In short, notions of what should remain "private" have altered radically in the last fifty years. (Remember when Lucy and Desi had to sleep in twin beds for the sake of televised decency?) Cultural historians may debate whether or not there was a "sexual revolution" in the late 1960s; what is undeniably true is that there was a revolution in sexual communication that started in the 1960s and has continued unabated into the present. Just as we all knew that women had pubic hair long before *Playboy* and *Penthouse* stopped airbrushing their photos, we all knew about sex and suspected sexual deviance. We would not have had red light districts or laws against bestiality if it were otherwise, but only recently have we confronted so explicit a degree of publicity about a collection of life activities that Pierre Hegy has termed "the libido factor" as is now the case.[3]

The media of mass communication have been the principal agents for a dramatic change in the realm of privacy on a global scale. This alteration makes the assertion that "religion is a private matter" less and less tenable. From Koresh in Waco to the pope kissing the tarmac in New York, from priests who are sexual molesters to priests who are freedom fighters, from the Ayatollah Khomeini to Archbishop Tutu: Religion is repeatedly thrust into the American public eye, hence the public arena, just as is other behavior that was once considered "private." We also know, of course, that American history is replete with evidence that religion has never in fact been private.[4] In issues large and small that have entered the public arena, religious considerations have been raised both explicitly and implicitly. From Sunday closing laws to "Away in a Manger" on supermarket public address systems, from abolition to the State of Israel, from the Salvation Army's kettle to "In God We Trust" on United States currency, religion's influence has been part of the agenda of American public life.

PRIVACY AND SYSTEMS

The "private matter" view of religion, however, is not unimportant, for it was connected to a form of cultural status politics that has been undergoing significant change. Karel Dobbelaere argues against the use of the "public–private" distinction in sociology as itself inherently political: "[T]he dichotomy 'private–public,'" he writes, "is not a structural aspect of society, but rather a legitimizing conceptualization of the world, an ideological pair used in conflicts by participants." In the social sciences its use, ironically, is actually rooted in ideological concepts used by [European] liberals and socialists in the nineteenth century to legitimate functional differentiation and the autonomization of "secular" institutions. . . . Later these concepts were used by workers to defend their political, religious or family options against possible sanctions and eventual dismissal by the management of Christian organizations (e.g., schools or hospitals), if they failed to behave according to ecclesiastical rules in matters of family life, politics or religion. They defended their "private" options, their "private" life, in what managers of ecclesiastical organizations called the "public" sphere.[5]

Dobbelaere suggests that Jürgen Habermas's distinction between "system" and "lifeworld" will be more helpful.[6] *Privatization* in religion, in this view, grew from an intention to shield the lifeworld of primary relationships from a superimposing system of ecclesiastical bureaucracy. In the United States, not "big church" but "big business" was often the system counterpart to privatization: Employees could do what they wanted during their "private" time. This view gained added credence from interpretations of the Free Exercise Clause that not only prohibited hiring/firing discrimination on the basis of "creed," but also established certain employee rights with regard to religious practices.

Coupled with the privacy aphorism was yet another: "A man's home is his castle." Note the non-gender-neutral language. It is important to the "libido factor" constellation of which Hegy speaks. Significant to the development of capitalism was the separation of the workplace from the homeplace; over time, this division also became relatively gender-segregated. Women stayed at home; men went "to work." Yet the aphorism affirms the power relationship of "the provider" as "head of household," hence the putative control over the private sphere by men. "Wait 'til your father gets home!" as a form of warning similarly affirms this relationship. Male headship was strongly structured into the system/lifeworld division of capitalist society well into the mid-twentieth century. It was taken for granted that parents certainly, fathers mostly, could make decisions about their children's welfare, including discipline, nutrition, health care, and education. The public school system, with attendant health care regulations, was the first intrusion of the American bureaucratic system into the lifeworld of its citizens. Not surprisingly, court cases about religious practices followed in its wake. Less explicitly acknowledged, but implicitly affirmed in myriad ways, was the authority of husbands over wives that would include sexual decision making and the possibility of corporal reprisal.

In *The Restructuring of American Religion* Robert Wuthnow points to the rise of the *state* as a corporate actor as the signal development for understanding changes in American religion since World War II.[7] The public educational system has been the major institutional expression of the state as corporate actor vis-à-vis "family life" or the homeplace. Beginning with *Brown v. Board of Education* (1954), on the one hand, and post-*Sputnik* fears, on the other, the federal government became more and more intimately involved with public education. Although education remains formally a responsibility of the individual states, increasing federal regulations dictate the parameters within which the states must exercise their responsibilities. The school is principally a system agency that has almost unmediated access to the lifeworld in any setting in which children may be involved.

As an instance of this, we may view the dramatic changes that have occurred in the *in loco parentis* doctrine. Prior to World War II, the schoolteacher was understood to be acting on behalf of the parent(s) of his or her charges. It was generally assumed that parents would exercise corporal punishment for various infractions; hence teachers employed corporal punishment similarly. From the 1950s forward, however, use of corporal punishment was eliminated in the public schools, then in many private institutions as well. From the early 1960s, for example, I can remember quite vividly that one of the principal distinctions between public and Catholic schools—perhaps the principal distinction to the children—was that "You get hit in Catholic school." Although Roman Catholic practice has changed dramatically on this point, there is still a general belief that corporal punishment is employed in the contemporary fundamentalist–evangelical Christian school movement; certainly there is evidence that parents from the fundamentalist-evangelical traditions are more likely to use corporal punishment.[8]

But it is the role of the teacher in the public school system vis-à-vis the parent that has changed most dramatically. Rather than supporting homeplace decisions about child discipline, the teacher is now in the position of system agent to report parents whose discipline or life-style is perceived as too harsh or aberrant. Rather than acting as the parents' agent in the process of child rearing, the teacher is now the state's agent of system development. Small wonder that conservative Christians in the United States—and religious conservatives throughout much of the West (e.g., British Muslims)—see the public school as the "enemy" on many fronts. To the issue of discipline may be added, for example, sex education and gender equality, the teaching of evolution, and some approaches to multiculturalism and diversity that imply that all value systems are equal.

The school is not the only system actor to impose itself increasingly on the lifeworld. The media similarly insert themselves into homeplace settings. In research I conducted on National Federation of Decency, now American Family Association (NFD/AFA), activists who led protests in the mid-1980s against convenience stores that openly sold sexually oriented magazines, one of the clearest dynamics of protest motivation was that the people felt their "safe" local neighborhoods were being invaded by system actors—in this case, economic profit makers protected by a "godless" state.[9] Although these activists certainly were not happy about hard-core pornography shops in city centers, they implicitly connected the city center with what would in Habermasean terms be system life: politics and economics. Against this they set the lifeworld of the homeplace, particularly epitomized by residence in a neighborhood that in their eyes created a haven from system life. Usually this was a suburban or semirural setting where families abounded. It was precisely because the *local* convenience store sold the magazines that the protest seemed appropriate to these activists, most of whom had not participated in similar protest activity previously. Their argument was enhanced by the claim of at least some local convenience store managers or owners that they had no control over what magazines were sold in the store or how they were displayed: "Don't blame me. It's the system."

Alongside this sit television and radio, which have been the major foci of NFD/AFA activity since the organization's inception. Again, the rationale of the protests is the "invasion" of the lifeworld or homeplace by money-hungry system agencies. The AFA rejects the idea that television and radio are private-choice options, that one can either "just turn it off" or not have one to begin with. In their view, the media represent an inherently public activity that no one can avoid. It is impossible for parents to watch children twenty-four hours a day, and school classes, even in private institutions, sometimes expect television viewing as a part of assignments. We can fairly anticipate that the Web will similarly become a part of the public culture of the rising generation. These media further serve to break down privacy in the home even as they also bring, for example, religious issues into public scrutiny. The mass media create a public culture that is different in kind, not merely degree, from that of prior epochs.

Inseparable from the school or the media is the role of law enforcement. Codes against both child and spousal abuse have altered how the police handle "domestic" complaints. Although children may not be explicitly urged to "rat" on their parents, they are aware that parental actions against them, or paternal actions against their mother, can lead to police involvement. Parents are equally aware that children can bring state agencies into the home and that discipline and other activities have to be conducted as at least semipublic activities: That is to say, parental actions in the homeplace are subject to system review. These refer not only to direct acts of violence but also to matters of neglect or impropriety. For example, inadequate restraint of time and place of parental sexual activity may be interpreted as a form of sexual abuse, at least at the investigatory level.

As a counter to the argument I am making, it may be urged that everything I am saying has to do with children. There is much truth to this; that is, that among "consenting adults" anything goes, hence privacy per se is not under attack. Similarly, Robert Mapplethorpe could have made any photos of adults he wanted and displayed them for adults at private galleries; the crucial offense was putting them in a public museum to which children could go. People may practice any religion they want as long as they don't impose it on their children: And here's the rub. At a critical juncture in the system/lifeworld debate comes the question of how adult (including parental) religious convictions are to be expressed around children and to what extent parents in particular have the right not only to hold religious convictions but to insist that those religious convictions make legitimate action demands upon them as stewards of (God's) creation in their role as parents.

This is clearly one of the places in which the underlying tension of religion and state opens to public view. In an increasing number of cases, usually involving groups on the conservative side of the spectrum, but not always, the treatment of children as a religious duty has been viewed with suspicion by the courts. So far, this has been restricted to religion in public places, on the one hand (e.g., school prayer), and religion and the body (e.g., withholding of medical care, imposing of severe corporal punishment), on the other. Nevertheless, it is not impossible to foresee the day when "mind pollution" might be lodged as a complaint against parents who attempt to inculcate a set of religious values into their children. Courts have already recognized in some cases other forms of what might be termed psychological abuse. Here, again, the potential for system shrinkage of the lifeworld is manifest.[10]

THE DEPRIVATIZATION OF RELIGION

Ironically, system prerogatives and lifeworld preservation are intercorrelated. That is, those who are most successful at the system level are relatively more capable of isolating their "private" sphere from system invasion. Though certainly no one is immune from lifeworld intrusion, those who are financially well off can make freer decisions about where to live, where to shop, where to send their children to school, where to seek medical assistance, and so on. System rejection of "irrational" criteria, for example, with respect to the rental or sale of real estate, leave the economic variable as the principal one to be employed in neighborhood selection. When we look at the work of James Davidson and his colleagues on religion and elite status, we may get an inkling of why it is that, relatively speaking, religious conservatives are more likely to be active in putting issues before the public eye than religious liberals: namely, religious conservatives as a group are significantly underrepresented at the top levels of system life. Going into the public arena and attempting to use the privacy of the ballot box as a mass-level alternative to lifeworld control by personal wealth may be the only course available to less elite, conservative groups. This is true not only in the United States, for example, but in the aborted election of Islamicists in Algeria. To note this is not to say that "religion is merely a matter of economics," but rather that economic disprivilege may force religious devotees in nonelite settings who wish to protect their lifeworld to take different steps from those available to people in higher strata.

To take an example not involving children, consider how "small business" people regularly claim the system—often phrased as "the government"—is creating obstacles to their success. Large corporations are almost entirely *publicly* held; hence they are used to revealing many of their operating processes. Although there are often scandals involving specific officers of corporations, the concept of public accountability of corporations is generally widely acknowledged.[11] Small business people, by contrast, see *private* enterprise being challenged by system regulation. In their view, private enterprise means something akin to "running my business the way I want to run it" and taking the consequences of financial success or failure. System restraints, regulations, and so on, appear to be undermining the fundamental American economic myth of private enterprise by narrowing the field on which individual decision making can play itself out. Changes in health care in the United States are but a case in point of this larger phenomenon, and the reshaping of the health care "industry" is one field where the historically *private* practice of medicine is most likely to influence lifeworld activities of the homeplace of the rest of us, including our religious convictions.

It can hardly be doubted that for many Americans today "public religion" conjures an image of the "New" Christian Right, but only historical myopia can obscure the fact that today's Christian Right arose in response to the Christian Left that moved from the civil rights movement to the anti–Vietnam War movement with hardly a breath to spare. There is more than a difference in political philosophy between these two Christian poles: The Christian Left is inherently inclusivist, and the Christian Right is inherently exclusivist. What this means is that the Christian Left could appeal to a set of values that it in effect claimed transcended Christianity, including all Americans within its purview: fundamental human rights given to us all by a benevolent Creator. For the Christian Right, however, nothing transcends Christianity; rather, Christianity is the transcendence of all human systems of action. Hence it is at least theoretically impossible for citizenship in the global or "world" community of humankind to be a value determining an individual's worth. Ultimately, his or her relationship to Jesus Christ is the final arbiter of all decisions.[12]

The issue of public religion and the narrowing of the private sphere thus are best cast in the global–local tension that is a crucial dynamic in globalization theory. Public religion in our time is *different* even from public religion in past eras of American history precisely because of the global character of system life, which has grown increasingly powerful since the end of World War II. Not merely as buzzwords, but as experience, multiculturalism and diversity con-

stantly break into the lifeworld. Various efforts to halt or slow immigration testify to this concern; yet, in fact, current immigration policy itself was part of a
movement to seize the global initiative by the United States in the 1960s. But the
global dynamic is also two-headed, because it creates a local counterpoint. Universalism and particularism are ideal types that in reality merge, as Roland
Robertson has put it, into two subalternatives: the particularization of the uni-
versal (particularistic universalism) and the universalization of the particular
(universalistic particularism).[13] The latter epitomizes movements of the Religious
Right that compete within the public arena with what often appears to be the secular center–Left coalition, in which the religious Left sounds often only faintly,
precisely because it shares many of the same universalistic values as the center–Left generally.

Although privatization may have characterized the secularization process at a
specific historical juncture, it now appears that perhaps as a corollary of the general theory of secularization as a self-limiting process, the invasion of the lifeworld that characterizes the system effects of high-technology multinational
capitalism brings religion back into the public forum, even though it may be in
an initially negative guise. Literally *any publicity of religion makes religion a
public issue,* hence legitimates a religious demand for access to the public arena.
The media play a crucial role here, for in an open society they have simultaneously a charismatizing and decharismatizing effect. Religious claims are radically relativized—but *so are all other claims.* Religion clearly loses as an
authority structure, but other ideological authority structures are simultaneously
undermined.[14]

In our culture, not surprisingly then, religion takes on a *therapeutic* rather
than an authoritative mode. Clergy are "helping professionals" whose occupation has become increasingly feminized—not simply that there are more
women among the clergy, but that what the clergy do is more like women's
work; indeed, the ministry became more like women's work *before* more
women became clergy.[15] This is a kind of privatization of religion, all religions
becoming a bit more like client cults, but at the same time doing therapy has
become more of a public activity—again running the ultimate risk of system
regulation.

A corollary of the therapeutic shift in the religious dimension is the frequent
distinction currently made between "religion" and "spirituality," with the latter
being the more positively valenced term. Religion is institutional, organized, apparently associated with the system. Spirituality is personalized, freer, a characteristic of the lifeworld. Nevertheless, people look to religious leaders
potentially to meet spiritual needs. "Spiritual life" opens a dimension for religious action that potentially stands apart from the public–private dichotomy. I
say "potentially" because at first blush "spirituality" can seem the apotheosis of

privatization: the "my own religion" of Sheilaism. The widespread seeking for spiritual "fulfillment," however, suggests that Sheilaism is not working for many people. Spirituality speaks to an inner dynamic, but it does not necessarily have to be private. Corporate action can meet the inner needs that the term seems to embody.

The spirituality–religion contrast marks an attempt to reassert the lifeworld against system encroachments. In the United States, religion is largely one and the same with "organized religion," and organization smacks of system. Persons can seek "spiritual fulfillment," by contrast, with a sense of control over their inner life that comes to replace the increasingly lost control over sectors of the lifeworld. A challenge to public religion, then, is to bridge the gap between system and lifeworld as a mediating structure. Religion as a public endeavor becomes potentially a way that "private" matters may be articulated in public settings—or that lifeworld may reassert itself vis-à-vis system. This is not to say that it will always be successful. Studies of the political victories of the Christian Right, for example, suggest that success is greatest in local elections—an outcome quite consistent with the theoretical argument that the Religious Right represents localistic protest against overarching global homogenization.

THE NEW PUBLIC RELIGION

In this view, public religion actually becomes the "carrier" of privacy. The role of public religion is to assert lifeworld prerogatives over against system demands. Public religion acts as a counterweight to the "iron cage" of bureaucratic rationalization that appears to move inexorably through high-technology multinational capitalism. One might say that the historic institutional role of religion is "turned on its head": whereas religion once imposed system constraints on believers, the New Public Religion offers its services to negotiate the sustenance of the lifeworld.

Obviously, such a dramatic role shift is going to take some getting used to; that is, not everyone, inside or outside religion, is going to accept this intermediary role for religion. Some within religion will assert that religion must stand for some "distinctives," hence religion cannot assert the right to privacy, or the preservation of the lifeworld, for everyone. But this has been a perennial problem in pluralistic society. Religious communities have pondered hard at best, fought at worst, about how to assert the specific truth claims of their "brand" of religion, while recognizing that everyone's truth claims must have some access to the public square if at some point anyone's truth claims are not put in jeopardy. Persons intentionally outside religious communities—or in marginal communities—will likely feel that any intrusion of religion into public discourse potentially threatens the Free Exercise Clause, hence is an attempt to impose a religious establishment. But again, this problem has been with us virtually since the beginning of the American experiment and is never likely to be resolved to everyone's satisfaction—the school prayer decision is a case in point (which, note, involves children again).

Clearly running against the role I am outlining for public religion is the current activism of both the Protestant Right and Roman Catholicism in protesting abortions in ways that directly confront the lifeworld of the mothers and physicians. It is perhaps this specific manifestation of religion in the public square that most creates resistance to the concept of public religion today. Accosting mothers and murdering physicians are quite different in character from street-corner preaching or sitting at a lunch counter or pouring duck's blood on draft files. Anti-abortion protestors who invade the lifeworld hark back to an era when religion was a system actor and religious action meant repressive action. Nevertheless, this one deviant case can be the exception against which proactive public religious movements may instead be cast: The New Public Religion is *not* what anti-abortion protestors do.

This does not mean that the New Public Religion must endorse all life-styles as equally valid. It should be possible to draw lines between life-style options that are good and not so good, without attempting to exclude those that are not so good from the public square. It should be possible for religious groups to say, if they choose, that abortion is absolutely morally wrong, without being thereby disposed to harassment, arson, and murder. It should be possible for religious groups to say, if they choose, that gay is not good, without gay bashing. Certainly if this is not possible, then religious groups must understand that they have no grounds for exemption from punishment for these actions and that these actions move beyond the limits of public *religion,* even though the actors involved may be inspired by religious texts—witness Nat Turner's rebellion.

On the other hand, in the spirit of multiculturalism and diversity, the New Public Religion has the right to demand that religion as a cultural expression of people's past experiences, present values, and future aspirations be included in school curricula. The exclusion or trivialization of religion as a part of the United States' history, literature, sociology, and so on, clearly represents an inaccurate, artificially limited presentation of these fields. It is quite possible to teach about, for example, Our Lady of Guadalupe without requiring students to believe in Our Lady of Guadalupe or the Blessed Virgin Mary or Jesus Christ. Not to teach about the Virgin of Guadalupe is intentionally to deny a significant aspect of Mexican–American history and culture. Of course, this will mean teaching about Shinto and Buddhism as well as Japanese American Christianity when Asian American peoples and their history and culture are up for discussion. If we could learn nothing else from the dynamics that led to the hostage taking of Americans in Iran and the deterioration of United States–Iranian relations, it should be that religion has to be taken seriously as a part of a people's culture in order to understand that people.

At its best, however, the New Public Religion should be able to contribute more than this to American public life. It should be able to develop pathways toward tolerance and forgiveness.[16] All of the principal world religions understand God as just and merciful. The specific doctrinal paths through which these attributes are worked out in practice certainly differ among the traditions, yet it is deeply regrettable that the primary public presences of religion are conflictful and negative. Religions going at each other or condemning specific behavior or groups do little to enhance the image of religions as public actors. Perhaps one of the most disastrous displays of Protestant unity in America, for example, was the passage of Prohibition legislation. The denouement of the Social Gospel movement as a religious endeavor may be marked by this effort, which was also strongly an anti-Catholic effort by majority Protestants. This was a signal case of religion operating as a system actor to invade the lifeworld; like the abortion issue in the present, it informs the historical consciousness of those who are skeptical of allowing religion a public role.

Public religion has been at its best, by contrast, when it has supported rights of conscience. Solidarity with conscientious objectors has been one instance of considerable public presence for religions. Regrettably, many religious bodies are still not prepared to take up the cause of those who object to military service on nonreligious, philosophical grounds. Doing so would show the New Public Religion has taken a great step forward. Support for the integrity of conscience in regard to military service, however, remains curiously negative: the right *not* to serve. Nevertheless, even this opens potential doors for conflict: the right *not* to take medicine(s) or surgery. Although this right is generally upheld for adults, it becomes, as we have seen, a ground for real confrontation with system priorities when it comes to children. The matter is a difficult one, but it has powerful consequences vis-à-vis the potential extension of the doctrine of "state's interest." Not to defend parental rights in this domain is latent agreement that parents in fact have no rights at all and that religious convictions are acceptable only when they underwrite existing system priorities.

It may be objected that this point of view places children at risk. My response is that children are already at risk, and there are no guarantees that system priorities protect them. To be alive is to be at risk. More to the point, however, celebrated cases notwithstanding and statistical evidence certainly not being perfect, there are far more cases of children being killed and maimed each year in connection with public school activities—from classroom shootings to school bus accidents to athletics—than there are associated with parents' religiously based decisions. Indeed, if risk were the real issue, statistics would speak for religious decisions and against the "experts" of state-based knowledge-class bureaucracies, including the public school system.

REGAINING PRIVACY

I now come back to where I began to raise again the question of how privacy rights have altered in the last fifty years. On paper, privacy rights seem to have been extended to adults for behavior "behind closed doors." Search warrant protections have been strengthened, as have rights with regard to police confrontation, though these are often honored in the breach. On the other hand, parental rights and rights with respect to the homeplace more generally are more and more narrowly circumscribed. Both by statute and by adjudication, it is now generally the case that all children are theoretically wards of the state; hence the state may step into the parent–child relationship at any time to restrain or reverse parental decisions. All homes are foster homes in this respect. Public school teachers represent the major agents for the enforcement of system prerogatives in respect to parent–child relations. Only those parents of relative means are partially exempt from this first line of offense—and in some states barely so, depending upon the degree of private school regulation, as all private schools now effectively operate at the total discretion of the state.

The child has become the demigod of a new state cult within American civil religion, wherein the state asserts that it knows what is best for children: parents must work within the limits authorized by the state, and religion may only be presented as a set of ideas that the parents think are important, but the child may reject at any time.[17] All practices in the name of religion when applied to children are potentially subject to state scrutiny. Allegations of abuse may be made and taken seriously not only concerning present but also past behavior, often without documentation. The homeplace, then, insofar as children are concerned, has lost a significant preemptive claim to privacy.

The homeplace has also lost a preemptive claim to privacy with regard to marital relations. Although in theory gender-neutral, contemporary spousal abuse laws tend to give wives immediate access to judicial redress not only for such direct spousal violence as wife beating but also for spousal rape. Whether or not these laws are capable of enforcement, they virtually destroy any claim by any religion to male headship and/or female submission. Any religious teaching that a male has certain rights in relation to his wife or a wife has duties to her husband may be laid aside by the state. Not only does the state allow divorce, but it actually criminalizes behavior in the homeplace regardless of religious teachings. Although the religious group may teach whatever it wants about sex role relations within marriage, these teachings may only be put into practice at the risk of state sanction, even if the marital partners have entered into a voluntary covenant as consenting adults and have the opportunity of a voluntary exit through the state's provision of divorce.

Religious rites themselves are also potentially assailable under the narrowing scope of Free Exercise as system extends to lifeworld. Although the Supreme Court ultimately upheld the right of Santeristas to engage in specific forms of animal sacrifice (not significantly different in performance from what happened on virtually every family farm in the United States a hundred years ago), religions are constantly subject to state scrutiny in their practices, both formal and informal. Charges of abuse, harassment, or molestation, in the present or the past, may be brought against religious professionals and/or their congregations. Whereas "behind closed doors" once meant that a person's conduct was not open to public observation and potential embarrassment, that his or her *privacy was protected,* the phrase takes on an increasingly sinister meaning as the lifeworld is diminished. Clergy and lay leaders often are now schooled on ways of avoiding privacy and counseled to act in ways that allow witnesses to be present.

The erosion of the lifeworld and attendant claims to privacy represents the extension of the principle of contract, rather than covenant, to the most intimate life relations; even where a written contract is not possible, the assumptions of contract law nevertheless remain the guiding ones for human relations: Absent a contract consent can never be proved; hence one is always potentially subject to legal presentment for one's actions.[18] The right to privacy is correspondingly reduced to *being alone;* in other words, one may do what one wants by oneself "behind closed doors" apparently without system interference, as long as one is not using illicit drugs or printing money. As soon as one enters into a social situation, system prerogatives begin to assert themselves. It should not be surprising, then, that Sheilaism—"my own religion"—should be on the rise, for religion as known heretofore is inherently social, hence subject to system intervention. Privacy in religion, as it has been defined in the past, increasingly comes to lose the possibility for corporate expression. Hence to be religious in any of the senses known within the world religions is to engage in some measure of *public* religion, even if unintendedly so.

The New Public Religion, then, in some ways makes manifest this latent truth: To practice the historical religions or to choose to create a corporate religious expression akin to these religions is to engage in public religion, because the private realm is devoid of social experience. To be religious is to relate to others in the search for and celebration of ultimate meaning. The challenge to existing religious bodies is to recognize that unless they assert their common cause in setting limits to the invasion of the lifeworld, only a hollow shell of religious life may remain.

Notes

CHAPTER 1

1. William James, *The Varieties of Religious Experience* (New York: Vintage Books, 1990[1902]), p. 17.

2. Elaborations of this definition appear in the multivolume works produced by the Fundamentalism Project and published by the University of Chicago Press. It is condensed, and the elaborations are anticipated in the introduction to the five volumes, Martin E. Marty and R. Scott Appleby (eds.), *Fundamentalisms Observed* (Chicago: University of Chicago Press, 1991), pp. vii–xi.

3. Wilfred Cantwell Smith, *The Meaning and End of Religion* (New York: Macmillan, 1963), pp. 15–50, 203–245.

4. Mircea Eliade (ed.), *The Encyclopedia of Religion* (New York: Macmillan, 1987ff.). The editors were Charles J. Adams, Joseph M. Kitagawa, Martin E. Marty, Richard P. McBrien, Jacob Needleman, Annemarie Schimmel, Robert M. Seltzer, and Victor Turner. Had we had to agree on a single definition of religion, we would never have gotten past "Aaron," the first entry. Winston L. King was given the assignment of addressing the subject and did so capably, without resolving debates on the matter (cf. "Religion," Vol. 12, pp. 282–293).

5. Chester E. Jorgenson and Frank Luther Mott (eds.), *Benjamin Franklin* (New York: Hill & Wang, 1962), p. 203.

6. William Lee Miller, *The First Liberty* (New York: Knopf, 1986), p. 28.

7. A pioneering work on this subject is John F. Wilson, *Public Religion in American Culture* (Philadelphia: Temple University Press, 1979).

8. Robert N. Bellah, "Civil Religion in America," *Dædalus* 96(1967), pp. 1–21.

9. Jorgenson and Mott, *Franklin,* p. 12.

10. Thomas Paine, *The Age of Reason* (1794), quoted in Page Smith (ed.), *Religious Origins of the American Revolution* (Missoula, Mont.: Scholars Press, 1976), p. 220; Thomas Jefferson to Ezra Stiles Ely, 25 June 1819; see Dickinson W. Adams (ed.), *The*

Papers of Thomas Jefferson: Jefferson's Extracts from the Gospels (Princeton, N.J.: Princeton University Press, 1983), pp. 386–387.

11. See Martin E. Marty, "Committing the Study of Religion in Public," *Journal of the American Academy of Religion* 57(1988), p. 1; also, Robert M. Healy, *Jefferson on Religion and Public Education* (New Haven, Conn.: Yale University Press, 1962), pp. 217, 219.

12. James, *Varieties,* p. 36.

13. Alfred North Whitehead, *Religion in the Making* (New York: Macmillan, 1916), p. 16.

14. John Dewey, *The Public and Its Problems* (New York: Holt, 1924), pp. 41, 49, 169–170; Walter Lippmann, *The Public Philosophy* (New York: Mentor, 1955), pp. 75–76.

15. John Dewey, *A Common Faith* (New Haven, Conn.: Yale University Press, 1934).

16. Walter Lippmann, *A Preface to Morals* (Boston: Beacon, 1960), pp. 327–328.

17. David Tracy, *The Analogical Imagination* (New York: Crossroad, 1981).

18. Catherine Albanese, *America: Religions and Religion,* 2nd ed. (Belmont, Calif.: Wadsworth, 1992), pp. 402–403, 405, 409, 417, 419, 422, 424, 429–430.

19. Ibid., p. 397.

20. Quoted in Ernest Gellner, *Legitimation of Belief* (Cambridge: Cambridge University Press, 1974), p. 147.

21. The mission statement of the Public Religion Project, a Pew Charitable Trusts–funded project at the University of Chicago.

22. Ronald T. Takaki, *A Different Mirror* (Boston: Little Brown, 1993); Henry Steele Commager, *The American Mind* (New Haven, Conn.: Yale University Press, 1950).

23. Stephen Covey, "The Beliefs We Share," *USA Weekend* (July 4–6, 1997), pp. 4–5.

24. See Martin E. Marty, *The Public Church* (New York: Crossroads, 1981), p. 3; the other references course through my writings along with other images and metaphors, but there is comment on each in Martin E. Marty, *The One and the Many* (Cambridge, Mass.: Harvard University Press, 1997).

25. Peter Burke, *Varieties of Cultural History* (Ithaca, N.Y.: Cornell University Press, 1997), pp. 196, 208.

26. David G. Hackett (ed.), *Religion and American Culture* (New York: Routledge, 1995); Walter H. Conser, Jr., and Sumner B. Twiss, *Religious Diversity and American Religious History* (Athens: University of Georgia Press, 1997); Harry S. Stout and D. G. Hart, *New Directions in American Religious History* (New York: Oxford, 1997); Thomas Tweed (ed.), *Retelling U.S. History* (Berkeley: University of California Press, 1997); Jonathan D. Sarna (ed.), *Minority Faiths and the American Protestant Mainstream* (Urbana: University of Illinois, 1998).

27. Bob Greene, "Can Bagels Get Any More Mainstream Than This?" *Chicago Tribune* (23 June 1998), section 5.

28. K. Anthony Appiah, "The Multiculturalist Misunderstanding," *New York Review of Books* (Oct. 9, 1997), pp. 30–36.

29. Richard Brookhiser, "All Nice, All the Time," *National Review* (May 4, 1998), pp. 54–56.

30. Louis Menand, "Being an American," *Times Literary Supplement* (Oct. 30, 1992), pp. 2–3.

CHAPTER 2

1. *Reynolds v. United States,* 98 U.S. 145 (1879) at 166.

2. *United States v. Ballard,* 322 U.S. 78 (1944) at 86.

3. 50 United States Code App. ¶ 456 [j], 1958 ed.

4. *United States v. Seeger,* 380 U.S. 163 (1965) at 166.

5. Stanley Ingber, "Religion or Ideology," *Stanford Law Review* 41(1989), p. 260; see *Walsh v. United States*, 398 U.S. 333 (1970) at 344.

6. Richard John Neuhaus, *The Naked Public Square* (Grand Rapids, Mich.: Eerdmans, 1984), p. 125.

7. Rick Bragg, "Judge Allows God's Law to Mix with Alabama's," *New York Times* (Feb. 13, 1997), p. A14.

8. *Bowers v. Hardwick,* 478 U.S. 186 (1985) at 211.

9. David A.J. Richards, *Toleration and Constitution* (New York: Oxford University Press, 1986), pp. 259, 273.

10. Edward B. Foley, "Political Liberalism and Establishment Clause Jurisprudence," *Case Western Reserve Law Review* 43(1993), p. 965.

11. Kyron Huigens, "Science, Freedom of Conscience and the Establishment Clause," *University of Puget Sound Law Review* 13(1989), pp. 67, 96; cf. Karl Popper, *The Logic of Scientific Discovery,* rev. ed. (London: Hutchison, 1968).

12. Huigens, "Science," p. 90.

13. Ibid., pp. 138–139.

14. Peter S. Wenz, *Abortion Rights as Religious Freedom* (Philadelphia: Temple University Press, 1992), p. 136.

15. Regarding Pfeffer, see Phillip E. Hammond, *With Liberty for All* (Louisville: Westminster John Knox Press, 1998), p. 4; regarding Bob Jones University, see *Bob Jones University v. U.S.,* 461 U.S. 574 (1983).

16. Stephen L. Carter, *The Dissent of the Governed* (Cambridge, Mass.: Harvard University Press, 1998), p. 29.

17. José Casanova, *Public Religions in the Modern World* (Chicago: University of Chicago Press, 1994), pp. 223, 233.

18. "No to 'Life Partners,'" *Catalyst* 25(May 1998), p. 11.

19. *Olmstead v. United States,* 277 U.S. 438 (1927) at 479.

CHAPTER 3

1. Cf. Henri Frankfort, *Kingship and the Gods* (Chicago: University of Chicago Press, 1978[1948]).

2. See ibid., pp. 337–344.

3. G. Ernest Wright, "The Faith of Israel," in *The Interpreter's Bible,* Vol. 1 (Nashville: Abingdon, 1952), p. 354.

4. In *Engel v. Vitale,* 370 U.S. 421 (1962) at 432, proscribing the recitation of official prayer in the public schools, the Court declared that "the Establishment Clause stands as an expression of principle on the part of the Founders of our Constitution that religion is too personal, too sacred, too holy, to permit its 'unhallowed perversion' by a civil magistrate."

5. *Walz v. Tax Commission,* 397 U.S. 644 (1970) at 669.

6. *Watson v. Jones,* 13 Wall. 679 (1872) at 728.

7. For a recent scholarly study on this theme, see Isaac Kramnick and R. Laurence Moore, *The Godless Constitution* (New York: Norton, 1996), in which the authors expound on and celebrate "the intentionally secular base on which the Constitution was placed" (p. 14).

8. Cf. *McCollum v. Board of Education,* 333 U.S. 203 (1948); *Zorach v. Clauson,* 343 U.S. 306 (1952); *Engel v. Vitale,* 370 U.S. 421 (1962); *Abington v. Schempp,* 374 U.S. 203 (1963); *Lee v. Wiseman,* 505 U.S. 577 (1992).

9. Lyman Beecher, "The Memory of Our Fathers"; quoted in Elwyn A. Smith, *Religious Liberty in the United States* (Philadelphia: Fortress, 1972[1827]), p. 89.

10. Alexis de Tocqueville, *American Democracy,* Vol. 1 (New York: Knopf, 1945[1835]), pp. 303–309.

11. G. K. Chesterton, *What I Saw in America* (New York: Dodd, Mead, 1922), p. 18; Sydney E. Mead, *The Nation with the Soul of a Church* (New York: Harper & Row, 1975).

12. Michael J. Perry, "Religious Arguments in Public Political Debate," *Loyola Law Review* 29(1996), p. 1421.

13. Reinhold Niebuhr, *The Irony of American History* (New York: Scribner, 1952).

14. Cf. Peter F. Drucker, "Organized Religion and the American Creed," *Review of Politics* 13(1956), p. 296.

15. Reinhold Niebuhr, *Pious and Secular America* (New York: Scribner, 1958).

16. Tocqueville, *American Democracy,* Vol. 1, pp. 303–309.

17. Francis Grund, "Religion and Morality Preside over Their Council" (1837), in Henry Steele Commager (ed.), *America in Perspective* (New York: Random House, 1947), pp. 85, 87.

18. *Zorach v. Clausen,* 343 U.S. 306 (1952) at 313–314. The negation of religion, Justice Douglas wrote, "would be preferring those who believe in no religion over those who do believe."

19. Drucker, "Organized Religion," p. 298.

20. See Robert T. Handy, *A Christian America* (New York: Oxford University Press, 1984); Mark A. Noll et al., *The Search for Christian America* (Colorado Springs, Colo.: Helmers & Howard, 1989). For a well-documented historical account of the pervasive influence of religion in American culture and society, see Jon Butler, *Awash in a Sea of Faith* (Cambridge, Mass.: Harvard University Press, 1990), in which the author recounts the advance of religious commitment in America between 1700 and 1865 and shows how America emerged after 1800 as an extraordinarily spiritual "hothouse" that far eclipsed the Puritan achievement of the seventeenth century, even as secularism triumphed in Europe with its pattern of established national churches.

21. Richard John Neuhaus, *The Naked Public Square* (Grand Rapids, Mich.: Eerdmans, 1984). Even more recently, still others see the absence of religion in American public life; cf. John W. Whitehead, *Religious Apartheid* (Chicago: Moody Press, 1994).

22. Kramnick and Moore, *The Godless Constitution,* pp. 173, 175.

23. H.R. Rep. No. 1693, 83d Cong., 2d Sess. (1954). "Almost simultaneously with the passage of the resolution, both houses passed another resolution" establishing a Capitol prayer room; see Anson P. Stokes and Leo Pfeffer, *Church and State in the United States* (New York: Harper & Row, 1964), pp. 568–570. "In God We Trust" was placed on all U.S. currency during the Civil War and has never been removed.

24. See Mark Silk, *Spiritual Politics* (New York: Simon & Schuster, 1988), pp. 96–100.

25. William Lee Miller, *Piety Along the Potomac* (New York: Houghton Mifflin, 1964).

26. Cf. A. Roy Eckardt, *The Surge of Piety in America* (New York: Association Press, 1958), and the more recent study, Barry A. Kosman and Seymour P. Lachman, *One Nation Under God* (New York: Harmony Books, 1993), which focuses on the considerable social impact and the importance of religion in American public life.

27. Neuhaus, *Naked,* p. 161.

28. See Arthur A. Cohen, *The Myth of the Judeo-Christian Tradition* (New York: Harper & Row, 1969).

29. See Leo Pfeffer, "The Deity in American Constitutional History," *Journal of Church and State* 23(1981), pp. 215–239.

30. Quoted in Edward F. Humphrey, *Nationalism and Religion in America, 1774–1789* (Boston: Chapman, 1924), p. 407.

31. From D. M'Allister, "Testimonies to the Religious Defect of the Constitution" (1874); quoted in Morton Borden, *Jews, Turks, and Infidels* (Chapel Hill: University of North Carolina Press, 1984), p. 59.

32. Ibid.

33. William Gribbin, *The Churches Militant* (New Haven, Conn.: Yale University Press, 1973), p. 34.

34. From M'Allister, "Testimonies," p. 59.

35. Ibid., pp. 47–48.

36. See James M. King, *Facing the Twentieth Century* (New York: American Union League Society, 1899), pp. 585–593; A. K. Weinberg, *Manifest Destiny* (Baltimore: Johns Hopkins University Press, 1935); H. Richard Niebuhr, *The Kingdom of God in America* (New York: Willett, Clark, 1937); Handy, *Christian America;* Ernest Lee Turveson, *Redeemer Nation* (Chicago: University of Chicago Press, 1968).

37. See Borden, *Jews, Turks, and Infidels,* pp. 53–74.

38. Bela Bates Edwards, *Writings of Professor B. B. Edwards,* Vol. 2 (New York: Jewett, 1892), p. 489.

39. Ezra Stiles Ely, *The Duty of Christian Freemen to Elect Christian Rulers* (Philadelphia: n.p., 1827), pp. 8, 11.

40. Horace Bushnell, *Reverses Needed* (1861), in Borden, *Jews, Turks, and Infidels,* p. 61. Having condemned the Founding Fathers for establishing a government even without mentioning even the name of God in the Preamble to the Constitution, Bushnell hoped the nation would succeed in "cutting off . . . the false theories under which we have been so fatally demoralized."

41. David McAllister, *The National Reform Movement* (1898), quoted in Leo Pfeffer, *Church, State, and Freedom,* rev. ed. (Boston: Beacon, 1967), p. 241.

42. Ibid.

43. *Congressional Record,* Feb. 14, 1951.

44. Ibid., Oct. 20, 1997; the amendment is frequently referred to at present as the Ishtook Amendment, so named for its primary sponsor in the House, Representative Ernest Ishtook (R.-Okla.).

45. Franklin H. Littell, *From State Church to Pluralism,* rev. ed. (New York: Macmillan, 1971), p. xxvi. Similarly, the Presbyterian Church (U.S.A.) has declared, "We have no right to claim that ours is and always has been a Christian nation"; see James E. Beumler, "Social Teachings of the Presbyterian Church," *Church and Society* (Nov./Dec. 1984), p. 83. Long identified with its advocacy of the separation of church and state, the National Council of Churches, composed of thirty-two member bodies, almost four decades ago expressed its opposition to any constitutional amendment that would declare that the United States is a "Christian Nation"; see "Opposition to the Christian Amendment Proposal," Policy Statement adopted by the General Board of the National Council of Churches of Christ in the U.S.A., June 4, 1959. Charles G. Adams, a national Baptist leader for some years identified with the Baptist Joint Committee on Public Affairs, wrote, "Baptists pervert their own heritage by clamoring for a . . . 'Christian nation'"; see Charles G. Adams, "The Scrutiny of History," *Baptist History and Heritage* 20(July 1985), p. 67.

46. *Engel v. Vitale* at 431.

47. This view was enunciated by the Court in its first major church–state case, *Reynolds v. United States,* 98 U.S. 145 (1878), and has been frequently reaffirmed.

48. *Lynch v. Donnelly,* 465 U.S.668 (1984) at 687–688.

49. Douglas Laycock, "The Free Exercise of Religion," *George Washington Law Review* 60 (March 1992), p. 843.

50. Although organized religion has the constitutional right to be involved in public affairs, its tax exemption may be denied if it fails to meet the "substantiality" test (i.e., "no substantial part of the activities of which is carrying on propaganda, or otherwise attempting to influence legislation"), engages in partisan politics, or endorses particular political candidates. Even with this disability of the loss of tax exemption, organized religion may still exercise its right to be involved in public affairs and the body politic.

51. Stephen L. Carter, *The Culture of Disbelief* (New York: Basic Books, 1993), p. 214. There are those who do hold that religious arguments have no place in public political speech: see Bruce A. Ackerman, *Social Justice in the Liberal State* (New Haven, Conn.: Yale University Press, 1980); Edward M. Gaffney, "Politics Without Brackets on Religious Convictions," *Tulane Law Review* 64(1990), pp. 1143–1194.

52. Perry, "Religious Arguments," p. 1424.

53. *United States v. Cruikshank,* 92 U.S. 588, 591 (1876). Expressed negatively, the Court said, "It was not, therefore, a right granted to the people by the Constitution of the United States."

54. *Stromberg v. California,* 283 U.S. 359 (1931).

55. See Cushing Strout, *The New Heavens and New Earth* (New York: Harpers, 1973); Patricia U. Bonomi, *Under the Cope of Heaven* (New York: Oxford University Press, 1986); Mark A. Noll (ed.), *Religion and American Politics from the Colonial Period to the 1980s* (New York: Oxford University Press, 1990).

56. *The Williamsburg Charter: A National Celebration and Reaffirmation of the First Amendment Religious Liberty Clauses* (Williamsburg, Va., 1988), p.19.

57. *Walz v. Tax Commission of the City of New York* at 670.

58. *McDaniel v. Paty,* 435 U.S. 618 (1978) at 640–641.

59. Richard Rorty, "Religion as a Conversation-Stopper," *Common Knowledge* 3(Spring 1994), pp. 1–3. According to Rorty, "The main reason religion needs to be privatized is that, in political discussion with those outside the relevant religious community, it is a conversation-stopper."

60. See Robert Audi and Nicholas Wolterstorff, *Religion in the Public Square* (Lanham, Md.: Rowman & Littlefield, 1997), for a vigorous debate and dialogue on the subject.

61. *Lee v. Wiseman* at 591.

62. Michael Perry, *Religion in Politics* (New York: Oxford University Press, 1997), p. 37.

63. Cf. Abner S. Greene, "The Political Balance of the Religion Clauses," *Yale Law Journal* 102(1993), pp. 1611–1644; Kent Greenawalt, *Private Consciences and Public Reasons* (New York: Oxford University Press, 1995). For a contrary view, see Perry, *Religion in Politics.*

64. Although arguments of the appropriateness or political effectiveness of such activity may well be offered as to make such alternatives implausible, the point being made here is that such activity is not constitutionally impermissible even though the particular religious movement or party may be advancing ideas contrary to those guaranteed in the Constitution.

65. This action was predicated on a reformed tax law of 1992 and based on the parliamentary "sect" report published in 1996; see news release of "Human Rights Without Frontiers," 30 June 1996 (Brussels).

66. Klaus Scholder, *The Churches and the Third Reich,* Vol. 1 (Philadelphia: Fortress, 1988), p. x.

67. See Robin W. Lovin, (ed.), *Religion and American Public Life* (New York: Paulist Press, 1986), pp. 7–28; cf. Martin Marty, *The Public Church* (New York: Crossroad, 1981). For a recent analysis of the prophetic tradition in American life, in which the author argues that the American "radical tradition" stems not from Aristotle, but from the prophets of the Hebrew Bible, see James Darsey, *The Prophetic Tradition and Radical Rhetoric in America* (New York: New York University Press, 1997).

68. See Daniel J.B. Hofrenning, *In Washington but Not of It* (Philadelphia: Temple University Press, 1995); for earlier studies of the involvement of religious lobbying in the nation's capital, cf. Luke E. Ebersole, *Church Lobbying in the Nation's Capital* (New York: Macmillan, 1951); James Lewis Adams, *The Growing Church Lobby* (Grand Rapids, Mich.: Eerdmans, 1970); Allen D. Hertzke, *Representing God in Washington* (Knoxville: University of Tennessee Press, 1988).

69. Gayraud S. Wilmore, *The Secular Relevance of the Church* (Philadelphia: Westminster, 1962), pp. 24–25.

70. In stating his own mission, Jesus declared, "The Spirit of the Lord is upon me, because he has anointed me to preach the good news to the poor; he has sent me to heal the brokenhearted, to preach deliverance to the captives, and recovery of sight to the blind, to free those whom tyranny has crushed" (Luke 4:18, quoting Isaiah 61:1–2).

71. Ronald J. McAllister, "Religion in the Public Arena," *Journal of Church and State* 30(1988), p. 30; cf. Dieter T. Hessel (ed.), *The Church's Public Role* (Grand Rapids, Mich.: Eerdmans, 1993).

72. See John Yoder, *For the Nations* (Grand Rapids, Mich.: Eerdmans, 1997).

73. J. David Bleich, "God Talk: Should Religion Inform Public Debate?" *Loyola of Los Angeles Law Review* 29(1996), p. 1518.

74. Scholder, *Churches and the Third Reich,* Vol. 2, p. ix.

75. See Dean M. Kelley, "The Rationale for the Involvement of Religion in the Body Politic," in James E. Wood, Jr. (ed.), *The Role of Religion in the Making of Policy* (Waco, Tex.: Baylor University J. M. Dawson Institute of Church–State Studies, 1991), pp. 159–189; James E. Wood, Jr., "Christian Faith and Political Society," in James E. Wood, Jr. (ed.), *Religion and Politics* (Waco, Tex.: Baylor University J. M. Dawson Institute of Church–State Studies, 1983), pp. 9–22.

76. Scholder, *Churches and the Third Reich,* Vol. 2, p. 222.

CHAPTER 4

1. Nathan Glazer, *We Are All Multiculturalists Now* (Cambridge, Mass.: Harvard University Press, 1997), p. 7

2. K. Anthony Appiah, "The Multiculturalist Misunderstanding," *New York Review of Books* 44 (Oct. 9, 1997), p. 32.

3. Andreas Glaeser, "Divided in Unity: The Hermeneutics of Self and Other in the Postunification Berlin Police" (doctoral dissertation, Harvard University, 1997).

4. Appiah, "Multiculturalist Misunderstanding," p. 31.

5. Alexis de Tocqueville, *Democracy in America* (Garden City, N.Y.: Doubleday, 1969), p. 279.

6. Seymour Martin Lipset, *American Exceptionalism* (New York: Norton, 1996), pp. 19–20; for a detailed contrast of the influence of church and sect religion in America, see

E. Digby Baltzell, *Puritan Boston and Quaker Philadelphia* (New York: Free Press, 1979).

7. Max Weber, *Economy and Society* (Berkeley: University of California Press, 1978), p. 1209.

8. Ibid.

9. See Perry Miller, *Roger Williams* (Indianapolis: Bobbs-Merrill, 1953), pp. 61–62; cf. Timothy L. Hall, *Separating Church and State: Roger Williams and Religious Liberty* (Champaign: University of Illinois Press, 1998).

10. Miller, *Williams*, p. 64.

11. Ibid.

12. Seymour Martin Lipset, *The First New Nation* (New York: Basic, 1963), pp. 164–165.

13. William Finnegan, "The Unwanted," *New Yorker* 73 (Dec. 1, 1997), pp. 62–63.

14. Ibid., p. 78.

15. Russell Stevens, review of *African Exodus, Key Reporter* 63 (Winter 1997–1998), p. 14.

16. Vaclav Havel, "The State of the Republic," *New York Review of Books* 45 (Mar. 5, 1998), p. 46.

17. Appiah, "Multiculturalist Misunderstanding," pp. 35–36.

18. Jürgen Habermas, *The Theory of Communicative Action,* Vol. 2 (Boston: Beacon Press, 1987).

19. William Dean, *The Religious Critic in American Culture* (Albany: State University of New York Press, 1994).

20. Portions of this essay have previously appeared in the September 1998 issue of the *Journal of the American Academy of Religion* and are included here in revised form with the kind permission of the editor, Glenn Yocum.

CHAPTER 5

1. Jacob Neusner (ed.), *World Religions in America* (Louisville: Westminster John Knox Press, 1994 [2nd ed., augmented, 1999]).

2. Jacob Neusner and William Scott Green (eds.), *The Religion Factor* (Louisville: Westminster John Knox Press, 1996).

3. *Lingua Franca* (September/October, 1995), pp. 61–66.

4. This part of the chapter began as an address at the University of Wyoming on April 7, 1997.

CHAPTER 6

1. Christian Coalition mission statement as quoted in Lori Forman, *The Political Activity of the Religious Right in the 1990's: A Critical Analysis* (New York: American Jewish Committee [pamphlet], 1994).

2. Max Stackhouse, "Theo-Cons and Neo-Cons on Theology and Law," *Christian Century* (Aug. 27, 1997), p. 760.

3. I am indebted for some of this material to Thad Williamson, a graduate student, for his paper submitted at Union Theological Seminary in New York, "True Prophecy? A Critical Examination of the Socio-Political Stance of the Mainline Churches."

4. Helen J. Mayer et al., "A Tide of Born-Again Politics," *Newsweek* 96 (Sept. 15, 1980), p. 32.

5. "Persecution Bill Is Contested," *Christian Century* (May 13, 1998), p. 495.

6. Benton Johnson, "Theology and the Position of Pastors on Social Issues: Continuity and Change Since the 1960s," *Review of Religious Research* 39 (1998), pp. 293–308.

7. Robert T. Handy, *A Christian America* (New York: Oxford University Press, 1984), p. 21.

8. See David Devlin-Foltz, *Take It on Faith?* (Aspen, Colo.: Aspen Institute, 1997), p. 43.

9. Justin Watson, *The Christian Coalition* (New York: St. Martin's Press, 1977).

10. Stephen L. Carter, *The Culture of Disbelief: How American Law and Politics Trivialize Religious Devotion* (New York: Basic Books, 1993), p. 3.

11. Quoted in Harvey Cox, "The Warring Visions of the Religious Right," *Atlantic Monthly* 276 (Nov. 1995), p. 63.

12. Donald E. Miller, *Reinventing American Protestantism: Christianity in the New Millennium* (Berkeley: University of California Press, 1997).

13. See Gustav Niebuhr, "Americans Say Religion and Politics Mix," *New York Times* (June 25, 1996), pp. A1, A18.

14. Michele Mitchell, "Onward Christian Whippersnappers," *New York Times* (June 23, 1997), p. A14.

15. Roger Shinn, "Christian Faith and Economic Practice," *Christian Century* (July 24, 1991), pp. 720–723.

16. Interfaith Alliance mail brochure, winter, 1998.

17. For the Hart and Gallup data, see Karl Zinsmeister, "Indicators," *American Enterprise* (Nov./Dec. 1995), p. 18; the Sojourners call was included in a mail flyer, "Let Your Voice Ring Out!" (Summer 1996).

18. *Network: A National Catholic Social Justice Lobby* (newsletter, Washington, D.C.) (May/June 1996), p. 6.

19. Frank Rich, "Godzilla of the Right," *New York Times* (May 20, 1998), p. A23.

20. See Laurie Goodstein, "Religious Right Frustrated, Trying New Tactic on G.O.P.," *New York Times* (March 23, 1998), pp. A1, A12.

21. In Devlin-Foltz, *Take It on Faith?*, p. 11.

22. Author's notes, April 1996.

23. "The New Liberation Theology: What's Wrong, and Right, with the Religious Right," *Harvard Magazine* (Nov./Dec. 1996), p. 36.

24. "Robertson Delivers Pep Talk to Coalition," *Christian Century* (Oct. 8, 1997), p. 865.

25. See Peggy L. Shriver, *The Bible Vote: Religion and the New Right* (New York: Pilgrim Press, 1981), p. 103.

26. Watson, *Christian Coalition,* p. 184.

CHAPTER 7

1. Kevin Phillips, *The Politics of Rich and Poor* (New York: Random House, 1990), p. 10.

2. Denny Braun, *The Rich Get Richer* (Chicago: Nelson-Hall, 1997); Andrew Hacker, *Money* (New York: Scribner, 1997).

3. *Statistical Abstracts of the United States* (Washington, D.C.: U.S. Department of Commerce, 1997), p. 470.

4. Holly Sklar, "Imagine a Country," in Paula S. Rothenberg (ed.), *Race, Class, and Gender in the United States,* 4th ed. (New York: St. Martin's Press, 1998), p. 192.

5. Daniel Kadlec, "How CEO Pay Got Away," *Time* (Apr. 20, 1997), p. 59.

6. James D. Davidson, "Theories and Measures of Poverty," *Sociological Focus* 18(1985), pp. 177–198.

7. Sklar, "Imagine," p. 192.

8. Lawrence Mishel and Jared Bernstein, *The State of Working America, 1992–1993* (Armonk, N.Y.: Sharpe, 1994), p. 258.

9. "The Forbes Four Hundred," *Forbes* 158(Oct. 14, 1996), pp. 108–295.

10. "The Forbes Four Hundred," *Forbes* 160(Oct. 13, 1997), pp. 147–378.

11. See William Ryan, *Equality* (New York: Pantheon Books, 1981); Phillips, *Politics of Rich and Poor;* Mishel and Bernstein, *State.*

12. Ryan, *Equality,* p. 173.

13. Stephen Hart, *What Does the Lord Require?* (New York: Oxford University Press, 1992).

14. See Robert C. Liebman and Robert Wuthnow, *The New Christian Right* (New York: Aldine de Gruyter, 1983); Stephen D. Johnson and Joseph B. Tamney (eds.), *The Political Role of Religion in the United States* (Boulder, Colo.: Westview Press, 1986); Charles Hall, "The Christian Left," *Review of Religious Research* 39(1997), pp. 27–45.

15. See Jeffrey K. Hadden and Charles Longino, *Gideon's Gang* (New York: Pilgrim Press, 1974); Bernard Evans, "The Campaign for Human Development," *Review of Religious Research* 20(1979), pp. 264–278; Hall, "Christian Left."

16. John Earle et al., *Spindles and Spires* (Atlanta: John Knox Press, 1976); Donald P. Smith, *Congregations Alive* (Philadelphia: Westminster Press, 1981); James R. Wood, *Leadership in Voluntary Organizations* (New Brunswick, N.J.: Rutgers University Press, 1981); Aldon Morris, *The Origins of the Civil Rights Movement* (New York: Free Press, 1984); David Roozen et al., *Varieties of Religious Presence* (New York: Pilgrim Press, 1984); Alan K. Mock, "Congregational Religious Styles and Orientations to Society," *Review of Religious Research* 34(1992), pp. 20–33; Carl S. Dudley and Sally A. Johnson, *Energizing the Congregation* (Louisville: Westminster John Knox Press, 1993); James D. Davidson et al., "Through the Eye of a Needle: Social Ministry in Affluent Churches," *Review of Religious Research* 38(1997), pp. 247–262.

17. See Earle et al., *Spindles;* John Wilson, *Religion in American Society* (Englewood Cliffs, N.J.: Prentice-Hall, 1978); James D. Davidson, "Captive Congregations," pp. 239–261 in Johnson and Tamney (eds.), *Political Role of Religion;* Keith Roberts, *Religion in Sociological Perspective* (Belmont, Calif.: Wadsworth, 1995).

18. See Hadden and Longino, *Gideon's Gang;* Morris, *Origins;* James D. Davidson, *Mobilizing Social Movement Organizations* (Storrs, Conn.: Society for the Scientific Study of Religion, 1985); C. Eric Lincoln and Lawrence H. Mamiya, *The Black Church in the African American Experience* (Durham, N.C.: Duke University Press, 1990); Hall, "Christian Left."

19. See Samuel Blizzard, *The Protestant Parish Minister: A Behavioral Science Interpretation* (Storrs, Conn.: Society for the Scientific Study of Religion, 1976); Philip Murnion, *New Parish Ministers* (New York: National Pastoral Life Center, 1992).

20. Davidson et al., "Through the Eye."

21. Dudley and Johnson, *Energizing.*

22. See David C. Leege, *Parish Organizations: People's Needs, Parish Services, and Leadership* (Notre Dame, Ind.: University of Notre Dame, 1986); Dudley and Johnson,

Energizing; James D. Davidson and Jerome R. Koch, "Beyond Mutual and Public Benefits," pp. 292–306 in N. J. Demerath et al. (eds.), *Sacred Companies* (New York: Oxford University Press, 1997).

23. See Dudley and Johnson, *Energizing;* Davidson et al., "Through the Eye."

24. Davidson et al., "Through the Eye."

25. See Wood, *Leadership;* Dudley and Johnson, *Energizing;* Davidson et al., "Through the Eye."

26. Davidson, *Mobilizing;* Davidson et al., "Through the Eye."

27. See Ryan, *Equality;* James R. Kluegel and Eliot R. Smith, *Beliefs About Inequality* (New York: Aldine de Gruyter, 1986).

28. See N. J. Demerath III, *Social Class in American Protestantism* (Chicago: Rand-McNally, 1965); Rodney Stark, "The Economics of Piety," pp. 483–503 in Gerald W. Thielbar and Saul D. Feldman (eds.), *Issues in Social Inequality* (Boston: Little, Brown, 1972); Donald J. Treiman, *Occupational Prestige in Comparative Perspective* (New York: Academic Press, 1977); Rodney Stark and William Sims Bainbridge, *The Future of Religion* (Berkeley, Calif.: University of California Press, 1985); Davidson, "Captive Congregations"; William McKinney and Daniel V. A. Olson, "Protestant Church Decision-Makers," pp. 295–301 in Constant H. Jacquet and Alice M. Davis (eds.), *Yearbook of American and Canadian Churches* (Nashville: Abingdon Press, 1991); Davidson et al., "Through the Eye"; Hacker, *Money.*

29. N. J. Demerath III and Philip Hammond, *Religion in Social Context* (New York: Random House, 1969); James R. Wood, "Authority and Controversial Policy," *American Sociological Review* 35(1970): pp. 1057–1069; Hadden and Longino, *Gideon's Gang;* Davidson, "Captive Congregations."

30. See Barbara Hargrove, *The Emerging New Class* (New York: Pilgrim Press, 1986); Davidson, *Mobilizing;* Davidson et al., "Through the Eye."

31. See Gail Kennedy (ed.), *Democracy and the Gospel of Wealth* (Boston: Heath, 1949); Norman Vincent Peale, *The Amazing Results of Positive Thinking* (Englewood Cliffs, N.J.: Prentice-Hall, 1959); Robert A. Schuller (ed.), *Robert Schuller's Life Changers* (Old Tappan, N.Y.: Revell, 1981); David Edward Harrell, Jr., *Pat Robertson* (New York: Harper & Row, 1987); Paul Zane Pilzer, *God Wants You to Be Rich* (New York: Simon & Schuster, 1995); Oral Roberts, *Expect a Miracle* (Nashville: Nelson, 1995); Jim Bakker, *I Was Wrong* (Nashville: Thomas, 1996).

32. See Max Weber, *The Sociology of Religion* (Boston: Beacon Press, 1964); Redmond Mullin, *The Wealth of Christians* (Maryknoll, N.Y.: Orbis, 1984); Hart, *What Does the Lord Require?*

33. See Reinhold Niebuhr, *Moral Man in Immoral Society* (New York: Scribner, 1960); Martin Luther King, Jr., *Why We Can't Wait* (New York: Mentor, 1964); James Cone, *Black Theology and Black Power* (New York: Seabury, 1969); Gustavo Gutiérrez, *A Theology of Liberation* (Maryknoll, N.Y.: Orbis, 1973); Ron Sider, *Rich Christians in an Age of Hunger* (Downer's Grove, Ill.: Inter-Varsity Press, 1977); Julio de Santa Ana, *Good News to the Poor* (Maryknoll, N.Y.: Orbis, 1979); Jesse Jackson, *Straight from the Heart* (Philadelphia: Fortress, 1987); Marie Augusta Neal, *The Just Demands of the Poor* (New York: Paulist Press, 1987); Jesse Jackson, *Keep Hope Alive* (Boston: South End Press, 1989); Jim Wallis, *The Soul of Politics* (San Diego: Harcourt Brace, 1995).

34. See Martin Marty, *Righteous Empire* (New York: Dial Press, 1970); Dean R. Hoge, *Division in the Protestant House* (Philadelphia: Westminster Press, 1976); Roozen et al., *Varieties;* Davidson, "Captive Congregations"; Mock, "Social Differentiation"; James D.

Davidson et al. (eds.), *Faith and Social Ministry* (Chicago: Loyola University Press, 1990); Dudley and Johnson, *Energizing;* Davidson et al., "Through the Eye."

35. See Benton Johnson, "Do Holiness Sects Socialize in Dominant Values?" *Social Forces* 39(1961), pp. 309–316; Weber, *Sociology of Religion;* Davidson, "Captive Congregations"; Nancy Tatom Ammerman, *Bible Believers* (New Brunswick, N.J.: Rutgers University Press, 1987); Margaret Poloma, *The Assemblies of God at the Crossroads* (Knoxville: University of Tennessee Press, 1989); Michael R. Roberts, "Nazarenes and Social Ministry," pp. 157–178 in Davidson et al., *Faith and Social Ministry;* Keith Roberts, *Religion;* Davidson et al., "Through the Eye."

36. See Cone, *Black Theology;* Joseph Gremillion (ed.), *The Gospel of Peace and Justice* (Maryknoll, N.Y.: Orbis, 1976); Peter J. Henriott et al., *Catholic Social Teaching: Our Best Kept Secret* (Maryknoll, N.Y.: Orbis, 1990); Lincoln and Mamiya, *Black Church;* United Methodist Church, *Social Principles* (Washington, D.C.: General Board of Church and Society, 1992).

37. See Liebman and Wuthnow, *New Christian Right;* Johnson and Tamney, *Political Role of Religion;* Hall, "Christian Left."

38. See K. Peter Takayama and Susan Darnell, "The Aggressive Organization and the Reluctant Environment," *Review of Religious Research* 20(1979), pp. 315–334; Davidson, *Mobilizing;* Hall, "Christian Left."

39. See Liston Pope, *Millhands and Preachers* (New Haven, Conn.: Yale University Press, 1942); Hadden and Longino, *Gideon's Gang;* Bruce C. Birch and Larry Rasmussen, *The Predicament of the Prosperous* (Philadelphia: Westminster, 1978); Davidson, *Mobilizing;* Davidson and Koch, "Beyond Benefits"; Davidson et al., "Through the Eye."

40. See James D. Davidson, "Religious Belief as an Independent Variable," *Journal for the Scientific Study of Religion* 11(1972), pp. 65–75; James D. Davidson, "Glock's Model of Religious Commitment," *Review of Religious Research* 16(1975), pp. 83–93; James D. Davidson, "Socio-Economic Status and Ten Dimensions of Religious Commitment," *Sociology and Social Research* 61(1977), pp. 462–485; James D. Davidson and Dean D. Knudsen, "A New Approach to Religious Commitment," *Sociological Focus* 10(1977), pp. 151–173; James D. Davidson et al., *The Lafayette Urban Ministry* (Lafayette, Ind.: Lafayette Urban Ministry, 1977); Davidson, *Mobilizing;* Davidson, "Captive Congregations."

41. See Kluegel and Smith, *Beliefs;* Mock, "Social Differentiation"; Ralph E. Pyle, "Faith and Commitment to the Poor," *Sociology of Religion* 54(1993), pp. 385–401; Davidson et al., "Through the Eye."

42. There is often a sizable gap between church teachings about economic inequality and members' attitudes about the same issues. Although liberal and mainline Protestant groups sometimes espouse support for social welfare and some redistribution of wealth, their members give these ideas a relatively cool reception, tending to favor individualistic explanations of poverty. Conversely, although sects often stress good fortune beliefs, individuals in conservative Protestant groups, especially persons in holiness and pentecostal groups, often harbor views of welfare and economic redistribution that are far more structural than their church's official teachings. Thus, members of socially prosperous, theologically liberal groups are not inclined to support equality as much as their church leaders would like, whereas persons in working-class, theologically conservative traditions are more inclined to favor it than their leaders might think. See Wood, *Leadership;* Pyle, "Faith and Commitment."

43. In our view, a majority of both mainline churches and working-class sects tend to perpetuate inequality; a minority of groups in both categories promote equality. This view challenges the assumption that sects are in "high tension" with the dominant culture. Although sects may be at odds with the dominant culture with regard to matters of personal and sexual morality, and churches may tend to affirm prevailing norms about personal and sexual matters, the pattern seems reversed when the issues turn to social inequality. See Pyle, "Faith and Commitment"; James D. Davidson et al., *The Search for Common Ground* (Huntington, Ind.: Our Sunday Visitor, 1997).

44. Wade Clark Roof and William McKinney, *American Mainline Religion* (New Brunswick, N.J.: Rutgers University Press, 1987), p. 217.

45. Hoge, *Division;* Davidson, *Mobilizing;* Davidson, "Captive Congregations."

46. See Davidson and Koch, "Beyond Benefits."

47. See Hurst, *Social Inequality;* Phillips, *Politics of Rich and Poor.*

48. Takayama and Darnell, "Aggressive Organization"; Davidson, *Mobilizing.*

49. Examples are Bruce Kenrick, *Come Out the Wilderness* (New York: Harper, 1962); Elizabeth O'Connor, *Call to Commitment* (New York: Harper & Row, 1963); George W. Webber, *The Congregation in Mission* (New York: Abingdon Press, 1964); Emma L. Greenwood, *How Churches Fight Poverty* (New York: Friendship Press, 1967); Rudiger Reitz, *The Church in Experiment* (Nashville: Abingdon, 1969); Edgar Trexler (ed.), *Creative Congregations* (Nashville: Abingdon, 1972); B. Carlisle Driggers (ed.), *Models of Metropolitan Ministry* (Nashville: Broadman, 1979).

50. See Dean R. Hoge and David Roozen (eds.), *Understanding Church Growth and Decline* (New York: Pilgrim Press, 1979); Ammerman, *Bible Believers;* R. Stephen Warner, *New Wine in Old Wineskins* (Berkeley: University of California Press, 1998); Ammerman, *Baptist Battles*; Roger Finke and Rodney Stark, *The Churching of America* (New Brunswick, N.J.: Rutgers University Press, 1992); David A. Roozen and C. Kirk Hadaway, *Church and Denominational Growth* (Nashville: Abingdon Press, 1993).

CHAPTER 8

1. Martin E. Marty, *The Public Church* (New York: Crossroad, 1981), pp. 10, 16.

2. Ibid., p. 16.

3. Martin E. Marty, *The One and the Many: America's Struggle for the Common Good* (Cambridge, Mass.: Harvard University Press, 1997).

4. Robert Nisbet, *Social Change and History* (New York: Oxford University Press, 1969), p. 6.

5. In the Quad-Cities region of Iowa, pro-life and pro-choice activists have, over the past two years, engaged in discussions to prevent any violence connected with Planned Parenthood's attempt to open an abortion clinic in the area. At the second national Common Ground Network for Life and Choice conference (described later) held May 14–17, 1998, in conjunction with the Program on the Analysis and Resolution of Conflicts at Syracuse University, Jeanne Wonio, a representative from the Catholic Diocese of Davenport, which supports the common ground dialogue, illustrated the criticism she had received with a spring 1997 editorial in *Life Activist News* entitled "Common Ground Crock" (p. 1). "Once again," it began,

some pro-lifers involved with the "Common Ground Network for Life and Choice" have been handing pro-life ground over to pro-aborts. The Common Ground Network, a collaboration of pro-lifers and pro-aborts, have been meeting to come to an agreement on "acceptable limits of protest" outside abortion centers. There are, however, no rules that are acceptable to pro-lifers for what can go on in-side the mills, only agreed rules for protesting. In other words, the compromising that is done in these Common Ground discussions is being done by the pro-lifers. It's outrageous. The Common Ground discussion forum prohibits discussion of whether the legal status of abortion should change, which automatically constitutes an implied acceptance of the current policy and tacit surrender of the pro-life position.

Even this early in our account, two points need making: (1) Whatever one might think about legal abortion, the *Life Activist* criticism of common ground is astute and must be incorporated into a meaningful characterization of common ground. (2) At the Common Ground conference, Marilyn Cohen, a clinic director who is seeking to open up the dis-puted abortion clinic, described the intense criticism *she* is receiving from *abortion rights colleagues* for *her* participation in Quad-Cities Common Ground. That both pro-life and pro-choice can object to the same common ground practices in itself makes the notion, at a minimum, interesting.

6. Joseph Bernardin and Oscar H. Lipscomb, *Catholic Common Ground Initiative: Foundational Documents* (New York: Crossroad, 1997), p. 34.

7. Marty, *Public Church*, p. 16.

8. Thomas J. Reese, *A Flock of Shepherds*: *The National Conference of Catholic Bishops* (Kansas City, Mo.: Sheed & Ward, 1992), p. 47.

9. Bernardin and Lipscomb, *Catholic Common Ground Initiative*, pp. 17–18.

10. For details, see *Initiative Report,* a quarterly newsletter published by National Pas-toral Life Center, 18 Bleecker Street, New York City 10012-2404. In my conclusion I de-scribe the papers prepared for the second conference, held March 6–8, 1998, attended by fifty-two participants expressly invited to mirror, in articulate ways, the diversity of Catholic thinking and acting regarding "the exercise and reception of authority in the church." I attended this meeting. I also attended the first conference and briefly served as executive secretary of the Initiative.

11. Gustav Niebuhr, "Beliefs," *New York Times* (Aug. 24, 1996), p. 7.

12. Yves Conger, "A Last Look at the Council," in Alberic Stacpoole (ed.), *Vatican II Revisited* (Minneapolis, Minn.: Winston Press, 1986), pp. 342, 351.

13. The material quoted from Avery Dulles, S.J., here and in the following paragraphs is from a typescript of the lecture distributed by him.

14. The "Internet" Webster Dictionary gives the date 1874 and the definition "A basis of mutual interest or agreement." The earliest use of the term that I have found is in John Henry Cardinal Newman's 1852 lectures *The Idea of a University*. Newman used it in the essentially pleasant and noncontroversial sense that a liberally educated person ought to be able to mix amiably with others from all stations of life. Thus, Newman identified the term with a gentleman's *civility*.

15. Personal interviews, 1991, 1996; cf. Cynthia Gorney, *Articles of Faith* (New York: Simon & Schuster, 1998), pp. 418–420, 443.

16. Puzder must be judged prescient. In their June 29, 1992, *Planned Parenthood of Southeastern Pennsylvania v. Casey* majority (five to four) joint opinion, Justices San-dra Day O'Connor, Anthony Kennedy, and David Souter wrote, "[W]e have concluded that the essential holding of *Roe* should be reaffirmed. Yet it must be remembered that *Roe v. Wade* speaks with clarity in establishing not only the woman's liberty but also the state's 'important and legitimate interest in potential life.' That portion of the decision in *Roe* has been given too little acknowledgment and implementation in its subsequent cases."

17. See James R. Kelly, "Truth, Not Truce: 'Common Ground' on Abortion, a Movement Within Both Movements," *Virginia Review of Sociology* 2 (1995), p. 218.

18. In the mid-1980s the late Anthony Lukas used it as the title for his acclaimed work on school integration in Boston, but he never explicitly explained the term, nor did he define it. Still, the title fits his sympathetic account of the different lifeworlds of three Boston families who diverged radically in their views of compulsory school busing but who shared the trait of a good-willed bafflement and a desire for a harmonious community for family life.

19. The Common Ground Network for Life and Choice's first award for Outstanding Common Ground Leadership was awarded to St. Louis Common Ground: Andrew Puzder, B. J. Isaacson, Loretto Wagner, and Jean Cavender. All served on the original steering committee.

20. Although St. Louis Common Ground boasts no dramatic breakthroughs, their idea soon became institutionalized in the Washington-based Common Ground Network for Life and Choice (CGNFLC), a division of Search for Common Ground. I'm on its advisory board.

21. The first use of the term in an authoritative Catholic document that I can find is ¶ 224 of the American Bishops 1983 Pastoral Letter *The Challenge of Peace,* where they teach that "non-violent resistance offers a common ground of agreement for those individuals who choose the option of Christian pacifism even to the point of accepting the need to die rather than to kill, and those who choose the option of lethal force allowed by the theology of just war. Non-violent resistance makes clear that both are able to be committed to the same objective: defense of their country." In their acknowledgment of the principled dispute between pacifists and just war adherents, the bishops also anticipated the Bernardin Catholic Common Ground Initiative: "The experience of preparing this pastoral letter has shown us the range of strongly held opinion in the Catholic community on questions of war and peace. . . . Not only conviction and commitment are needed in the Church, but also civility and charity" (¶ 12). This is not to say that pro-choice and pro-life premises can fit the same moral framework. But it's also worth noting that in *The Challenge of Peace* the bishops acknowledged, "Millions join us in our 'no' to nuclear war, in the certainty that nuclear war would inevitably result in the killing of millions of innocent human beings, directly or indirectly. Yet many part ways with us in our efforts to reduce the horror of abortion and our 'no' to war on innocent human life in the womb, killed not indirectly, but directly" (¶ 287). This is at least implied or incipient common ground, since the bishops, and the Catholic laity, can contribute to peace initiatives only in cooperation with those who do not share their teaching on abortion. *The Challenge of Peace* can be found in David J. O'Brien and Thomas A. Shannon (eds.), *Catholic Social Thought* (Maryknoll, N.Y.: Orbis Books, 1992), and in many other sources, often with different pagination, but the paragraph numbering, which is used here, is constant.

22. Thomas G. Fuechtmann (ed.), *Joseph Cardinal Bernardin: Consistent Ethic of Life* (Kansas City, Mo.: Sheed & Ward, 1988), p. 24. Bernardin was referring to the "meeting ground of principle and practice between civil rights and pro-life advocates" that emerged as disability groups and abortion opponents joined to protest the decision made by parents and doctors to forgo a lifesaving operation on a neonate who had Down's syndrome, "Baby Doe."

23. Bernardin, for example, offered a ten-point interpretation of a November 1989 National Conference of Catholic Bishops' resolution on abortion and Catholic politicians; see Joseph Bernardin, "The Consistent Ethic of Life After Webster," *Origins* 19 (April 12, 1990), p. 6.

24. See Charles J. Fahey and Mary Ann Lewis (eds.), *The Future Of Catholic Institutional Ministries* (New York: Third Age Center, Fordham University, 1992).

25. "News Summary," *New York Times* (Mar. 2, 1993), p. A2.

26. "You Too Can Be a Centrist," *Time* (Aug. 7, 1995), p. 16.

27. "President's Success Lay in Ability to Co-Opt Republican Issues," *New York Times* (Nov. 6, 1996), p. A1; Maureen Dowd, "Yin Hails Yang," *New York Times* (Nov. 7, 1996), p. A33.

28. Katha Pollitt, "A Dangerous Game on Abortion," *New York Times* (June 18, 1996), p. A23.

29. Terry's newsletter is undated. Similarly, in her March 9, 1993, *National Right to Life News* column, the National Right to Life Committee (NRLC) president, Wanda Franz, advised the activists in three thousand NRLC chapters that common ground was a "clever pro-choice" strategy seeking "to gain acceptance of the pro-abortion position as morally equivalent (or morally superior!) to the pro-life position."

30. On April 27, 1998, a pro-life member of the Steering Committee, Marilyn Kopp, resigned from the Common Ground Network for Life and Choice (CGNFLC). She wrote:

When I am NOT GIVEN the opportunity to address or confront these issues (gross injustice) adequately (and this, for me, is my calling to "love my neighbor"), then staying in the situation, for me, is almost abusive and intolerable. I can accept the fact that if I present my case, there will be individuals who will not agree with me. My role as an activist is just to move on then and present the case to other people. I see the abortion issue as no different from the slavery issue or women's rights issues.

Besides the important point that individuals can reach, in prudence and integrity, the limits of common ground it should be noted that the director of CGNFLC, Mary Jacksteit, circulated Kopp's letter of resignation to Steering Committee and Advisory Board members.

31. Michael J. Perry, *Love and Power: The Role of Religion and Morality in American Politics* (New York: Oxford University Press, 1991), ch. 3.

32. Marty, *Public Church,* p. 76. In an early paper I argued that the failure of the American churches to produce anything close to a satisfactory public theology of abortion is related to their ecumenical failure to dialogue on abortion before producing confessional statements; see James R. Kelly, "Ecumenism and Abortion: A Case Study of Pluralism, Privatization and the Public Conscience," *Review of Religious Research* 30 (March, 1989): pp. 225–235. In retrospect, American Catholicism showed the least interest. But things have changed: cf. *The Ecumenical Dialogue on Moral Issues: Potential Sources of Common Witness or of Divisions* (Geneva: World Council of Churches, 1995), a study document of the Joint Working Group between the Roman Catholic church and the World Council of Churches.

33. Cf. Talcott Parsons, *The Social System* (Glencoe, Ill.: Free Press, 1951); Talcott Parsons et al., *Working Papers in the Theory of Action* (Glencoe, Ill.: Free Press, 1953); Talcott Parsons, *Societies* (Englewood Cliffs, N.J.: Prentice-Hall, 1971); Talcott Parsons, *Action Theory and the Human Condition* (New York: Free Press, 1978).

34. Nisbet, *Social Change and History,* p. 283.

35. Kieran Flanagan, *The Enchantment of Sociology: A Study of Theology and Culture* (New York: St. Martin's Press, 1996), p. 19.

36. Paul Ricoeur, *Lectures on Ideology and Utopia* (New York: Columbia University Press, 1986). Ricoeur describes his method as a "genetic phenomenology, a regressive analysis of meaning, digging beneath surface levels of meaning to a more fundamental

level." Because he rejects the possibility of an "objective" spectator view of human behavior, Ricoeur insists that "understanding envelops explanation."

37. Cf. Dennis Hamm, "Unity an Option? Seventh Sunday of Easter," *America* (May
12, 1998), p. 31.

38. Joseph Bernardin, *The Gift of Peace* (Chicago: Loyola University Press, 1997), p.
130.

39. Martin E. Marty, "Our Joseph," *Chicago* (Jan. 15, 1997), pp. 35–36.

40. Richard P. McBrien, *Caesar's Coin: Religion and Politics in America* (New York:
Macmillan, 1987), p. 168; Bernardin's Fordham and Georgetown addresses can be read in
John P. Langan, *Joseph Cardinal Bernardin* (Washington, D.C.: Georgetown University
Press, 1998).

41. Marty, *Public Church,* p. 89.

42. Ricoeur, *Lectures,* pp. 252–253.

43. Ibid.

44. Patricia Zapor, "Bishops to Clinton: Let's Work Together," *Tablet* (Mar. 13, 1993),
p. 6.

45. The other presenters and their titles were Philip Selznick, "Authority in America";
Joseph A. Komonchak, "Authority and Its Exercise"; and James A. Coriden, "Church Authority in American Culture: Cases and Observations."

46. The text of this paper by Dulles is available from the Catholic Common Ground
Initiative.

CHAPTER 9

1. Alan Wolfe, *One Nation, After All* (New York: Viking, 1998), pp. 39–87.

2. Ibid., p. 74.

3. *Family News from Dr. James Dobson* (July 1998), p. 5.

4. See Samuel J. Preuss, *Explaining Religion* (New Haven, Conn.: Yale University
Press, 1987), for an analysis of how religion has been historically defined and ex-
plained; cf. Daniel L. Pals, *Seven Theories of Religion* (Oxford: Oxford University
Press, 1996).

5. Emile Durkheim, *The Elementary Forms of the Religious Life* (New York: Free
Press, 1965[1912]).

6. See Robert Bellah, "Civil Religion in America," *Dædalus* 96(1967), pp. 1–21;
Robert Bellah, *The Broken Covenant,* 2nd ed. (Chicago: University of Chicago Press,
1992[1975]); Robert Bellah and Phillip Hammond, *Varieties of Civil Religion* (San Francisco: Harper & Row, 1980); for a bibliographical summary of research on civil religion,
James A. Mathisen, "Twenty Years After Bellah," *Sociological Analysis* 50(1989), pp.
129–146.

7. Thomas Luckmann, *The Invisible Religion* (New York: Macmillan, 1967), p. 48.

8. Robert Bellah has been particularly critical of this privatistic turn, or what he calls
"expressive individualism": cf. Robert Bellah et al., *Habits of the Heart* (Berkeley: University of California Press, 1985.)

9. Peter L. Berger, *The Sacred Canopy* (Garden City, N.Y.: Doubleday, 1967).

10. See Linell E. Cady, *Religion, Theology, and American Public Life* (Albany: State
University of New York Press, 1993), p. 23.

11. José Casanova, *Public Religions in the Modern World* (Chicago: University of
Chicago Press, 1994).

12. See R. Stephen Warner, "Work in Progress Toward a New Paradigm for the Sociological Study of Religion in the United States," *American Journal of Sociology* 98(1993), pp. 1044–1093.

13. Peter L. Berger, interview in *The Christian Century* (Oct. 29, 1997), p. 974.

14. Casanova, *Public Religions,* p. 5.

15. This kept political power in male hands. Ann Douglas, *The Feminization of American Culture* (Garden City, N.Y.: Doubleday, 1988), reflects on how the feminization of culture arose from the dominance of women in the "private" sphere, which produced a sentimental culture, impoverishing both the private and public realms. Cf. Susan Moller Okin, *Justice, Gender, and the Family* (New York: Basic Books, 1989) for an economic analysis of the "private" work of women in the homeplace.

16. The Christian Right has used the private/public dichotomy to rationalize and discriminate against women and their participation in public life. At their 1998 Annual Convention, Southern Baptists, the nation's second largest denomination (after Roman Catholics), revised their statement of Baptist Faith and Message relating to family relations: "The husband and wife are of equal worth before God, since both are created in God's image. The marriage relationship models the way God relates to His people. A husband is to love his wife as Christ loved the church. He has the God-given responsibility to provide for, to protect and to lead his family. A wife is to submit herself graciously to the servant leadership of her husband even as the church willingly submits to the headship of Christ. She, being in the image of God as is her husband thus equal to him, has the God-given responsibility to respect her husband and to serve as his helper in managing the household and nurturing the next generation." *SBC Bulletin,* "Baptist Faith and Message 'Family' Article," Southern Baptist Convention, Salt Lake City, Utah, July 9–11, 1998.

17. Phillip E. Hammond, *With Liberty for All* (Louisville: Westminster John Knox Press, 1998), p. 106.

18. Casanova, *Public Religions,* p. 229.

19. Examples in liberal Protestantism include Walter Winks, *Engaging the Powers* (Minneapolis: Fortress Press, 1992); cf. Ched Myers, *Who Will Roll Away the Stone?* (Maryknoll, N.Y.: Orbis Books, 1994). Both use liberation theology to confront unjust social patterns in the United States.

20. For more details on the agenda of Christian Reconstructionists, see Mark Juergensmeyer, "Christian Violence in America," in *Annals* 558(1998), pp. 88–100.

21. The theological agenda of the Christian Right is powerful and well organized. The rhetoric follows a fourfold stereotypical pattern: (1) There is a chronological series of events that are described as brought by the perversion of Christian culture—the Equal Rights Amendment, the decision to legalize abortion, the rise of the homosexual movement. (2) Groups are blamed—secular humanists, feminists, gay right activists, or such branches of the federal government as the Supreme Court, the Congress, or the Internal Revenue Service. (3) The historical and cultural results of these events and groups are depicted—a permissive society, a culture open to "alternative life-styles." (4) The final step is the agenda, which is relatively straightforward: pro-life, pro-family, pro-moral, and pro-American. See Casanova, *Public Religions,* p. 154.

22. See Didi Herman, *The Antigay Agenda* (Chicago: University of Chicago Press, 1997).

23. David Gary Comstock, *Unrepentant, Self-Affirming, Practicing* (New York: Continuum, 1996), p. 13.

24. Herman, *Antigay Agenda,* pp. 137–169.

25. Mel White describes his own journey from conservative anti-gay Christian to a pro-gay Christian minister in *Stranger at the Gate* (New York: Plume/Penguin Group, 1994). White also covers the threats of violence against him and other gays and lesbians in the name of religion (p. 233).

26. The fourfold typology that I use in this discussion is a modified version used in Comstock, *Unrepentant,* pp. 13–14.

27. Keith Hartman, *Congregations in Conflict* (New Brunswick, N.J.: Rutgers University Press, 1996), p. 180.

28. Joseph Ratzinger, "Letter to the Bishops of the Catholic Church on the Pastoral Care of Homosexual Persons (1986)," in Jeffrey S. Siker (ed.), *Homosexuality in the Church* (Louisville: Westminster John Knox Press, 1994), p. 40.

29. Ibid., p. 43.

30. John J. McNeill writes about his own experience of being a gay priest who was silenced and rejected by the Roman Catholic church in his book *The Church and the Homosexual* (Boston: Beacon Press, 1993).

31. For a moderate religious approach to American family issues see Don Browning et al., *From Culture Wars to Common Ground* (Louisville: Westminster John Knox Press, 1997); more liberal approaches to the American family include Arlene Skolnick, *Embattled Paradise* (New York: Basic Books, 1991), and Judith Stacey, *Brave New Families* (New York: Basic Books, 1990).

32. The first sign of schism is in the United Methodist church, in which eighteen conservative clergy and twenty-five laypeople, in the spring of 1998, asked to be allowed to separate from their regional body, the California–Nevada Annual Conference (*Christian Century* [April 22–29, 1998], p. 421).

33. Wolfe, *One Nation,* pp. 39–87.

34. Information on the Creech trial was taken from the *United Methodist Information,* official website of the United Methodist church, http://www.umc.org.

35. In *Presbyterian Outlook* (Apr. 13, 1998), p. 15.

36. Richard B. Hays, "Awaiting the Redemption of Our Bodies," in Siker, *Homosexuality,* pp. 3–47.

37. The Presbyterian church struggled with the issue of marriage and divorce and at midcentury changed the Westminster Confession to permit divorce and remarriage on grounds other than adultery and desertion (*Minutes,* Presbyterian Church U.S.A., 1953:43–44; *Minutes,* Presbyterian Church U.S.A., 1959:68–70).

38. Wolfe, *One Nation,* p. 78.

39. Comstock, *Unrepentant,* p. 14.

40. See *Stanton v. Righter,* 1996, Archives of the Episcopal Church, Austin, Texas, for the details of the trial.

41. Peter J. Gomes, *The Good Book* (New York: Morrow, 1996), p. 162.

42. Ibid., p. 146.

43. Stanley Hauerwas, *Dispatches from the Front* (Durham, N.C.: Duke University Press, 1994), pp. 153–154.

44. See Choon-Leong Seow, "A Heterosexual Perspective," in Choon-Leong Seow (ed.), *Homosexuality and the Christian Community* (Louisville: Westminster John Knox Press, 1996), pp. 14–27; Sylvia Thorson-Smith et al., *Called Out With* (Louisville: Westminster John Knox Press, 1997); Jane Adams Spahr, (ed.), *Called Out* (Gaithersburg, Md.: Chi Rho Press, 1995).

45. Thorson-Smith, *Called Out With,* p. 22.

46. Hartman, *Congregations,* p. 179.

47. See Max L. Stackhouse, "The Heterosexual Norm," in Seow, *Homosexuality,* pp. 141–142.

48. A theological and ethical framework for the ordination of homosexuals is articulated in Kathy Rudy, *Sex and the Church* (Boston: Beacon Press, 1997). Rudy argues from an evangelical perspective that the scriptural canon lacks a fundamental ethic of sexuality. She goes beyond simply laying down rules for right behavior and attempts to propound criteria for judging what is morally good and bad sex.

CHAPTER 10

1. Martin E. Marty, "The Twentieth Century," in Mark Noll (ed.), *Religion and American Politics* (New York: Oxford University Press, 1990), p. 324.

2. Martin E. Marty, "Transpositions," *Annals* 480(1985), p. 17.

3. See Herbert Richardson, *Constitutional Issues in the Case of Reverend Moon* (Lewiston, N.Y.: Mellen, 1984); James T. Richardson, "Public Opinion and the Tax Evasion Trial of Reverend Moon," *Behavioral Sciences and the Law* 10(1992), pp. 53–63.

4. Carleton Sherwood, *Inquisition* (Washington, D.C.: Regnery, 1990).

5. James T. Richardson, "The Religious Freedom Restoration Act," in Chris Barringar and David Sinacore-Guinn (eds.), *Religion, Pluralism, and the Law* (Atlanta: Scholars Press, 1999).

6. See Dick Anthony, "Religious Movements and Brainwashing Testimony," in Tom Robbins and Dick Anthony (eds.), *In Gods We Trust,* 2nd ed. (New Brunswick, N.J.: Transaction, 1990), pp. 295–344; James T. Richardson, "Cult/Brainwashing Cases and the Freedom of Religion," *Journal of Church and State* 33(1991), pp. 55–74.

7. See James T. Richardson, "Legal Status of New Religions in the United States," *Social Compass* 42(1995), pp. 249–264; James T. Richardson, "Minority Religions ('Cults') and the Law," *University of Queensland Law Journal* 18(1995), pp. 183–207.

8. See Richardson, "Cult/Brainwashing Cases."

9. See Richardson, "Legal Status."

10. See Rex Davis and James T. Richardson, "The Organization and Functioning of the Children of God," *Sociological Analysis* 37(1976), pp. 321–339.

11. See James T. Richardson and Rex Davis, "Experiential Fundamentalism," *Journal of the American Academy of Religion* 51(1983), pp. 397–425.

12. See James T. Richardson, "New Religions and Religious Freedom in Eastern and Central Europe," in Irena Borowik and Grzegorz Babiński (eds.), *New Religious Phenomena in Central and Eastern Europe* (Krakow: Nomos, 1997), pp. 257–282.

13. See James T. Richardson, "Social Control of New Religions," in Susan Palmer and Charlotte Hardman (eds.), *Children in the New Religions* (New Brunswick, N.J.: Rutgers University Press, 1998).

14. See Amy Cuhel-Schuckers, "Ecumenism in the Unification Church," *Entre* (May 1991), pp. 16–18.

15. Kathy Winnings, personal communication to the author, Sept. 2, 1997.

16. See Anson Shupe and David Bromley, *The New Vigilantes* (Beverly Hills, Calif.: Sage, 1980).

17. Jonathan Wells, "Excommunication Without a Trial," unpublished typescript; Jonathan Wells, "Theological Witch-Hunt," *Journal of Unification Studies* 1(1997), pp. 23–41.

18. The report is all the more curious inasmuch as the Southern Baptist Convention is not itself a constituent member of the NCC. Roman Catholic scholars also participated in constructing the report, though the Catholic church is not a constituent body of the NCC. A 1987 cover letter sent with the document to persons who expressed interest in receiving it also makes reference to "the office within the Southern Baptist Convention that deals with cults" and advises that "it would be useful" to readers "to be in touch with them." See Wells, "Witch-Hunt," pp. 24, 40–41.

19. See James T. Richardson and John DeWitt, "Christian Science Spiritual Healing, the Law, and Public Opinion," *Journal of Church and State* 34(1992), pp. 549–561.

20. See James A. Beckford, *Cult Controversies* (London: Tavistock, 1985).

21. Jehovah's Witnesses' advertisement, *New York Times* (July 1, 1998), p. 12.

22. See Beckford, *Cult Controversies;* James T. Richardson and Barend van Driel, "New Religions in Europe," in Anson Shupe and David Bromley (eds.), *Anti-Cult Movements in Cross-Cultural Perspective* (New York: Garland, 1994), pp. 129–170.

23. Not all European countries have become involved of late in the serious efforts to exert control over newer and smaller faiths. For instance, the Netherlands, Italy, and Denmark have not shown the same level of concern. Why these differences occur is not well understood, but they are noteworthy. Such actions probably cannot occur without the tacit blessing of dominant religious groups in Germany, France, and Belgium. This implies that when governments and legal systems do not take action toward newer faiths, the dominant ones must not be pushing them to do so (or if they are, they are doing so ineffectively).

24. See Richardson, "Minority Religions."

25. Ibid.

26. See Richardson, "New Religions and Religious Freedom."

27. See Marat S. Shterin and James T. Richardson, "Local Laws Restricting Religion in Russia," *Journal of Church and State* 40(1998), pp. 319–341.

28. See ibid.; also James T. Richardson and Marat S. Shterin, "Religious Minorities and Religious Freedom in Russia," in Peter Danchin (ed.), *The Protection of Religious Minorities in Europe* (New York: Columbia University Press, 1998).

CHAPTER 11

1. See Rhys H. Williams, "Constructing the Public Good," *Social Problems* 42(1995), pp. 124–144; "Religion as Political Resource," *Journal for the Scientific Study of Religion* 35(1996), pp. 368–378.

2. Benedict Anderson, *Imagined Communities* (London: Verso, 1991).

3. Anthony P. Cohen, *The Symbolic Construction of Community* (London: Tavistock, 1985).

4. See Michele Lamont and Marcel Fournier (eds.), *Cultivating Differences* (Chicago: University of Chicago Press, 1992); cf. Rhys H. Williams (ed.), *Cultural Wars in American Politics* (Hawthorne, N.Y.: Aldine de Gruyter, 1997), pp. 283–295.

5. See Williams, "Constructing"; Rhys H. Williams, "Covenant, Contract, and Communities," *International Issues* 30(1994), pp. 31–50; Rhys H. Williams, "Visions of the Good Society and the Religious Roots of American Political Culture," *Sociology of Religion* 59(1999), pp. 1–34; and Rhys H. Williams and Timothy J. Kubal, "Movement Frames and the Cultural Environment," *Research in Social Movements, Conflict and Change* 21(1999), pp. 225–248.

6. See Richard Madsen, "Contentless Consensus," in Alan Wolfe (ed.), *America at Century's End* (Berkeley: University of California Press, 1991), pp. 440–460.

7. Robert N. Bellah et al., *The Good Society* (New York: Knopf, 1991).

8. Emile Durkheim, *The Elementary Forms of Religious Life* (New York: The Free Press, 1995[1912]).

9. For examples, see Rhys H. Williams, "Movement Dynamics and Social Change," in Martin E. Marty and R. Scott Appleby (eds.), *Accounting for Fundamentalisms* (Chicago: University of Chicago Press, 1994), pp. 785–833.

10. Two classic expressions of American pluralist thinking are David Truman, *The Governmental Process* (New York: Knopf, 1951), and Robert Dahl, *Who Governs?* (New Haven, Conn.: Yale University Press, 1961).

11. Emile Durkheim, *The Division of Labor in Society* (New York: Free Press, 1933[1893]); Durkheim, *Elementary Forms.*

12. David I. Kertzer, *Ritual, Politics, and Power* (New Haven, Conn.: Yale University Press, 1988).

13. Clifford Geertz, *The Interpretation of Cultures* (New York: Basic Books, 1973); see especially the chapters "Ideology as a Cultural System," "Religion as a Cultural System," and "Ritual and Social Change in Java."

14. For an analysis of religiously based cultural resources and their use by a variety of political actors in municipal politics, see Rhys H. Williams and N. J. Demerath III, "Religion and Political Process in an American City," *American Sociological Review* 56(1991), pp. 417–431.

15. N. J. Demerath III and Rhys H. Williams, "Civil Religion in an Uncivil Society," *Annals* 480(1985), pp. 154–166.

16. Robert N. Bellah, "Civil Religion in America," *Dædalus* 96(1967), pp. 1–21; see also Russell E. Richey and Donald G. Jones, *American Civil Religion* (New York: Harper & Row, 1974).

17. See Williams, "Constructing"; Williams and Demerath, "Religion and Political Process."

18. See, for example, A. James Reichley, *Religion in American Public Life* (Washington, D.C.: Brookings Institution, 1985); John F. Wilson, *Public Religion in American Culture* (Philadelphia: Temple University Press, 1979).

19. See, for example, Sacvan Bercovitch, "The Ends of American Puritan Rhetoric," John Bender and David E. Wellbery (eds.), *The Ends of Rhetoric* (Stanford, Calif.: Stanford University Press, 1990), pp. 171–190.

20. Kertzer, *Ritual, Politics, and Power.*

21. Williams, "Constructing."

22. For empirical examples, see N. J. Demerath III, "The Moth and the Flame," *Sociology of Religion* 55(1994), pp. 105–117; Williams and Demerath, "Religion and Political Process."

23. Williams and Demerath, "Religion and Political Process"; Williams, "Constructing"; cf. Fred Kniss, "Ideas and Symbols as Resources in Intrareligious Conflict," *Sociology of Religion* 57(1996), pp. 7–24.

24. Antonio Gramsci is credited with developing "hegemony" as a sociopolitical concept. Gramsci, however, was a practical political organizer and was writing from prison, so his conceptual development is not always precise or systematically developed; see Antonio Gramsci, *Selections from the Prison Notebooks* (New York: International Publishers, 1971).

25. Steven Lukes, *Power* (London: Macmillan, 1974).

26. David D. Laitin, *Hegemony and Culture* (Chicago: University of Chicago Press, 1986).

27. Daniel T. Rodgers, *Contested Truths* (New York: Basic Books, 1987).

28. C. B. McPherson, *The Political Theory of Possessive Individualism* (Oxford: Oxford University Press, 1962).

29. See Gwyneth I. Williams and Rhys H. Williams, "'All We Want Is Equality,'" in Joel Best (ed.), *Images of Issues,* 2nd ed. (New York: Aldine de Gruyter, 1995), pp. 191–212.

30. Rhys H. Williams and Jeffrey Neal Blackburn, "Many Are Called but Few Obey," in Christian Smith (ed.), *Disruptive Religion* (New York: Routledge Publishers, 1996), pp. 167–185.

31. Williams, "Constructing."

32. See Warren I. Susman, *Culture as History* (New York: Pantheon, 1984).

33. See, for example, Robert T. Handy, *A Christian America,* 2nd ed. (New York: Oxford University Press, 1984).

34. Clyde Wilcox, "Premillennialists at the Millennium," in Steve Bruce et al. (eds.), *The Rapture of Politics* (New Brunswick, N.J.: Transaction, 1995), pp. 21–39.

35. Both the political rhetoric and the social reality behind the "culture war" are analyzed in Williams, *Cultural Wars.*

36. See Robert Wuthnow, *The Restructuring of American Religion* (Princeton, N.J.: Princeton University Press, 1988).

37. I use the term rather loosely, following Will Herberg, *Protestant–Catholic–Jew* (New York: Harcourt Brace, 1955).

38. Examples abound, but see Ralph Reed, *Politically Incorrect* (Dallas: Word, 1994).

39. This is the "majoritarian" solution to the tension between our highly religious political culture and our formally secular political institutions; see Williams and Demerath, "Religion and Political Process."

40. Williams, *Cultural Wars,* pp. 283–295.

41. For example, see Williams, "Movement Dynamics."

42. Williams, "Religion as Political Resource."

43. An earlier version of this chapter was presented to the annual meeting of the Religious Research Association, San Diego, California, in November 1997. I wish to thank Katherine Jahnige, Ezra Kopelowitz, Paul Lichterman, Martin Marty, and the editors for comments on the earlier draft.

CHAPTER 12

1. Max Weber, *Economy and Society* (Berkeley: University of California Press, 1978), pp. 576–610.

2. Cf. Cynthia Crossen, "Dare We Say It?" *Wall Street Journal* (Mar. 31, 1998), pp. A1, A14.

3. Pierre Hegy, "The Libido Factor," *Research in the Social Scientific Study of Religion* 2(1990), pp. 31–46.

4. Both Wittgensteinians and Durkheimians, of course, would object that the idea that "religion" could be "private" is a contradiction in terms. These theoretical considerations must be laid aside for the moment.

5. Karel Dobbelaere, "Secularization," *Encyclopedia of Religion and Society* (Walnut Creek, Calif.: AltaMira Press, 1998), p. 453.

6. See Jürgen Habermas, *The Theory of Communicative Action,* Vol. 2 (Boston: Beacon Press, 1987).

7. Robert Wuthnow, *The Restructuring of American Religion* (Princeton, N.J.: Princeton University Press, 1987), pp. 314–322.

8. See Christopher Ellison, "Conservative Protestantism and the Corporal Punishment of Children," *Journal for the Scientific Study of Religion* 35(1996), pp. 1–16; Christopher Ellison et al., "Conservative Protestantism and the Parental Use of Corporal Punishment," *Social Forces* 74(1996), pp. 1003–1028.

9. See William H. Swatos, Jr., "Picketing Satan Enfleshed at 7-Eleven," *Review of Religious Research* 30(1988), pp. 73–82.

10. See Thomas Robbins, "Church-and-State Issues in the United States," *Encyclopedia of Religion and Society* (Walnut Creek, Calif.: AltaMira Press, 1998), pp. 87–89.

11. To say that a corporation is publicly accountable does not mean that it operates "in the public interest," but it does mean that the corporation provides audited financial records through annual reports, follows federal and state guidelines for employment and other workplace practices, interacts with the media at some level through "spokespersons," and so on.

12. On considerations of religiopolitical alignments, particularly among American Christians, see, e.g., Benton Johnson and Mark A. Shibley, "How New Is the New Christian Right?" in Jeffrey K. Hadden and Anson D. Shupe (eds.), *Secularization and Fundamentalism Reconsidered* (New York: Paragon House, 1989), pp. 178–198; Eugen Schoenfeld, "Militant Religion," in William H. Swatos, Jr. (ed.), *Religious Sociology* (New York: Greenwood Press, 1987), pp. 125–137; William H. Swatos, Jr., "On Being 'Right' and Religious," in Steve Bruce et al. (eds.), *The Rapture of Politics* (New Brunswick, N.J.: Transaction, 1994), pp. 137–146.

13. Roland Robertson, *Globalization* (London: Sage, 1992).

14. Cf. Ronald M. Glassman, "Manufactured Charisma and Legitimacy," in Ronald M. Glassman and William H. Swatos, Jr. (eds.), *Charisma, History, and Social Structure* (New York: Greenwood Press, 1986), pp. 122–128.

15. See Paula D. Nesbitt, *The Feminization of the Clergy in America* (New York: Oxford University Press, 1997); William H. Swatos, Jr., "The Feminization of God and the Priesting of Women," in William H. Swatos, Jr. (ed.), *Twentieth-Century World Religious Movements in Neo-Weberian Perspective* (Lewiston, N.Y.: Mellen Press, 1992), pp. 283–298.

16. As an example of some of the kinds of issues that could be addressed here, see Donald Shriver, *An Ethic for Enemies* (New York: Oxford University Press, 1995).

17. Writing of the English case in which the establishment of the Church of England continues to promote a geographical residential parish system, Edward Bailey similarly describes children "as the *wilful divinities* of the parish's implicit religion"; Edward I. Bailey, *Implicit Religion in Contemporary Society* (Kampen, Netherlands: Kok Pharos, 1997), p. 211.

18. Cf. David G. Bromley, "Remembering the Future," *Sociology of Religion* 58(1997), pp. 105–140.

Selected Bibliography

Appiah, K. Anthony. "The Multiculturalist Misunderstanding." *New York Review of Books* 44(Oct. 9, 1997): 30–36.

Audi, Robert and Nicholas Wolterstorff. *Religion in the Public Square.* Lanham, Md.: Rowman & Littlefield, 1997.

Bellah, Robert N. "Civil Religion in America." *Dædalus* 96(1967): 1–21.

———. *The Broken Covenant,* 2nd. ed. Chicago: University of Chicago Press, 1992[1975].

Bellah, Robert N., Richard Madsen, William M. Sullivan, Ann Swidler, and Steven M. Tipton. *Habits of the Heart.* Berkeley: University of California Press, 1985.

Borden, Morton. *Jews, Turks, and Infidels.* Chapel Hill: University of North Carolina Press, 1984.

Bruce, Steve, Peter Kivisto, and William H. Swatos, Jr. (eds.). *The Rapture of Politics.* New Brunswick, N.J.: Transaction Books, 1994.

Butler, Jon. *Awash in a Sea of Faith.* Cambridge, Mass.: Harvard University Press, 1990.

Carter, Stephen L. *The Culture of Disbelief.* New York: Basic Books, 1993.

———. *The Dissent of the Governed.* Cambridge, Mass.: Harvard University Press, 1998.

Casanova, José. *Public Religions in the Modern World.* Chicago: University of Chicago Press, 1994.

Cohen, Arthur A. *The Myth of the Judeo-Christian Tradition.* New York: Harper & Row, 1969.

Davidson, James D., Alan K. Mock, and C. Lincoln Johnson. "Through the Eye of a Needle." *Review of Religious Research* 38(1997): 247–262.

Dean, William. *The Religious Critic in American Culture.* Albany: State University of New York Press, 1994.

Gaffney, Edward M. "Politics Without Brackets on Religious Convictions." *Tulane Law Review* 64(1990): 1143–1194.

Glazer, Nathan. *We Are All Multiculturalists Now.* Cambridge, Mass.: Harvard University Press, 1997.

Habermas, Jürgen. *The Theory of Communicative Action,* Vol. 2. Boston: Beacon Press, 1987.

Hadden, Jeffrey K. and Anson D. Shupe (eds.). *Secularization and Fundamentalism Reconsidered.* New York: Paragon House, 1989.

Hall, Charles. "The Christian Left." *Review of Religious Research* 39(1997): 27–45.

Hammond, Phillip E. *With Liberty for All.* Louisville: Westminster John Knox Press, 1998.

Handy, Robert T. *A Christian America.* New York: Oxford University Press, 1984.

Herberg, Will. *Protestant–Catholic–Jew.* New York: Harcourt Brace, 1955.

Hessel, Dieter T. (ed.). *The Church's Public Role.* Grand Rapids, Mich.: Eerdmans, 1993.

Johnson, Stephen D. and Joseph B. Tamney (eds.). *The Political Role of Religion in the United States.* Boulder, Colo.: Westview Press, 1986.

Kelley, Dean M. "The Rationale for the Involvement of Religion in the Body Politic." In James E. Wood, Jr. (ed.), *The Role of Religion in the Making of Policy,* 159–189. Waco, Tex.: Baylor University J. M. Dawson Institute of Church–State Studies, 1991.

Kosmin, Barry A. and Seymour P. Lachman. *One Nation Under God.* New York: Harmony Books, 1993.

Kramnick, Isaac and R. Laurence Moore. *The Godless Constitution.* New York: Norton, 1996.

Liebman, Robert C. and Robert Wuthnow. *The New Christian Right.* New York: Aldine de Gruyter, 1983.

Lipset, Seymour Martin. *American Exceptionalism.* New York: Norton, 1996.

Lovin, Robin W. (ed.). *Religion and American Public Life.* New York: Paulist Press, 1986.

Marty, Martin E. *The Public Church.* New York: Crossroad, 1981.

———. *The One and the Many.* Cambridge, Mass.: Harvard University Press, 1997.

———. "Public Religion." *Encyclopedia of Religion and Society,* 393–394. Walnut Creek, Calif.: AltaMira Press, 1998.

Marty, Martin E. and Edith L. Blumhofer. *Public Religion in America Today.* Chicago: Public Religion Project, 1997.

Mead, Sydney E. *The Nation with the Soul of a Church.* New York: Harper & Row, 1975.

Miller, William Lee. *The First Liberty.* New York: Knopf, 1986.

Neuhaus, Richard John. *The Naked Public Square.* Grand Rapids, Mich.: Eerdmans, 1984.

———. *America Against Itself.* Notre Dame, Ind.: University of Notre Dame Press, 1992.

Neusner, Jacob, and William Scott Green (eds.). *The Religion Factor.* Louisville: Westminster John Knox Press, 1996.

Niebuhr, Reinhold. *The Irony of American History.* New York: Scribner, 1952.

———. *Pious and Secular America.* New York: Scribner, 1958.

Noll, Mark A. (ed.). *Religion and American Politics from the Colonial Period to the 1980s.* New York: Oxford University Press, 1990.

Perry, Michael. *Love and Power: The Role of Religion and Morality in American Politics.* New York: Oxford University Press, 1991.

———. *Religion in Politics.* New York: Oxford University Press, 1997.

Pfeffer, Leo. *Church, State, and Freedom,* rev. ed. Boston: Beacon Press, 1967.

———. "The Deity in American Constitutional History." *Journal of Church and State* 23(1981): 215–239.

Reed, Ralph. *Politically Incorrect.* Dallas: Word, 1994.

Richardson, James T. "Cult/Brainwashing Cases and the Freedom of Religion." *Journal of Church and State* 33(1991): 55–74.

———. "Legal Status of New Religions in the U.S." *Social Compass* 42(1995): 249–264.

———. "Minority Religions ('Cults') and the Law." *University of Queensland Law Journal* 18(1995): 183–207.

Robbins, Thomas. "Church-and-State Issues in the United States." *Encyclopedia of Religion and Society,* 87–89. Walnut Creek, Calif.: AltaMira Press, 1998

Roof, Wade Clark and William McKinney. *American Mainline Religion.* New Brunswick, N.J.: Rutgers University Press, 1987.

Shriver, Donald. *An Ethic for Enemies.* New York: Oxford University Press, 1995.

Shriver, Peggy L. *The Bible Vote.* New York: Pilgrim Press, 1981.

Silk, Mark. *Spiritual Politics.* New York: Simon & Schuster, 1988.

Smith, Page (ed.). *Religious Origins of the American Revolution.* Missoula, Mont.: Scholars Press, 1976.

Stokes, Anson P. and Leo Pfeffer. *Church and State in the United States.* New York: Harper & Row, 1964.

Swatos, William H., Jr. (ed.). *Religious Sociology.* New York: Greenwood Press, 1987.

Tinder, Glenn. *The Political Meaning of Christianity.* San Francisco: Harper & Row, 1991.

Tocqueville, Alexis de. *Democracy in America.* Garden City, N.Y.: Doubleday, 1969[1835].

Warner, R. Stephen. "Work in Progress Toward a New Paradigm for the Sociological Study of Religion in the United States." *American Journal of Sociology* 98(1993): 1044–1093.

Williams, Rhys H. "Constructing the Public Good." *Social Problems* 42(1995): 124–144.

———. "Religion as Political Resource." *Journal for the Scientific Study of Religion* 35(1996): 368–378.

——— (ed.). *Cultural Wars in American Politics.* Hawthorne, N.Y.: Aldine de Gruyter, 1997.

Wilson, John F. *Public Religion in American Culture.* Philadelphia: Temple University Press, 1979.

Wolfe, Alan. *One Nation, After All.* New York: Viking, 1998.

Wood, James E., Jr. "Christian Faith and Political Society." In James E. Wood, Jr. (ed.), *Religion and Politics,* 9–22. Waco, Tex.: Baylor University J. M. Dawson Institute of Church–State Studies, 1983.

Wuthnow, Robert. *The Restructuring of American Religion.* Princeton, N.J.: Princeton University Press, 1988.

Index

About the Contributors

ROBERT N. BELLAH is Elliott Professor of Sociology, Emeritus, at the University of California, Berkeley. Achieving recognition early on through the publication of his Harvard bachelor's thesis, he acquired national prominence as a result of his article "Civil Religion in America" in *Dædalus* in 1967, followed by *The Broken Covenant* in 1975, and the lead authorship of *Habits of the Heart* in 1985. He continues to work on a major study of religious evolution, a topic on which he wrote early in his career.

JAMES D. DAVIDSON is Professor of Sociology at Purdue University and has spent much of his career studying the relationship between social stratification and religion. He has been executive officer of the Society for the Scientific Study of Religion, editor of the *Review of Religious Research,* and president of the Religious Research Association. He is best known popularly for his contributions to a series of volumes on American Catholic laity.

WILLIAM SCOTT GREEN is Dean of the College and Director of the Program in Judaic Studies at the University of Rochester. With Jacob Neusner he has edited *The Religion Factor* and has also edited the Brown Judaic Studies series volumes *Approaches to Ancient Judaism.*

PHILLIP HAMMOND is D. Mackenzie Brown Professor of Religious Studies and Sociology at the University of California, Santa Barbara. His latest book, *With Liberty for All,* was published in early 1998, and a book on the Soka Gakkai

Buddhist sect in America is due in 1999. He has been editor of the *Journal for the Scientific Study of Religion* and subsequently president of the SSSR.

JAMES R. KELLY is Professor and sometime Chair of Sociology at Fordham University. Primarily an essayist, he writes widely in both the social scientific literature and such semischolarly religious periodicals as *America, Commonweal,* and *The Christian Century.* He has also been consistently active in ecumenical affairs and was involved in the Catholic Common Ground Initiative from its beginnings as a national endeavor. Kelly served as president of the Association for the Sociology of Religion in 1998.

MARTIN E. MARTY is Fairfax M. Cone Professor Emeritus of Modern Christianity at the University of Chicago and Director of the Public Religion Project. In addition to editorial relationships to *Church History, The Christian Century,* and his own widely read newsletter *Context,* Marty is the author of dozens of books and has been the recipient of over fifty honorary degrees. He has been recognized by the Society for the Scientific Study of Religion with a lifetime career achievement award and by the American Academy of Religion by an award named in his honor.

JACOB NEUSNER is Distinguished Research Professor of Religious Studies at the University of South Florida and Professor of Religion at Bard College. A specialist in rabbinic Judaism and prolific author, he has recently published *The Price of Excellence: Universities in Conflict During the Cold War Era.*

RALPH E. PYLE completed his doctorate at Purdue University in 1995 under Jim Davidson's direction and is now a member of the faculty of Michigan State University. His first book, *Persistence and Change in the Protestant Establishment,* was published by Praeger in 1997 and has been accompanied by articles in the journals of the various professional societies in the social scientific study of religion.

JAMES T. RICHARDSON, holding doctorates in both sociology and law, is Professor of Sociology at the University of Nevada—Reno and Director of its renowned Master's Program in Judicial Studies. He began his research focusing on the Jesus Movement and subsequently turned to new religious movements in general, increasingly centering on law and religion. He was president of the Association for the Sociology of Religion in 1986 and is currently president of the American Association of University Professors (AAUP).

PEGGY L. SHRIVER is a past president of the Religious Research Association and is currently a professional church leadership administrator and researcher, principally with the National Council of Churches, but also with the Presbyterian Church (U.S.A.) and Union Seminary in New York City. She was among the first to write a book on the rise of the new Christian Right in America; she lectures widely and is also the author of several volumes of poetry.

WILLIAM H. SWATOS, JR., is Executive Officer of the Association for the Sociology of Religion and of the Religious Research Association. From 1989 to 1994 he was editor of *Sociology of Religion,* the official journal of the ASR; he is also editor-in-chief of *The Encyclopedia of Religion and Society.* He has edited, coedited, authored, or coauthored over a dozen books, principally in the sociology of religion.

JAMES K. WELLMAN, JR., completed his Ph.D. in religion at the University of Chicago in 1995 and has served as associate pastor of Fourth Presbyterian Church, Chicago and is now a lecturer in the Comparative Religion Program at the University of Washington. His first book, *Gold Coast Church and the Ghetto: Christ and Culture in Mainline Protestantism,* will be published in 1999.

RHYS H. WILLIAMS is a member of the sociology faculty of Southern Illinois University, with a principal interest in the sociology of religion in the context of the sociology of culture. He has written extensively in academic journals and with Jay Demerath has coauthored the award-winning *A Bridging of Faiths: Religion and Politics in a New England City.*

JAMES E. WOOD, JR., is Simon and Ethel Bunn Distinguished Professor of Church–State Studies and Director of the J. M. Dawson Institute of Church–State Studies at Baylor University. He is also Founding Editor of the *Journal of Church and State,* a position he held for twenty-five years. He has edited dozens of volumes and written several monographs on aspects of church–state relations, principally in the United States but also internationally.